D1342899

Literary Lives

General Editor: **Richard Dutton**, Professor of English, Lancaster University

This series offers stimulating accounts of the literary careers of the most admired and influential English-language authors. Volumes follow the outline of the writers' working lives, not in the spirit of traditional biography, but aiming to trace the professional, publishing and social contexts which shaped their writing.

Published titles include:

Ce 'ric C. Brown
J' .N MILTON

. . Davison
C.)RGE ORWELL

chard Dutton
LLIAM SHAKESPEARE

. a Fergus
NE AUSTEN

oline Franklin
ON

es Gibson
MAS HARDY

neth Graham
NRY JAMES

' Hammond
N DRYDEN

a Hopkins
RISTOPHER MARLOWE

avid Kaye
JONSON

Lago
FORSTER

n Machann
THEW ARNOLD

sdair D. F. Macrae
B. YEATS

Joseph McMinn
JONATHAN SWIFT

Kerry McSweeney
GEORGE ELIOT

John Mepham
VIRGINIA WOOLF

Michael O'Neill
PERCY BYSSHE SHELLEY

Leonée Ormond
ALFRED TENNYSON

Harold Pagliaro
HENRY FIELDING

George Parfitt
JOHN DONNE

Gerald Roberts
GERARD MANLEY HOPKINS

Felicity Rosslyn
ALEXANDER POPE

Tony Sharpe
T. S. ELIOT
WALLACE STEVENS

Peter Shillingsburg
WILLIAM MAKEPEACE THACKERAY

Grahame Smith
CHARLES DICKENS

Janice Farrar Thaddeus
FRANCES BURNEY

Linda Wagner-Martin
SYLVIA PLATH

Nancy A. Walker
KATE CHOPIN

Gary Waller
EDMUND SPENSER

Cedric Watts
JOSEPH CONRAD

John Williams
MARY SHELLEY
WILLIAM WORDSWORTH

Tom Winnifrith and Edward Chitham
CHARLOTTE AND EMILY BRONTË

John Worthen
D. H. LAWRENCE

David Wykes
EVELYN WAUGH

Literary Lives
Series Standing Order ISBN 0–333–71486–5 hardcover
Series Standing Order ISBN 0–333–80334–5 paperback
(*outside North America only*)

You can receive future titles in this series as they are published by placing a standing order. Please contact your bookseller or, in case of difficulty, write to us at the address below with your name and address, the title of the series and one of the ISBNs quoted above.

Customer Services Department, Macmillan Distribution Ltd, Houndmills, Basingstoke, Hampshire RG21 6XS, England

Christopher Marlowe

A Literary Life

Lisa Hopkins
Senior Lecturer in English
Sheffield Hallam University

First published 2000 by
PALGRAVE
Houndmills, Basingstoke, Hampshire RG21 6XS and
175 Fifth Avenue, New York, N. Y. 10010
Companies and representatives throughout the world

PALGRAVE is the new global academic imprint of
St. Martin's Press LLC Scholarly and Reference Division and
Palgrave Publishers Ltd (formerly Macmillan Press Ltd).

ISBN 0–333–69823–1 hardback
ISBN 0–333–69825–8 paperback

This book is printed on paper suitable for recycling and
made from fully managed and sustained forest sources.

A catalogue record for this book is available
from the British Library.

Library of Congress Cataloging-in-Publication Data
Hopkins, Lisa, 1962–
    Christopher Marlowe—a literary life / Lisa Hopkins.
        p. cm. — (Literary lives)
    Includes bibliographical references and index.
    ISBN 0–333–69823–1
    1. Marlowe, Christopher, 1564–1593. 2. Dramatists, English—Early
    modern, 1500–1700—Biography. I. Title. II. Literary lives (New York,
    N.Y.)
    PR2673 .H59 2000
    822'.3—dc21
    [B]   00–041514

10   9   8   7   6   5   4   3   2   1
09   08   07   06   05   04   03   02   01   00

Printed and bound in Great Britain by
Antony Rowe Ltd, Chippenham, Wiltshire

For Chris and Sam

Contents

Preface   ix

Acknowledgements   xi

1 Introduction   1

2 1580–1587: Canterbury and Cambridge   23

3 1587–1589: London and the World   43

4 1589–1592: Daring God out of Heaven   65

5 1592–1593: Tobacco and Boys   103

6 A Great Reckoning: From 1593 to Immortality   135

Notes   147

Index   173

Preface

The aim of this book is not in any sense to produce a conventional biography of Marlowe (a virtually hopeless task) but to consider his works in the light of some relevant-seeming aspects of what can be known or guessed about his own life. In particular, I have tried to relate his *oeuvre* to what seem to me to be two dominant and linked concerns: the English colonial enterprise, and Marlowe's insistently sceptical view of familial and social structures and of what they do to the individuals trapped within them. Throughout Marlowe's works, I have thought I have detected this dual exploration of how people orient themselves within both the macrocosm and microcosm, and of how the external landscape is always coloured by the landscape of the mind: in the words of one of Marlowe's most tormented characters, Mephistophilis in *Doctor Faustus*, 'Hell hath no limits, nor is circumscribed/In one self place, for where we are is hell' (II.i.123–4). Marlowe, who is always acutely conscious of literacy and the literary, spends his whole writing life on formal and thematic innovation, daringly widening and widening the range of what can be written about and thus, literally, 'circumscribed', but here he starkly acknowledges what always remains elusive.

Many other people have written on Marlowe. In recent years, what used to be a steady but slow trickle of work on him has turned into a positive spate. Writing on Marlowe ranges from the nonsense of the authorship conspiracy theorists to brilliant explorations of his individual works or of his career as a whole. The latter has been most recently and most importantly explored in Patrick Cheney, *Marlowe's Counterfeit Profession: Ovid, Spenser, Counter-Nationhood* (Toronto: University of Toronto Press, 1997). Another good recent survey of Marlowe's whole *oeuvre* is Fred B. Tromly, *Playing with Desire: Christopher Marlowe and the Art of Tantalization* (Toronto: University of Toronto Press, 1998). There are some excellent essays on various plays in *Two Renaissance Mythmakers*, edited by Alvin Kernan (Baltimore and London: The Johns Hopkins University Press, 1977), and also in *Christopher Marlowe and English Renaissance Culture*, edited by Darryll Grantley and Peter Roberts (Aldershot: Scolar Press, 1996) and *Marlowe, History, and Sexuality*, edited by Paul Whitfield White (New York: AMS Press, 1998). Among older work, Harry Levin's *Christopher Marlowe: The Overreacher* (London: Faber & Faber, 1961) remains a classic. There are numerous excellent editions of collected and individual plays, but I have found Mark Thornton Burnett's Everyman edition of the complete plays the most convenient, and have taken all my quotations from there (with quotations from *Doctor Faustus* from the A-text unless otherwise stated) except for those from *Hero and Leander*, which are from *Christopher Marlowe: The Complete Poems and Translations*, edited by Stephen Orgel (Harmondsworth: Penguin Books, 1971). In the case of *Edward II*, I have also consulted the notes in Charles R. Forker's Revels edition of the play (Manchester: Manchester University Press, 1994).

LISA HOPKINS

Acknowledgements

This book was made possible by research leave supported by the Arts and Humanities Research Board and by the Cultural Research Institute at Sheffield Hallam University, for which I would like to thank Judy Simons and Mick Worboys. I owe much to the collegial and friendly atmosphere created by my colleagues at Sheffield Hallam; in particular, Ian Baker has, as always, been an invaluable support, and Matthew Steggle has also been of great assistance. I am also greatly indebted to the inter-library loans staff of the Mary Badland Library at Sheffield Hallam University. My postgraduate student Annaliese Connolly was an immense help in exploring novelisations of Marlowe's life, and many other students have illuminated *Doctor Faustus* for me in seminars. Richard Dutton has been a magnificent series editor, whose assistance has gone well beyond the call of duty, and the early support of Charmian Hearne at Macmillan was vital to the project. Roy Flannagan helpfully read the manuscript and offered valuable suggestions, and Martin Wright operated a one-man cuttings service for Marloviana. My parents procured books and photocopies from Valletta library, and the joint award of the Hoffman Prize for Distinguished Publication on Marlowe in 1994 enabled me both to revisit Malta myself and also to visit the King's School, Canterbury, where I was very hospitably received. Constance Brown Kuriyama provided invaluable initial encouragement of some of my first ideas on Marlowe, S.P. Cerasano shared some of her research on Edward Alleyn, and David Farley-Hills, Alison Findlay, Roma Gill, Clare Harraway, and Carolyn Williams all graciously provided me with copies of their work. As always, I owe most of all to my husband Chris and my son Sam.

Earlier versions of parts of chapters 2, 3 and 4 appeared in *Papers on Language and Literature*, *Early Modern Literary Studies* and *(Re)Soundings* respectively, and are reproduced here by kind permission of the editors.

1
Introduction

The biographer of Marlowe has more than the usual reasons for caution. Although everyone agrees that Marlowe was born in Canterbury in 1564 (the same year as Shakespeare), that is, sadly, not only the first but also almost the last fact about his life for which there is sound documentary evidence and universal critical consensus. We know very little about his early life, though that has not deterred people from speculating: his father, the shoemaker John Marlowe, for instance, has, on the basis of what can be reconstructed about his finances, been variously interpreted as a solid enough tradesman and as an improvident and violent man who scarred his sensitive son for life, causing him to centre all his plays on violently Oedipal fantasies. At an unusually late stage in his life, the young Marlowe re-enters documented history by being enrolled as a pupil at the King's School, Canterbury, but we do not know what if any education he had before that, or whether his admission at King's should be, as has sometimes been suggested, attributed to his displaying unusual promise. He thence proceeded to Corpus Christi College, Cambridge, but was absent from it for increasing periods of time on what seems to have been government business. This last has inevitably given rise to a good deal of feverish speculation, with Marlowe sometimes seen as a sort of Elizabethan James Bond, but the only thing we know for certain about his apparent career in espionage is that he and Richard Baines, who was later to be his chief accuser when he was arrested shortly before his death, managed to get themselves detained for forging a coin in the Low Countries, an exploit for which each promptly blamed the other.

Forging a coin might well suggest poverty, and perhaps one of the greatest mysteries about Marlowe's career is his finances. He himself noted in his poem *Hero and Leander* that scholars were always poor, and certainly no playwright in Elizabethan England, however successful, could expect to live comfortably simply by selling their works. If Marlowe is indeed the young man represented in the portrait at Corpus Christi sometimes supposed to be of him (though there is no evidence for this beyond guesswork, and the fact that the sitter is the right age), he would have had money then, as is shown by the abundant display of expensive cloth and buttons, but there is no sign of his ever having any again, until, perhaps, the last year of his life, when he seems to have acquired the patronage of Thomas Walsingham, at whose country house at Scadbury, near London, he was reported to be staying when he died. It seems probable, then, that he must indeed have continued to work for the government in some capacity in tandem with his literary career.

It is, of course, for that literary career that he is famous, but even then details are tantalisingly vague. He probably, as I shall discuss in more detail below, started writing at Cambridge, though opinion is sharply divided on what exactly he wrote there. In the same year that he left, the first part of *Tamburlaine* burst onto the London stage, quickly followed by the second. So closely is Marlowe associated with *Tamburlaine* that it comes as a surprise to discover that there is no contemporary written statement which declares or confirms that he is the playwright. Indeed, in the seventeenth century the literary biographer Edward Phillips, Milton's nephew, categorically denied that Marlowe *did* write it, but nobody else has ever seriously doubted the ascription; certainly contemporaries refer to him unequivocally as being himself a '*Tamerlan*', and one plausible explanation of his ultimate arrest links it with the appearance shortly before of a threat against foreigners pinned on the wall of the Dutch churchyard and signed 'Tamburlaine'. It need not surprise us that Marlowe never bothered to assert his authorship of this wildly successful play. One very obvious explanation would be that the fact was simply too well known to need saying, and publication of plays was still in its infancy and very haphazard; not until Ben Jonson did any Renaissance English playwright publish his own work, and Jonson was thought pretentious for doing so. There is certainly no reason to suppose either that Marlowe was not the author of *Tamburlaine* or that the absence of written evidence on the subject constitutes grounds for any sort of conspiracy theory about his authorship of either this or anything else.

Tamburlaine, Part Two was written very quickly after the first play in response to its overwhelming popularity, and it was followed – in what order is not certainly known – by the other great works of his maturity: *The Jew of Malta, Edward II, Doctor Faustus, The Massacre at Paris* and the poem *Hero and Leander*. These, together with the *Tamburlaine* plays and the lyric poem 'The Passionate Shepherd to his Love', and to a lesser extent *Dido, Queen of Carthage* and translations of Ovid and Lucan, all of which Marlowe had probably written while still at Cambridge, form the basis of his claim to literary fame. It is certainly an extraordinary and very exciting *oeuvre*, with an emotional range matched in size and ambition only by the extent of the geographical range covered. However, both the canon and the range are small in comparison with that of his contemporary Shakespeare, and one might well wonder if Marlowe would have remained a figure of such compelling interest on the strength of his works alone without the added *frisson* given by the rumours about his life.

Even less is known about Marlowe's life after Cambridge than before. Thanks to the vagaries of record-keeping and document survival, his name does occasionally crop up, sometimes in unexpected contexts. As well as the coining incident, we hear of him reading a will on a visit home to Canterbury, or being reproached as a scoffer by the dying Robert Greene. There are rumours that he might have contemplated going to Scotland, and there are tantalising glimpses of some of the many forms of his name (Marley, Merlin, Marlow and Morley are all just as common as the version on which we have now standardised) as far apart as on a spying mission in Utrecht and tutoring Lady Arbella Stuart at Hardwick Hall, though it does not look as though either of these can have been the right Marlowe. Most of all, in the last few months of his life we hear of him becoming increasingly embroiled in violence. He falls out with a tailor in Canterbury and assaults him with his dagger, and two constables in the ward where he is living take the extraordinary step of making a formal complaint that they are scared of him. (One dreads to think what you need to do to make the police scared of you.) Finally, in

May 1593, in a private house in Deptford, Marlowe was stabbed to death in what has variously been interpreted as a drunker brawl or a calculated murder (or, by the wildest of the conspiracy theorists, as a cover story for him to be spirited away and assume a new identity as William Shakespeare).

As with the question of the authorship of *Tamburlaine*, however, despite the scantiness and unsatisfactoriness of much of the information, many more things are widely supposed about Marlowe's life than are actually known. By some mysterious process, it is, for instance, widely current that Marlowe was homosexual, and also that he was an atheist and a smoker. (It is not the least of the ironies of Marlowe's life and afterlife that while his own age could not forgive him for two of these, many of us now could not forgive him for the third; he is never going to fit comfortably into any form of conventional morality.) Again, as with the authorship of *Tamburlaine*, there is no confirmation of Marlowe's homosexuality, but again nobody doubts it, though some modern scholars would dispute the appropriateness of the term homosexual in this context, as discussed below. His choice of Edward II as a hero, his introduction of episodes of same-sex love or eroticism into *Dido, Queen of Carthage* and *Hero and Leander*, and his alleged remark 'All they that love not tobacco or boys be fools' all point in the same direction. The same reported remark is also the authority for his alleged smoking, and forms part of a longer series of accusations which include substantial comments about blasphemies and claims of atheism, which Marlowe is said to have uttered. Again, though one might want to be cautious about accepting all these at face value, Marlowe does seem to have been exactly the kind of person who would shy away from conventional pieties, and many of his plays can be read as asking searching questions about the existence of a divine power and the nature of religious belief.

It is doubtless because of this singularly spectacular biography that, although in any assertion about the life of Marlowe one is almost never on safe ground, critics have nevertheless been drawn irresistibly to that ground, and have wanted to interpret the plays, and above all their heroes, in the light of what they knew, or thought they knew, about the man who wrote them. In an article on 'Marlowe and the Critics', Irving Ribner mischievously cited the

1865 comments of Hippolyte Taine on Marlowe's work, before going on to observe that

> What is remarkable about this view of Marlowe is that the biography upon which it is based is a tissue of rumour and misinformation, almost every item of which has since been proved false, and that this highly dubious biography is used to throw light upon the plays which in turn are used to support the conjectures of the biography. For Taine, and for some critics even of our own time, Tamburlaine, Barabas, Faustus all speak with the voice of Marlowe himself.

Ribner himself is sure that 'the facts ... reveal something other than the dissolute bohemian who could have written the plays Taine read';[1] but Taine's belief that something of Marlowe himself was visible in his heroes has been a very widespread one, as, indeed, has the assumption that all the heroes are essentially the same character (which would in effect render any kind of biographical approach to Marlowe redundant, since he had already repeatedly performed the task of writing his own life himself).[2] Don Cameron Allen, for instance, claims that 'Marlowe is essentially a rhétoriqueur. If one goes by the speeches and never looks at the left-hand margin, one would have difficulty separating the men from the women or even the men from the men'.[3]

This view that the plays' characters are all the same, and all Marlowe, has led to a whole series of readings which simply conflate his life and works. Ribner notes that another eminent Marlovian, Paul Kocher, who argued that 'Marlowe really had only one great theme: himself', is 'as much concerned with Marlowe the man as with Marlowe the dramatist, and in the last analysis he is unable or unwilling to separate these two concerns'. But though Ribner is nervous about biographical readings, he nevertheless also castigates the diametrically opposite approach of Douglas Cole:

> If Romantic critics had tended to overemphasize biographical considerations in studying the plays, Cole goes to the opposite extreme, for he ignores biography entirely. It would be very convenient if this could be done, but with a writer like Marlowe it simply is not possible.

Somehow, then, a middle way must be found – though such an undertaking does not seem easy when Ribner goes on to observe of the current state of Marlowe criticism, 'no one of the three dominant approaches now current is in any real way compatible with either of the other two'.[4]

Few have shared Cole's unwillingness to consider the life in relation to the works, and indeed Marlowe himself seems almost to encourage one to do so since, as Harry Levin pointed out, the prologue to *Doctor Faustus* 'presents character in biographical synopsis'.[5] In Eugene Waith's view, 'if he was an atheist, a homosexual, a spy, a scoffer, and a quarreller, it seems more than a coincidence that he chose for principal characters an atheistical warrior, a scholar who sold his soul to the devil, a homosexual king, a Machiavellian schemer'.[6] J.M. Robertson, in the course of an extraordinary attempt to claim for Marlowe the authorship of much of the early Shakespeare canon, declares that 'obviously, the first stage is a circumspect notation and study of Marlowe's life' (though he himself becomes rather less than circumspect when he recounts an alleged encounter with Marlowe's ghost, which, rather unexpectedly, complains of the prevalence of cricket, football, tennis and golf in modern English life).[7] On a more sober note, David Bevington concurs with Una Ellis-Fermor of *Tamburlaine* and *Doctor Faustus* that 'both plays are deeply personal for the dramatist and that *Doctor Faustus* in particular is a play about Marlowe's own agony of loss'. He notes, however, that

> [t]he biographical hypothesis is problematic, of course, in part because of the uncertain reliability of the so-called Baines note and other testimonials to Marlowe's heterodoxy at the end of his life and in part because of the danger of making too simplified an equation between biography and art. It is tempting nonetheless to agree with Paul Kocher that Marlowe's own heterodoxy is, on the whole, beyond doubt.[8]

Marlowe's biography seems, then, to be a legitimate area of speculation, but, as so often with Marlowe, it will not do to posit any simple correlation between it and his plays.

If the facts of Marlowe's life allow room for debate, so too does the composition of his canon. Quite apart from the big names which everyone knows and associates with Marlowe, such as *Tamburlaine* and *Doctor Faustus*, an extraordinary number of plays both lost and extant have at one time or another been attributed to him. J.M. Robertson claims for him lost plays on Hannibal, on the basis of the reference in the Prologue to *Doctor Faustus* to Thrasimene and the Carthaginians, and on Scanderbeg. He argues that Marlowe wrote all his own plays (including *The Massacre at Paris*, in which he thinks Kyd collaborated) by 1590, and, moreover, composed with great ease and readiness. Marlowe would, therefore, also have had time, Robertson argues, to produce most of *1, 2* and *3 Henry VI* (in which he was 'too chivalrous' for popular taste in his treatment of Joan of Arc), some of *Titus Andronicus*, almost all of *The Comedy of Errors, Richard III* (with Kyd and Heywood) and the originals of *Henry V* and of *Julius Caesar*. Robertson further asserts that there are signs of Marlowe's hand in *The Troublesome Raigne of King John, Alphonsus Emperor of Germany, The Taming of a Shrew* and *Edward III*, as well as *A 'Larum for London, Arden of Faversham, Richard II, Romeo and Juliet, The Merchant of Venice* and *Macbeth*. Of this astonishing *oeuvre*, Robertson serenely declares '*Richard III* is his last play'.[9]

Perhaps the most surprising thing about the extraordinary catalogue of achievement which Robertson thus ascribes to Marlowe is that Robertson continues to subscribe to the 1593 death date. Others have not thus limited themselves.[10] The American enthusiast Calvin Hoffman notoriously suggested that Marlowe, having written all his 'own' plays before he was twenty (not to mention *Locrine, Edward III* and *The Spanish Tragedy*), went on to be smuggled abroad and then wrote all of Shakespeare's, and spawned a whole authorship industry dedicated to proving that Marlowe was Shakespeare.[11] There is, however, no evidence for such a theory other than wishful thinking, coupled all too often either with a predilection for conspiracy theories or a refusal to believe that a great playwright could have been anything so shocking as either a homosexual or an atheist.[12] There are, of course, more intelligent reasons for thinking that Marlowe could not have been either of these things, in the shape of modern critical arguments that neither identity was fully available in the sixteenth century, with atheism as we might now understand it intellectually inconceivable and homosexuality defined not as a separate and exclusive preference but as on a continuum of a range of behaviour patterns. While I see the force of these arguments, I do think that if there was *anyone* in the sixteenth century who would have taken the extremest possible position in both cases, it was Marlowe.

The canon generally accepted as Marlowe's is of course much smaller than that proposed by Robertson. Tucker Brooke, for instance, dismissed the possibility that either the old *King John* or *Titus Andronicus* might have been Marlovian, as well as *Richard III*, *The Taming of a Shrew* and the Manwood epitaph, though he conceded the possibility of both a Marlovian and a Kydian presence in *Arden of Faversham*, and maybe even in *Lust's Dominion*.[13] Amongst conventional scholars, perhaps the best claim for addition to the accepted canon comes from some or all of the *Contention Between the Houses of York and Lancaster* and *The True Tragedie of Richard Duke of York*,[14] which are variously thought to be Shakespeare's first drafts for the first two parts of *Henry VI*,[15] bad quartos of those plays, or quite separate Marlovian plays which may or may not have had other collaborators and may or may not have been revised by Shakespeare.[16] Other critics have detected Marlowe's hand in the *Henry VI* plays themselves, which like *The Jew of Malta* were for Strange's Men and seem to date from or before 1592,[17] though many would continue to give these to Shakespeare alone.[18]

It is indeed easy to detect in the *Henry VI* plays a note which seems unmistakably Marlovian, though it is of course equally easy to detect others which do not; indeed Margaret E. Owens suggests that '[s]o insistent is the verbal and visual imagery of decapitation in *2 Henry VI* that one might be tempted to speculate that the dramatist(s) took a deliberate risk, indulging in an exercise in theatrical audacity of a kind we more typically associate with Marlowe'.[19] It is certainly a possibility that, as Owens suggests, a Marlovian note may be present in the plays not because Marlowe himself wrote them, but because someone else is deliberately imitating him. However that may be – and the question is probably impossible to resolve – it certainly does seem as though the three *Henry VI* plays, and the first of them in particular, pit a Marlovian aesthetic and mode of dramatisation against a very different, rather more restrained one, which would later become particularly associated with Shakespeare.

If we go looking for Marlowe in the *Henry VI* plays, we find him early. The mighty line resonates in the opening of the first of the three, with what J.B. Steane calls its 'Marlovian attack' and '[v]ery Marlovian lines, with the strong verb placed at the beginning of the line':[20]

> Hung be the heavens with black, yield day to night!
> Comets, importing change of times and states,
> Brandish your crystal tresses in the sky,
> And with them scourge the bad revolting stars
> That have consented unto Henry's death![21]

We also hear obvious echoes of *Tamburlaine* in Charles' words to Pucelle, 'Thou hast astonished me with thy high terms' (*I*, I.2.93) and in her reply that 'Assigned am I to be the English scourge' (*I*, I.2.129), while the Master Gunner of Orléans' shooting of Salisbury (*I*, I.4) recalls the death of the Governor of Babylon in *Tamburlaine 2*, and Charles' question 'Was Mahomet inspired with a dove?' (*I*, I.2.140) shows a typically Marlovian awareness of other religions. The animus against Elizabeth in the daring terming of the Pucelle 'Astraea's daughter' (*I*, I.6.4) and the suggestion that she is pregnant by Alençon (the name of Elizabeth's most persistent French suitor) (*I*, 5.4.73) is also characteristic of Marlowe, as I shall discuss below, and not at all of Shakespeare, who not only barely refers to Elizabeth I, but seems to develop positive strategies to avoid her.[22] Towards the beginning of *The Comedy of Errors*, Egeon tells the Duke, 'A heavier task could not have been imposed / Than I to speak my griefs unspeakable'.[23] Egeon here is virtually translating the opening lines of Aeneas' tale to Dido, which, as *Hamlet* shows us, Shakespeare knew and remembered: 'Infandum, regina, iubes me renovare dolorem'. There is, however, a word which Egeon does not say, and that is 'queen'. *The Comedy of Errors* is, for all its classical source and improbable plot, a play surprisingly interested in political issues: we hear of the major political powers Ireland, Scotland, Spain, the New World and France making war against her heir, Henry of Navarre (III.2.122ff), and it has been suggestively argued that a central concern of the play is, as in *Edward II*, the doctrine of the monarch's two bodies.[24] We certainly come close to the discourses of contemporary politics in Antipholus of Syracuse's comments on Luciana:

> But her fair sister,
> Possessed with such a gentle sovereign grace,
> Of such enchanting presence and discourse,

> Hath almost made me traitor to myself.
> But lest myself be guilty to self-wrong,
> I'll stop mine ears against the mermaid's song.
>
> (III.2.167–72)

'Sovereign' and 'traitor' both drift in the direction of Elizabeth's sister queen, Mary, Queen of Scots, who was indeed portrayed as a mermaid, emblem of ensnaring, destructive sexuality. This indirect approach is, though, as near as we ever get to Elizabeth herself; here as at the beginning, 'queen' remains the name that the text will not speak. The riskiness of the references to Elizabeth in *1 Henry VI* certainly finds no echo here.

In the second part of *Henry VI* there are further signs suggestive of Marlovian authorship. Gloucester's attempt to calm himself by 'walking once about the quadrangle' sounds like a reminiscence of university days, characteristic and widespread in Marlowe but absent perforce in Shakespeare, who did not go to university (*II*, I.3.150–1). Suffolk's punning death by water is doubly reminiscent of *Edward II* both in the interest in water (which I discuss in chapter 5 on 'Tobacco and Boys') and in the use of a pun on letters to procure death, and the water imagery so characteristic of *Edward II* recurs again when the Lieutenant calls Suffolk 'Sir Pool! Lord Pool! / Ay, kennel, puddle, sink, whose filth and dirt / Troubles the silver spring where England drinks' (*II*, 4.1.70–2). The world of *Edward II* is further evoked in the references to 'Killingworth' (*II*, 4.4.39 and 44). Part Three also features some distinctly Marlovian-sounding lines, as when Richard exclaims, 'father, do but think / How sweet a thing it is to wear a crown; / Within whose circuit is Elysium / And all that poets feign of bliss and joy' (*III*, I.2.28–31).

Equally, however, there are lines that are indelibly associated with Shakespeare, such as 'Here had the conquest fully been sealed up, / If Sir John Falstaff had not played the coward' (*I*, I.1.130–1; Falstaff is also mentioned at *I*, I.4.35), and 'Froissart, a countryman of ours, records, / England all Olivers and Rowlands bred / During the time Edward the Third did reign' (*I*, I.2.29–31), which, in the light of the recent acceptance of *Edward III* into the Shakespearean canon, looks closer to Shakespeare's interests than to Marlowe's. (Though some computer tests would actually attribute *Edward III* as readily to Marlowe as to Shakespeare.) The stichomythia between Margaret and

Suffolk (*I*, 5.3) also looks Shakespearean, though Marlowe by the end of his career was beginning to experiment with shorter blocks of speech, as too does the Cardinal's guilt on his deathbed (*II*, 3.3), York's 'Bid'st thou me rage? why, now thou hast thy wish: / Wouldst have me weep? why, now thou hast thy will' (*III*, I.4.143–4), with its echo of Sonnet 135, and King Henry's 'What time the shepherd, blowing of his nails' (*III*, 2.5.3), so reminiscent of *Love's Labour's Lost*.

Neither of the references to Falstaff is, however, integral to the narrative; the name could easily have been subsituted for another, and indeed if this had been written by Shakespeare one would more readily have expected to find the earlier form 'Oldcastle' here. The very mention of Falstaff is thus suggestive of a process of revision, something which indeed seems to be confirmed by the titles of the second and third parts, *The Second Part of King Henry the Sixth, with the Death of the Good Duke Humphrey: earlier called The First Part of the Contention Betwixt the Houses of York and Lancaster* (*II*, p. 5), and *The Third Part of King Henry the Sixth with the Death of the Duke of York: earlier called The Second Part of the Contention Betwixt the Houses of York and Lancaster* (*III*, p. 5). Alteration of some sort is also clearly signalled by the fact that throughout 3.2 Margaret is consistently called Eleanor, even by herself. Indeed there even places where it seems possible to discern a chaffing rivalry between two dramatists of different geographical origins:

> *Say.* You men of Kent, –
> *Dick.* What say you of Kent?
> *Say.* Nothing but this; 'tis 'bona terra, mala gens.'
>   (I, 4.7.50–2)

Might this be Shakespeare, characteristically making a terrible pun on 'say', poking affectionate fun at another man of Kent?[25] And might the compliment to Kent at *III*, I.2.40–2, be a riposte? Moreover, it certainly seems as though someone is flaunting their knowledge of Warwickshire when Somerville informs us, 'It is not his, my lord; here Southam lies: / The drum your honour hears marcheth from Warwick' (*III*, 5.1.12.13). Might we conceivably be hearing the traces here of two dramatists, one (like Marlowe) from Kent, and one (like Shakespeare?) from Warwickshire, engaged in friendly geographical and professional rivalry?

We cannot, and perhaps we never will be able to, settle the multifarious debates surrounding the composition of the three parts of *Henry VI*. We do not even know what order they were written in – many critics would suggest that Part 1 postdates Part 2, and perhaps Part 3 as well[26] – let alone precisely who worked on them and when. I think, as do the most recent computer tests, that it is quite likely that Marlowe had a hand in them, and that, as Bakeless suggested,[27] he may well have done so in conjunction with Shakespeare. Nevertheless, I have not chosen to make much of them as part of his overall *oeuvre*, not only because of the uncertainty over their authorship, but also because I think they tell us relatively little about the development of Marlowe's thought. If he worked on them at all, they undoubtedly came late in his career, and though the imagery of water, the emphasis on decapitation and the turn to English history certainly chime with his known preoccupations at that stage of his career, then by the same token they tell us nothing that we did not know before, unless perhaps accepting them into his canon makes us readier to see him as a dramatist willing and able to collaborate with others. I would hesitate to call them hack-work, but the ways in which they echo rather than develop the ideas of *Edward II* constitute something not usual in the Marlowe canon, for Marlowe, though a relentless regurgitator of specific phrases, is nothing if not formally and thematically innovative, and tends to move on from his own work rather than repeat it. (Individual lines he frequently repeats, but structures, on the whole, he does not.) Though I am by no means convinced that Shakespeare's share of the writing was significantly larger than Marlowe's, I would nevertheless see the plays as much more integral, shaping and influential a part of Shakespeare's literary life than of his predecessor's, affording him a solid foundation in handling sweeps of time and mood and in dramatising the fate of the nation through its specific individuals.

Of the other plays sometimes attributed to Marlowe, perhaps the most mysterious and tantalising is the supposedly lost play on Scanderbeg, the existence of which is inferred from Gabriel Harvey's reference to him as a 'Scanderbegging wight'. I wonder, however, whether the allusion was actually prompted by *Tamburlaine Part Two*, which uses episodes from the life of Scanderbeg.[28] Scanderbeg, the Albanian hero who was born Giorgio Castriota but was called

'Iscander Bey', 'Lord Alexander', by his Turkish foes, was born in 1403, a year after Tamburlaine had defeated Bajazeth, and he and Tamburlaine, both enemies of the Turks, were often thought of together, as in Thomas Randolph's remark that 'I will be the Scanderbeg to this company, the very Tamburlaine of this ragged route'.[29] Equally, I wonder whether the idea of a supposed lost play on Hannibal, derived from the reference in the opening chorus of *Doctor Faustus* to 'the fields of Thrasimene', does not come from a misunderstanding. Might this actually allude to *Dido*, who was famous as a prototype and foreshadower of Hannibal[30] – and thus, incidentally, supplying us with evidence that *Dido* really was composed (and probably even performed) before *Tamburlaine*? Perhaps the 'lost plays' on Hannibal and Scanderbeg need to be relegated to the same corner of obscurity as the fragment 'I walkt along a stream', in *England's Parnassus* (1600), which Tucker Brooke confidently identified as Marlovian and as probably of the same date as *Hero and Leander*, but which has now been identified as a passage from *Devoreux* (1597).[31] Marlowe was also supposed to have written verses in Latin and a book against the Trinity which was too dangerous to be published, but nothing of these is now known to survive.

As well as considering what Marlowe did write, however, perhaps some attention should also be paid to what he did *not*. Though he is often seen as being in conscious rivalry with Spenser and later with Shakespeare, and seems to have been on the margins of the Sidney circle, he did not imitate them by producing a Petrarchan sonnet sequence, a curious and striking omission. Diana Henderson, indeed, argues that 'Marlowe … rejects Petrarchism entirely', and this, to his contemporaries, would probably have been a significant difference in attitude from those around him.[32] Since Petrarchism was associated with the impulse to idealise and also, by and large, with exclusively heterosexual love, Marlowe's avoidance of it perhaps provides further evidence not only for his homosexuality but also for the cynicism. We could perhaps link the absence of Petrarchan thought and imagery in his work with his equally marked avoidance of any obvious didactic or moralising intent, and with the way in which even the sublimest of his characters' urges towards abstract beauty, perfection or idealism are invariably deflated by bathos (the most famous and striking example of this being Tamburlaine's 'That perfect bliss and sole felicity, / The sweet fruition of an earthly crown' [*I*, II.viii.28–9]). Idealism of any sort cannot survive in the Marlovian world.

Uncertainty about the composition of the Marlovian canon only adds to the already myriad other uncertainties about the chronology of Marlowe's *oeuvre*. Michael Warren warns:

> [i]n all arguments concerning artistic, moral, or psychological development we are inclined to impose the shape that pleases us: we presume natural progresses in straight lines, or in curves, or else we conceive of a writer returning to former themes. But they are all our constructions, and Marlowe, whose life is surrounded with mystery and intrigue, is not an easy subject for such domestication into limited shapes of career.[33]

There are, broadly speaking, two main kinds of shape proposed for Marlowe's overall literary career. One model assumes him to have followed the usual contours of an artist's development by seeing him as progressing steadily to better and better work, culminating in the magnificent assurance and control of comic tone of *Hero and Leander* and in the play which is generally agreed to be his greatest, *Doctor Faustus*. The other offers a more awkward, less usual, less predictable and less explicable career shape, but one which is not, perhaps, out of keeping with so perverse and iconoclastic a playwright. There are considerable variations within what I am grouping together as this second pattern – *Hero and Leander*, *Dido, Queen of Carthage* and the translation of Lucan are all particularly prone to find themselves placed at either extreme of his writing life – but what seems to me to characterise it is principally a willingness to experiment with the received norms of artistic development and to imagine Marlowe producing odd things at odd times.

The crunch point in the perception of Marlowe's overall career is the problematic placing of *Doctor Faustus*. Robertson's wilder fantasies aside, most scholars are agreed in seeing *Tamburlaine* as Marlowe's first major play, written perhaps while the author was still at Cambridge,[34] and probably preceded by *Dido, Queen of Carthage*[35] (of which Marlowe may or may not have been sole author), *The Passion-ate Shepherd to his Love*,[36] and his translations of the first book of Lucan's *Pharsalia* and of the first three of Ovid's *Amores*[37] – which are often seen as being not merely apprentice pieces, but centrally linked to the overall development of his career in their twin emphases on love[38] and war and in their explorations of the values of ancient Rome. Clifford Ronan, for instance, sees echoes of the Lucan in particular in both *Edward II* and *The Massacre at Paris*, and comments in general that '[n]o author's plays are more Romanized than Marlowe's, a corpus marked by what Knoll calls "Caesarism"',[39] while Boas remarks that Lucan breaks epic conventions in discarding supernatural machinery and not allowing for any intervention by the gods, something that would surely have appealed to one of Marlowe's alleged temperament, and 'poured forth a wealth of geographical and ethnographical detail which was not lost on the author of *Tamburlaine*'.[40] There may, too, have been a translation of Colluthus's *Rape of Helen*, which had already been put into Latin by Thomas Watson, whom we know to have been Marlowe's friend during his early years in London; this is usually dated to 1587.[41] Tucker Brooke was inclined to place both the surviving translations as early poems and *Dido* as the first of the plays; he suggested that 'Marlowe wrote the play while still at college', although he also pointed out that '[e]vidently the text was printed from a theatre manuscript', and concluded:

> the feeling remains that *Dido* is early work. But adherents of this theory are on safer ground when they trust to general evidence of style and spirit than when they attempt formal demonstration.[42]

This reliance on instinct is also shared by the many critics who have felt that the title page's ascription of joint authorship of the play to Nashe must be intuitively disregarded.[43] Tucker Brooke felt himself, however, on surer ground with *Tamburlaine*:

> [s]ince the prologue to *Tamburlaine II* (lines 2317–19) specifically states (what the structure of the second part confirms) that the poet began the later drama only as a result of the confirmed success of the first part on the stage, production of part two before the end of March, 1588, would imply that part one can hardly have been written later than the beginning of 1587. It probably belongs to Marlowe's last year at Cambridge.

But what followed? Many, such as Tucker Brooke and David Bevington, would see *Doctor Faustus* as coming after *Tamburlaine*, though they acknowledge that there is a startling change of subject matter and style.[44] Bevington remarks,

> [w]hether *Doctor Faustus* is the immediate successor to *Tamburlaine*, as argued by a majority of scholars today, or Marlowe's last great play, it can be looked at as *Tamburlaine*'s polar opposite; one play stresses virtually unlimited opportunities for self-assertion ... , while the other begins with self-assertion only to brood despondently on human limitation and failure.[45]

However, the gulf between *Doctor Faustus* and *Tamburlaine* is not so great as all that: Sidney Homan remarks that '[m]uch of Tamburlaine ... remains in the Faustus who greets us in the opening scenes',[46] and as A.D. Nuttall has recently pointed out, 'Christ's blood, streaming in the firmament, is like, for those that remember, the black streamers which Tamburlaine would have set in the firmament to "signify the slaughter of the gods"', and '[a] little before he utters Christ's words, *consummatum est*, Faustus cuts his arm. Tamburlaine also cuts his arm and asks his sons to search the wound.'[47] Equally, Francis Johnson observes that *Doctor Faustus* and the two parts of *Tamburlaine* are 'the three dramas in which [Marlowe] makes greatest use of astronomical imagery',[48] while Paul Kocher remarks that '[m]ost of the poet's recourse to cience ... comes in his early plays, *Tamburlaine* and *Faustus*',[49] and John Mebane sees both as profoundly influenced by Neoplatonic philosophy.[50] On similar lines, Susan Richards suggests that 'Death is a kind of Mephostophilis to Tamburlaine's Faustus – the servant who gives unlimited power only to become the master'.[51] Putting *Faustus* next to *Tamburlaine* has thus enabled several critics to see both plays better.

The older tradition was certainly always in favour of a date early in Marlowe's career for *Doctor Faustus* (and so, for what it's worth, is Shakespeare in *Shakespeare in Love*). Austin K. Gray, arguing that '[i]n 1587 Brussels, Antwerp and the Prince of Parma had become the centre of interest', suggested that the genesis of *Doctor Faustus* might lie in a spying mission to the Netherlands while Marlowe was still at Cambridge, which would presumably mean an early date.[52] Beatrice

Daw Brown similarly thought the play was informed by Marlowe's student years, but was troubled by other considerations:

> [t]he argument for an early date, 1588–89, is based by its proponents largely on internal evidence, the academic quality of the play and the learned references, which seem to bring it near to Marlowe's Cambridge period. The reflection of further reading in ecclesiastical literature recorded in this paper might seem to favor this hypothesis. At the same time the maturity of thought in *Dr. Faustus* precludes the theory of an extremely early date.[53]

More recently, others have felt strongly that this cannot be an early play, and have argued for a date of 1592 or even 1593,[54] partly on the grounds that, as Edward Snow puts it, '[w]hatever the actual chronology of Marlowe's plays, no work of art – not even *The Tempest* – communicates more powerfully the *sense* of a "last work" than does *Doctor Faustus*',[55] but mainly because of W.W. Greg's insistence that the English *Faust Book*, Marlowe's main source, had not been published before 1592, and therefore Marlowe could not have borrowed from it before that date (though Greg also conceded that it might have been the revisers of the play who were responsible for the debt, rather than Marlowe himself).[56] Irving Ribner, working from the tidy-minded premise that in Marlowe's canon as a whole 'it is possible to trace a development not only in dramatic technique but also in philosophical scope', suggests *Edward II* as the penultimate play and *Doctor Faustus* as the last, with *The Massacre at Paris* immediately preceding them,[57] while Nicholas Brooke flatly asserts that '*Dr Faustus* was written at the end, not at the beginning, of Marlowe's career'.[58]

The vexed question of the date of *Faustus* is greatly complicated by the survival of the play in two variant texts, and not least by the fact that while the A-text seems to borrow from *A Looking Glass for London and England*, which was printed in 1592, and so must precede that, some at least of the B-text clearly postdates Marlowe's life, and also by the fact that, as Michael Warren points out, '[p]roponents of the A-text favor an early date around 1590, while proponents of the B-text, influenced by Greg, tend to favor a later date around 1592–1593, although they are far from uniform'.[59] The crucial issue, though, is as Greg identified, the date of the English *Faust Book*, but that may not be as clear-cut as Greg believed. Paul H. Kocher has argued that there is 'evidence tending to show that there was an edition of the English *Faust Book* at least as early as 1590, and that this edition was first printed at Cambridge', and has also adduced other strong reasons for the early date. He pointed to 'a reference to "Faustus" in Henry Holland's dialogue, *A Treatise Against Witchcraft*, published at Cambridge in 1590'. It is not clear whether this reference to 'Faustus' is to Marlowe's play or to something else such as, perhaps, a poem, but Kocher points out that the page referring to 'Faustus' also carries a marginal reference to 'Drunken Dunstan', and he suggests that '*Drunken Dunstan* may provide a key to the problem, on the theory that what *Dunstan* is, *Faustus* is likely to be, since they are cited side by side. But *Drunken Dunstan* eludes identification. No such title appears in the Stationers' Register at any time before 1591.'[60]

I too know of no possible candidate before 1590, but it may perhaps be suggestive that *A Knack to Know a Knave*, which was, Curt Zimansky says, 'written by a man who has Marlowe's verse rhythms in his head', features Archbishop Dunstan raising a devil to obtain information from him.[61] According to Henslowe, the first performance of *A Knack to Know a Knave* was 10 June 1592. Zimansky uses this information, and the play's apparent indebtedness to Marlowe, to argue that *Doctor Faustus* must therefore have been complete before this date, and, concomitantly, before the publication of the first known edition of the English *Faust Book* in May 1592. He further suggests that since the date of publication of the *Faust Book* must thus be a red herring in fixing the first possible date of Marlowe's play, we ought to revert to the older date of 1588–9 for *Faustus*. I certainly wonder whether there is not some now probably irretrievable connection between *A Knack to Know a Knave*, some earlier Dunstan work and that 1590 marginal annotation which would prove him right.[62] One further possible piece of evidence which might conceivably have some bearing on the argument is the possibility of a relationship between *Doctor Faustus* and the sermons of William Perkins, who was a popular Calvinist preacher during Marlowe's time at Cambridge. Observing how close the play is to the world of Marlowe's studies, G.M. Pinciss also points out that the theological complexities of the play are not to be found in the English *Faust Book*, and

> can perhaps best be understood by referring to what Perkins himself wrote in a work that, as Ian Breward notes, 'grew out of

sermons in the 1590s ...' According to Perkins, the practice of witchcraft is like the sin in Eden of desiring to become a god.[63]

Was Marlowe influenced by Perkins; or was Perkins, just possibly, influenced by Marlowe, further suggesting an early date for *Faustus*? Moroever, Michael Keefer points out that the reference in the English *Faust Book* to Pope Sixtus in the present tense seems to suggest that the translation was completed before his death in August 1590, and that Marlowe could perhaps have read it in manuscript,[64] as we know he did parts of Spenser's *Faerie Queene* and Paul Ive's treatise on fortification, which were both quoted in *Tamburlaine* before they had been published. Finally, Scott McMillin and Sally-Beth MacLean have recently argued that specific echoes and a general anti-Marlowe bias in *The Troublesome Reign of King John*, printed in 1591, show that *Doctor Faustus* must already have been on the stage.[65] In recent years, then, the pendulum seems to have been swinging back towards an early date,[66] and I would certainly favour that, because to read *Doctor Faustus* as early makes it so much more charged and more exciting: we may condemn the hero's blasphemy, but at the time when the threat to England from the Prince of Parma was still real or at least recent, we must equally strongly sympathise with his proposed anti-Parma manoeuvres, thus giving the play yet another pull of nervously balanced choices and divided allegiances.

Other areas of Marlowe's career are, mercifully, marginally less controversial. *The Jew of Malta* is often dated to 1589 or 1590[67] – it was certainly being acted in February 1592, and seems then not to have been new[68] – and is frequently thought to have been followed by *Edward II* – Tucker Brooke suggests late 1591/early 1592 for the latter, arguing that it can be no later because after that references to it begin to appear in contemporary literature – and Henslowe noted *The Massacre at Paris* as new in January 1593, which would make it Marlowe's last play.[69] This gives rise to schemas such as that of Harold Brooks, who declares:

> No one doubts that *Edward II* came late in Marlowe's career, cut short on 30 May 1593. His career in the drama perhaps did not continue beyond January, when *The Massacre at Paris* was 'new' for Henslowe. During the rest of his life, the theatres were closed because of plague; one imagines him working at *Hero and Leander* rather than for the paralysed London stage.[70]

This possibility may be strengthened by the apparent connection between *Edward II* and *The Comedy of Errors*, which seem to share a concern with the idea of the King's two bodies,[71] along with a detailed examination of the effect of real or supposed infidelity on the marriage, and the way in which the behaviour of the innocent spouse deteriorates as well as that of the guilty one. R.A. Foakes points to *The Comedy*'s apparent borrowing of the question 'What, will you murder me?' (IV.iv.107) from *Edward II*;[72] there is also the similarity between Mortimer's 'I cannot, nor I will not; I must speak'[73] and Adriana's 'I cannot nor I will not hold me still. / My tongue, though not my heart, shall have his will' (IV.2.17–18), and that between the brutal barbering of Edward and that of Dr Pinch (V.1.172–3).

Unfortunately, it is impossible to date *The Comedy of Errors* with greater precision than between 1589 and 1593, though R.A. Foakes argues for 'the supposition that *The Comedy of Errors* was written not long before or immediately after the long spell of plague which caused all acting to be prohibited in London throughout most of the year 1593, and which probably turned Shakespeare to writing his narrative poems'.[74] If Foakes is right, this would strengthen the argument for dating *Edward II* too to this period.

It is usually accepted that *Hero and Leander* is the last of all Marlowe's works and was quite possibly left unfinished at his death. Even this apparent note of certainty, though, reintroduces some other difficulties into the chronology, for M.C. Bradbrook, insisting on the parallels between *Hero and Leander* and *Dido*, is sure that at least one scene of the latter must have been written at the same time as the poem,[75] which presumably implies that Marlowe at the very end of his life was simultaneously producing his last work and revising what may well have been his earliest.[76] Clifford Leech similarly grouped the two together, suggesting that '*Dido* and *Hero and Leander* may have been worked at during Marlowe's Cambridge years, though the maturity of the style makes that difficult to credit; they may, on the other hand, date from the end of his short career'.[77]

Given these difficulties, I have not even attempted to argue with any degree of certainty for the dating of any of the plays. I do, though, see them as naturally falling within a series of three groupings: *Dido, Queen of Carthage* and *Tamburlaine*, centrally concerned with the encounter of ethnically different individuals; *The Jew of Malta* and *Doctor Faustus*, both also bearing traces of this interest, but most obviously focused on questions of religion and of faith; and finally *Edward II*, *The Massacre at Paris* and *Hero and Leander*, all of which have, at their heart, sexuality. (As it happens, my belief in the early date for *Doctor Faustus* means that this structure conforms to what I believe to be the chronological development of Marlowe's drama, but my discussion of the plays is not underpinned by a dependence on chronology.) Without wanting to become schematic, these, therefore, are the groupings with which I have chosen to work, and which I see as related to three crucial aspects of Marlowe's own life and career: his relationships with those involved in the English colonial enterprise, his views on Christianity and his own sexuality. Moreover, since the most securely established facts of his problematic career do seem to point fairly reliably to *Tamburlaine* and *Dido* as early work and to *Hero and Leander* as late, I have chosen to treat them in this order, with *The Jew of Malta* and *Doctor Faustus* thus naturally slotting into the middle. In each case, though, the major preoccupation of one 'phase' is foreshadowed in the previous phase or phases, where it is sounded as a minor note; and since Marlowe in moving on to a new concern never entirely loses sight of the old, such an approach will also, I hope, help me to illuminate the increasing richness and multidimensionality which accrues to his works throughout his career.

Whether Marlowe himself would have thought of the trajectory of his plays, poems and translations as constituting a literary career of any sort is a different matter. In an important recent book, Patrick Cheney has argued vigorously that he would have done, and that indeed he deliberately followed an Ovidian *cursus* in carefully planned contradistinction to the espousal of a Virgilian one by Spenser, from whom, Cheney insists, he differed both temperamentally and politically. For Cheney, 'Marlowe manages a complex, multigenre idea of a literary career, in direct professional rivalry with England's great national poet, in order to pen a poetics of counter-nation-hood'[78] (though Richard Rambuss suggests that 'Spenser's career goals are far more various and never strictly Virgilian').[79] Cheney's schema is not wholly convincing: it requires him to date the Lucan late, and though he is not entirely unique in so doing,[80] the consensus is against him. Nevertheless, his idea is a very suggestive one. Critics have often commented on the similarities and differences between Marlowe and Spenser,[81] against whom Marlowe does indeed seem to have an animus – it is, after all, a member of the

Despenser family, to which Spenser famously (and Marlowe may well have thought pretentiously) claimed to be related, who says in *Edward II* 'stab as occasion serves', which one might well read as a dig at the New Poet's doings in Ireland. One might even suggest that just as the books of Spenser's *Faerie Queene* are designed each to celebrate a different virtue, so the seven plays of Marlowe seem almost each to explore a different vice, with *Dido, Queen of Carthage*, in which Venus and Cupid preside over the action, focusing on lust; *Tamburlaine* 1, where all his opponents are so sure they can beat him, on pride; *Tamburlaine* 2 on sloth, of which Calyphas is an obvious emblem; *Doctor Faustus*, which is full, as will be seen later, of oral imagery, represting gluttony; *The Jew of Malta* on avarice; *Edward II* on envy (by the nobles, of Gaveston and then of Spencer); and *The Massacre at Paris* on wrath (the basic motivation of almost everyone in it). Of course this is overly schematic, but I find it nevertheless an interesting paradigm to contemplate, if only for the reason that it may alert us to the extent to which the interest and energies of Marlowe's plays are, contrary to popular belief, not always lodged entirely in the hero.

Cheney's other very interesting suggestion is that Marlowe not only had an idea of the literary but also advertised the fact, becoming 'the first playwright on the new European stage to *author* himself forcibly into his plays', something that Cheney sees as underlined by Marlowe's obsessive habit of self-quotation. I would strongly agree that Marlowe does, indeed, show a marked sense of literariness and writtenness. Thomas Healy argues that 'Faustus's evocation of the Trojan War exemplifies Marlowe's interest in characters who desire to take on roles from the past, even when they pose destructive consequences',[82] and many of Marlowe's characters seem radically configured by an exceptionally acute awareness of their previous literary incarnations. In this view, Marlowe not only led a literary life; he also constructed it out of the writing of literary lives. It is above all in this sense, rather than in seeking any simple one-to-one correspondences between the heroes and their author, that I want to trace the relationship of Marlowe's individual works to his overall literary life.

2
1580–1587: Canterbury and Cambridge

Christopher Marlowe, whose name was later to become virtually synonymous with atheism, was born, in the first of the many contradictions of his life, in the spiritual capital of England, and it is sometimes suggested that the visual splendour of Canterbury, and the history of the Cathedral's changing fortunes during the Reformation, are both inscribed in Marlowe's drama.[1] His fondness for stage spectacle, which might be seen as prompted by the rituals and splendour of the premier seat of the English Church, has been often remarked upon.[2] This is perhaps most particularly evident in *Doctor Faustus*[3] and in *Tamburlaine*, of which Muriel Bradbrook observes that

> [t]he first great poetic drama of the English stage is a pageant of iconoclasm and of iconoclastic ruthlessness. The shepherd conqueror who spurns kings' crowns from off their heads, and tramples emperors beneath his feet, recalls Foxe's picture of Henry VIII throned and making a footstool of the Pope; Marlowe's *Tragical discourses of Tamburlaine the Great* is a triumph of the secular, culminating in the burning of 'Mahomet's' sacred books by the blasphemer.

Certainly, the language of icons is strongly present in *Tamburlaine*: Bradbrook points out that 'the divine Zenocrate weeps, like Mary, tears of pearl' and that her coronation blasphemously parodies that of the Virgin. Thus, she says, 'Marlowe is a true son of the Henrican Reformation', which had of course operated with particular force in the spiritual capital of England.[4]

We know facts about Marlowe's childhood as the son of a Canterbury shoemaker and freeman – the births, names and ages of his sisters (one of whom, like her famous brother, was accused, after his death, of being a blasphemer),[5] the births and deaths of various brothers – but little of its flavour, though guesswork, as always with Marlowe, has not been wanting. Andrew Butcher, for instance, has recently speculated that a young boy called Christopher Mowle, who was said by one Elizabeth Dyer to have witnessed an assault on her, was the dramatist, even though the age Dyer gave for the child-witness would be wrong. The boy Mowle was specifically said by Dyer to have been living with John Roydon, the man she claimed to have assaulted her, rather than with his own parents, which would presumably point to some family difficulty – Butcher suggests that '[a]s recent immigrants to the city, Christopher Marlowe's mother and father faced extreme difficulties of social adaptation', and speculates on the effect that possibly witnessing the assault might have had on the boy.[6] The discrepancies in name and age, however, mean that the identification must remain highly uncertain.

Others have been quick to suggest that family life in the Marlowe household was unhappy. Constance Brown Kuriyama argues that '[h]is plays suggest...that Marlowe perceived his shoemaker father as aggressive yet weak, dominated by a wife of stronger character',[7] and William Urry pointed to the litigiousness and financial irregularities of Marlowe's father John,[8] though Andrew Butcher suggests that 'there may recently have been too great an insistence on John Marlowe's modesty of means, lack of business competence and social marginality', and that the family's frequent moves may have signalled upward mobility rather than impecuniousness.[9] Nevertheless, we have no evidence of family difficulties, and the intermittent evidence that survives from law-suits and accounts of will-reading shows that far from leaving for London for ever, as was once thought, Marlowe continued to visit Canterbury until shortly before his death, and was thus presumably in contact with his family.

It is, however, true that all his plays are littered with family groups shattered and destroyed, either through their own actions or those of others.[10] Sometimes the disharmony is limited to family disagreements or ideological disunity within the family group; at other points it becomes more extreme, leading to internecine betrayal and even murder. As Frank Ardolino suggests, 'the composite roles family members play as both fathers and sons, mothers and daughters, husbands and wives, brothers and sisters provide Marlowe with rich sources of complex interactions and the opportunity to portray the tensions created by the shifting roles, to limn, in short, the dynamics of power as established within the microcosm of the family'.[11] One might well feel, however, that Marlowe does more than simply 'limn' these: he seems not only to portray families, but also to provide a sharply focused and detailed critique of the problematics of familial interaction. Moreover, contrary to modern, psychoanalytically-driven theorising of the family, he sees these as arising fundamentally not from inherent inter-generational struggle, nor from the kinds of mythic model proposed by Ardolino – who sees the plays as radically informed by the Uranus–Jupiter–Saturn model – but as an aberration caused by particular aspects of social injustice and malaise.

In what seems likely to have been his earliest play, *Dido, Queen of Carthage*, the issue of family features very strongly. Margo Hendricks points out that 'even before he begins his dramatization of the "tragedy" of Dido, Marlowe chose to rehearse the lineage of Aeneas',[12] and he also stresses upbringing by inventing the character of Dido's nurse, living emblem of the forces which have conditioned her. The play opens, with characteristic Marlovian double-edgedness and with a striking departure from his Virgilian source, on what looks like a traditional scene of family life: a man with a boy on his lap. We rapidly discover, though, that this is not a scene of a father and a son, but an older man (albeit a god) and the boy whom he uses for his pleasure. Moreover, Jupiter promises to subordinate the interests of his real family to those of his lover Ganymede: he gives the boy the jewels which his wife Juno wore on her wedding day, and plucks a feather from the wing of his son Hermes.[13] The family conflict presaged here is actualised when Jupiter's daughter, Venus, enters – not in her traditional role as goddess of love, but, very pointedly, in her capacity as a mother, and, by implication, in the even less likely role, for a sex symbol, as grandmother. (This point is stressed again later in the characters' repeated references to the kinship ties between herself, Aeneas, Ascanius and her other son, Cupid.) Jupiter's infatuation with Ganymede, she claims, has had repercussions throughout the family, in that it has prevented him from paying proper attention to the welfare of her son Aeneas. Thus an initial lack of proper conjugal relations between husband and wife has apparently escalated into a situation which also affects both Jupiter's daughter and his grandson, and which will have serious implications too for his great-grandson Aeneas. We may, after all, remember, as David Farley-Hills reminds us in relation to *Tamburlaine*, that Jupiter usurped and killed his own father.[14]

The speech which Jupiter then makes to Venus assures her that she is wrong, and that he still has Aeneas' interests at heart:

> Content thee, Cytherea, in thy care,
> Since thy Aeneas' wand'ring fate is firm,
> Whose weary limbs shall shortly make repose
> In those fair walls I promised him of yore.
>
> (I.i.82–5)

In fact, however, the play itself proves Venus to be very accurate in her diagnosis of strains within the family. She has less insight into the cause, though, for she is herself complicit in it. When she visits the son for whom she has professed so much affection, she appears in disguise to him; only after she has left does he detect her identity, and he then proceeds to lament the lack of a closer relationship between them. Here we seem to be invited to discern that Jupiter's own poor parenting skills have, in one of the classic patterns of child abuse, been transmitted in turn to his daughter, who fails to mother her son as he would wish.[15] This is made very clear in Aeneas' moving comments as he realises the identity of the disguised figure with whom he has been talking:

> Achates, 'tis my mother that is fled:
> I know her by the movings of her feet.
> Stay, gentle Venus, fly not from thy son!
> Too cruel, why wilt thou forsake me thus?
> Or in these shades deceiv'st mine eye so oft?
> Why talk we not together hand in hand,
> And tell our griefs in more familiar terms?
> But thou art gone and leav'st me here alone,
> To dull the air with my discoursive moan.
>
> (I.i.240–8)

Here the familiar relationship between Aeneas and his mother, indicated in the fact that he can recognise her from so minor a detail as 'the movings of her feet', forms a sad counterbalance to her unexplained unwillingness voluntarily to reveal her identity to him – apparently, from his use of the term 'so oft', a regular feature of her behaviour to him.

Despite – or perhaps because of – Aeneas' sensitivity to his mother's lack of trust in him, he too is revealed as a poor parent. Ascanius early shows a strong sense of kinship: when Aeneas imagines that a rock he sees is Priam, Ascanius assures him that it cannot be, 'For, were it Priam, he would smile on me' (II.i.36). Perhaps it is this sense of a lost family – Aeneas has, after all, literally mislaid his wife, Creusa – which makes the child at once accost Dido with 'Madam, you shall be my mother' (II.i.96). (Richard Proudfoot points out that 'Marlowe's Dido, unlike Chaucer's, doesn't count pregnancy among her claims on Aeneas';[16] instead she is presented throughout the play as poignantly childless, anxious to mother.) Dido too has had a troubled family background: not only is she a widow, but in Virgil's original telling of her story, which Marlowe for the most part follows closely, her husband died at the hands of her brother, and she has also lost her father. Finally, like Jupiter and Venus before him, Aeneas in turn proves so indifferent to the fate of his offspring that he actually proposes at one point to leave Ascanius behind with Dido – his protestation that he couldn't have been about to depart because he would have had to leave his son behind is savagely undercut by the audience's awareness that that was in fact precisely what he was planning. Even Aeneas' denial is couched in worrying terms: 'Hath not the Carthage Queen mine only son?' (IV.iv.29) suggests that Ascanius' importance to his father may be at least as much dynastic as personal – as the only son of a widower, he forms a unique and temporarily irreplaceable link in the chain of succession; the implication, however, is that had he brothers, he might prove expendable, as Tamburlaine's son Calyphas is later to be. The inclusion of four generations in *Dido* allows us to see very clearly how the cycle of bad parent–child relationships renews and perpetuates itself.

Even when fewer generations are considered, however, the pattern is still discernible. *Tamburlaine* Part One both opens and closes with families (indeed Marlowe invented a relationship between Zenocrate and the Sultan to stress the extent to which it does so), and Lawrence Danson points out that family differences lie at the heart of the play in ways which offer an implicit critique of the hero:

> Tamburlaine takes a somewhat sordid family quarrel – the picture of Jove throwing his 'heavenly' father out of his chair is neither heroic nor pretty – as the model for his project of world conquest. The ironic iteration of the words 'heaven' and 'heavenly' would make it especially difficult for an alert member of the audience not to compare this example of filial revolt with the Christstory of love, obedience, and reconciliation.[17]

The reference to the mythological story of Ops's rebellion against his father (*I*, II.vii.13–14) is supplemented by Tamburlaine's information that the Scythians adore the statues of Pylades and Orestes (*I*, I.ii.242–3), who collaborated to kill Orestes' mother Clytemnestra; and the story of the House of Atreus, with its numerous internecine killings, is again invoked by the fact that Mycetes' 'Brother Cosroe, I find myself aggrieved' (*I*, I.i.1) seems to echo the words of Menalaus in John Pikeryng's *Horestes*, 'I finde my self agrevid to be, / That on such sort my systers slayne as all your gracis se'.[18] (Mycetes is so disillusioned with brotherhood that he interestingly images the soldiers sown from the dragon's teeth as 'the cruel brothers of the earth' [*I*, II.ii.47].) And a third ominous mythological reference comes from Zabina: 'may this banquet prove as ominous / As Procne's to th'adulterous Thracian King / That fed upon the substance of his child!' (*I*, IV.iv.25–6). Moreover, to be a Scythian was in some sense always already to be without family, to be rootless.[19]

At the level of plot, as well as that of allusion, families are also fissured and troubled.[20] The sharp differences between Cosroe and Mycetes open up questions of heredity, family resemblances and the nature/nurture debate, which is of course raised again in even more radical form by the victories won over kings by the mere son of a Scythian shepherd; and the end of the play sees both a marriage – providing an unusually comic form of closure to so violent a story – and also the reunion between Zenocrate and her father (though our sense of a comic conclusion may be somewhat lessened by the fact that Zenocrate must almost certainly have had to double up as one of the Virgins of Damascus,[21] so that we will just have seen the same boy actor killed as well as married). Family is thus signalled as an issue of some importance, and it becomes even more so in Part Two, where we observe closely Tamburlaine's three boys. We see the rivalry between them, brought about primarily by the very fact that they, unlike Ascanius, are members of a family instead of isolated heirs; we witness the effect on them of their mother's early death – indeed Calyphas' effeminacy, although clearly present from the beginning, could be interpreted as perhaps becoming exacerbated by a subconscious attempt to take over the role within the family of a lost mother;[22] and, as with Cosroe and Mycetes in Part One, we see also the radical differences amongst brothers which result eventually in the ultimate example of family fragmentation, Tamburlaine's infanticide.

Tamburlaine's killing of Calyphas is difficult to decode. It has often been seen as in some sense exemplary, in the light of Renaissance educational theory.[23] T.M. Pearce argues that it is indeed precisely a response to such theory:

> Here is portrayed a father who is at once a man of arms and a lover of poetry and worshipper of beauty, now faced with the problem of bringing up boys, his sons. The entire passage might have been written by Marlowe after reading Sir Thomas Elyot's *Boke Named the Governour* (1531), which appeared some fifty years earlier.[24]

Pearce sees in Marlowe's portrayal of Tamburlaine's immovability a response to twin stimuli: the attack by Gosson (like Marlowe, a former pupil of the King's School, Canterbury) on a lack of proper moral fibre in the theatre, and the attack by Sir Humphrey Gilbert on modern educational methods and their failure to prepare for military service. Tamburlaine, Pearce suggests, embodies the very virtues which both Gosson and Gilbert were, in their different ways, advocating, and in nothing is this more apparent than his stoic sacrifice of his own son. Paul Kocher similarly sees in Tamburlaine's stabbing 'an act of military discipline ... from the Elizabethan point of view Tamburlaine is merely heroic in this',[25] and suggests, moreover, that Tamburlaine's action is also rendered glorious by its association with the story of the Roman consul Manlius Torquatius, who similarly slew his son for disobeying orders. But such readings are, as Carolyn Williams recognises, counterintuitive; and, more importantly, they are notably not shared by the on-stage audience of dignitaries.

Infanticide also occurs elsewhere in the play, in Olympia's very differently motivated decision to kill her son, and crops up again in two more of the plays, *The Massacre at Paris* – where it is threatened rather than actual, since Catherine never needs to carry out her resolve to kill one or both of her sons – and *The Jew of Malta*. Here Barabas' initial affection for the daughter whose name means, ironically, 'the father's joy' is violently transmuted by her conversion to Christianity – her adoption, it could perhaps be argued, of a different father-figure – into a murderous hate whose momentum not only wipes out Abigail and her entire convent of nuns, but is also echoed in the kind of mock infanticide in which Barabas kills Ithamore, who, he so often stresses, has assumed the position of his heir. Family fragmentation is, of course, further emphasised in the play by the recurring presence of the two bereaved parents, Ferneze and Katherine, both of whom are apparently partnerless as well as childless. Moreover, Jeremy Tambling points to further elements in the play of fury directed at literal and symbolic members of its families when he comments on Barabas' stress on the nuns' frequent pregnancies, his identification of Abigail with the original exemplar of sibling rivalry, Cain, and the ways in which his celebrated image of 'infinite riches in a little room' (I.i.37), 'parodying the idea of Christ in the womb, suggest[s] a pre-Oedipal desire for identification with the mother'.[26]

In others of the plays matters never reach the pitch of family self-destruction seen in *The Jew of Malta* and *Tamburlaine*; but very often this is because in them, families are never formed in the first place. It is notable that one of the few things Mephostophilis denies Faustus is a wife: thus the scholar, whom we assume to have long since drifted apart from the 'base stock' from which he was sprung, is afforded no opportunity to recreate a family unit, something for which he perhaps compensates in his marked affection for his friends and even for Wagner, and, arguably, in his desire to please the pregnant Duchess of Vanholt. For William Blackburn, Faustus' incorrect citation of the laws of inheritance 'conceals the man's wilful ignorance of his own relationship with God the Father... Faustus is the son who disinherits himself',[27] while John P. Cutts suggests that Faustus is 'compensating for the father he never knew, allowing big brother Mephostophilis to keep giving him gifts and rewards to make up for childhood deprivation and for his low class estate'.[28]

Indeed, Michael Keefer sees Faustus' project as being 'a self-begotten rebirth into divine form' which ultimately leads him to 'an abject attempt to surrender his bodily integrity in a disgusting reversal of birth ... The bargain proposed – of resorption into a dismembering womb, and of regurgitation and dispersal, in exchange for the salvation of his soul – is the most violent expression of despair in the play'.[29] And Judith Weil comments on the appropriateness of the B-text's 'oeconomy', which, even if a misreading of *on kai me on*, may well be seen as registering a sensitive response to some of the dominant concerns of the play.[30]

Despite these desperate attempts at incorporation, Marlowe pointedly withholds from his hero personal participation in a family unit, even though the Faustus of his sources married Helen and fathered a son by her. In a brilliant analysis of the play, Kay Stockholder demonstrates Faustus' unease with his own sexuality and the ways in which his approaches to heterosexuality are thwarted by powerful patriarchal figures which, together with the presence of the strongly developed cuckoldry theme she shows to be present in the play, indicates to a psychoanalytically-oriented reader a deeply unresolved Oedipus complex.[31] And ironically, in another demonstration of the impossibility for him of attaining to a family life, the woman he is offered instead of a wife is Helen – the legendary marriage-breaker of mythology, the woman who abandoned her husband Menelaus and her daughter Hermione for the seducer, Paris.

Family even becomes an issue in the pageant of the Seven Deadly Sins. Pride 'disdain[s] to have any parents' (II.iii.116), Wrath 'had neither father nor mother' (II.iii.130), Gluttony's 'parents are all dead' (II.iii.145–6), while all the rest cite ill-matched couplings as their source of origin. Once again it is possible to discern a suggestion that fractured or non-existent family structures lie behind the darkest events of the play. Similarly in *Dido, Queen of Carthage* there is a strong sense of the fact that in coming together these two, widow and widower respectively, would be able to restore the family structure that each has lost – something that seems strongly signalled in Dido's desire effectively to reconstitute her former marriage by rechristening Aeneas Sichaeus, and by her enthusiastic response to Ascanius' request that she should function as a replacement mother for him. It is one of the most savage ironies of the play that it is family strife amongst the gods, specifically between Juno and Venus, which prevents this dream of a new family from reaching fulfilment, just as it has previously devastated the family of Priam and Hecuba.

Family breakdown is, then, repeatedly stressed as a recurring motif in Marlowe's plays, and its impact is heightened by the use of vignettes of happy families which provide both contrast and pathos. Obvious examples are Zabina and Bajazeth in *Tamburlaine Part One*, whose mutual affection, undiminished by the brutal circumstances of their captivity, could be seen as strongly reminiscent of the marriage of affection and mutual support proposed by Protestant ideology, and Olympia and her family in *Tamburlaine Part Two*, where again conjugal and filial devotion triumphantly survives external disasters. It is also noteworthy that Marlowe has rearranged chronology in *The Massacre at Paris* by deferring the death of Jeanne of Navarre until after her son's wedding, which allows us a tragically brief glimpse of the happy life she could apparently have led with her son and her new daughter-in-law (who is presented as markedly affectionate and deferential to her mother-in-law). And in his other late play, *Edward II*, Marlowe not only represents such patterns but also moves on to offer a sustained and sophisticated analysis of their underlying causes.

In *Dido, Queen of Carthage* it might be possible to argue that it is Jupiter's homosexual attachment to Ganymede which is seen as the initial spark for family disunity[32] (though in fact this idea is largely exploded by Jupiter's account of strife between him and Juno reaching much farther back, as when she harmed Heracles, and by the unpleasant insight into her character we are offered during her meeting with Venus). In *Edward II*, however, the question of whether or not homosexuality gives rise to family disruption is addressed head on, and answered with a resounding negative: in Stephen Orgel's formulation, '[b]oth politically and morally, the power-hungry nobles and the queen's adultery with Mortimer are as destabilising as anything in Edward's relationship with his favorite'.[33] The issue is highlighted from the very first lines of the play: '"My father is deceased; come, Gaveston, / And share the kingdom with thy dearest friend"' (I.i.1–2). Here we could, perhaps, see a suggestion that individual happiness can be enabled only by a breakdown of family structure, at least for Edward and for Gaveston; and undoubtedly Edward's preference for Gaveston has soured relations between himself and Isabella. Homosexuality seems, however, to have been seen in the Renaissance period not as an exclusive alternative to heterosexuality, but rather as on a sort of continuum with it, so that the breakdown of the marriage need not necessarily have been attributable solely to Edward's sexual preferences,[34] and as Claude J. Summers points out, 'while the word "unnatural" occurs frequently in the play to describe rebellion and anarchy and dissembling, it is never applied as a sufficient definition of homosexuality'.[35] Certainly Gaveston's undoubted homosexuality very markedly fails to have any deleterious effect on his marriage to Edward's niece;[36] and family ties other than the marriage bond are shown in the play to be totally unaffected by homosexuality. There is strong affection between Spenser and his father, between Edward and his brother, and, most notably of all, between Edward and his son. There is no trace, in the conduct of the homosexual king, of the poor parenting which characterised that supreme example of heterosexuality, the Queen of Love, let alone of the infanticidal rage of a Tamburlaine or a Barabas. If we judge by the devotion to him evinced by his son, Edward II is the best parent in the plays.

If it is not extra-familial erotic desires that undermine the stability of the family, then, what does? Perhaps part of the answer may lie in Marlowe's depiction of power relationships within the affected families; as Dympna Callaghan suggests of *Edward II*, 'sexuality is always overtly bound up with dominant institutions and practices of power'.[37] The children who suffer most badly in these plays are all royal children, or, what I take to be effectively analogous, the children of gods. Venus, Hermes, Aeneas, and Ascanius, in *Dido, Queen of Carthage*, are all divine or of divine ancestry; the son of the Guise in *The Massacre at Paris*, forced to view his father's murdered body, is the child of perhaps the foremost political figure in the country. Tamburlaine's troubled brood have as father 'the scourge of God', conqueror of half the world, and Jill Levenson points to the way in which the concept of Tamburlaine's kingship is insistently reinforced by the play's language.[38] The young Edward III is son and nephew not only of a king, but also, and perhaps even more importantly, of a queen, a power-broker between nations and in the internal political affairs of England, who shares in the responsibility for the brutal murder of his father. Even Abigail comes to grief only when her father has acquired so much wealth and power that he will soon be able to put himself forward as a serious candidate for the governorship of Malta: before his development of such ambitions, their relationship seems solid enough.[39]

As Simon Shepherd points out, the parenting of royal offspring was felt to be an especially difficult issue.[40] In cases like these the usual disadvantages of patriarchy – the discrepancy between the prospects of the eldest son and those of the other children – are significantly increased: for the eldest boy a crown, for the others the unenviable position of needing to be kept alive as possible successors, but equally of representing an ever-present threat, as is illustrated in the situations of Henry III and Henry IV in *The Massacre at Paris*, and in the strife between Cosroe and Mycetes in *Tamburlaine Part One*. (This question of the situation of potential heirs to thrones could, of course, have been an issue particularly highlighted for Marlowe himself and for his audiences by Elizabeth I's refusal to name her successor and by the consequent intrigues surrounding the various possible claimants such as the Grey sisters, Arabella Stuart and James VI of Scotland.) For the daughters, moreover, there was the unappetising prospect of being married off to seal a diplomatic treaty: this was the fate that awaited Zenocrate before her capture by Tamburlaine, and we are reminded of the fact when, towards the end of Part One, we briefly meet her first fiancé.

The usual fate of princesses is also figured in *The Massacre at Paris* in the person of Marguerite of Valois, who is treated with surprising sympathy – the racier aspects of her rather scandalous history, which included taking several lovers who reputedly included the Duke of Guise, are suppressed, and she is turned into the model daughter-in-law – and perhaps also in that of the Duchess of Guise, trapped in a loveless marriage which she owed to her high birth and her relationship to the royal family of France, who is seen as inextricably enmeshed in the structures of the family which simultaneously enable her and cripple her. She is saved from death at the hands of her jealous husband through the fact of her pregnancy, thus keeping the family unit (however unhappily) together. But she is also, like Venus in *Dido, Queen of Carthage*, complicit in the replication of her own unhappy situation by producing children born into an atmosphere of violence, suspicion and bloodshed, as we see only too clearly when her young son is forced to look at his murdered father's body. In her case, then, mothering, which would be seen by contemporary and indeed present-day audiences as the fulfilment of the most natural of all possible instincts, is also, from another per-spective, blameworthy and inevitably disastrous. (The potential consequences of family bonds are made further apparent within the Guise clan when, having murdered the Duke himself, the assassins make sure of his brother the Cardinal, whose only apparent crime lies in the fact of the relationship, while the Duke himself has, iron-ically, earlier stabbed a preacher called Loreine while addressing him as 'Dearly beloved brother' [Scene Seven, 5].)

It seems, then, that it is primarily the question of power, and per-haps more specifically of patriarchal power, that is involved in the production of unhappy marriages and fractured families. The more unequal the distribution of power within the family grouping, and the greater the concentration of it within the hands of the patriarch, the greater the risks of family break-up and disharmony. In this con-text it is perhaps significant that although Edward II is a king, and thus in theory a wielder of near-absolute power, it is in fact made very clear to us from an early stage in the play that his power is so seriously qualified by the disaffection of his barons that it amounts to virtually nothing. Whereas his brother-in-law of France, more secure on his throne, turns his back on the request for help which he receives from his sister and nephew, Edward never forgets his affection for his son and ultimately resigns his crown – and with it, inevitably, his life – in order to ensure the boy's succession to a throne which might otherwise have been bid for by Mortimer. It is equally noteworthy that the Earl of Kent forsakes his brother when he sees a chance for his own political star to gain the ascendant, but returns to a blind and indeed ultimately stupid loyalty to him when he loses his influence with Mortimer and Isabella. Isabella herself may also be an example of this phenomenon. Historically, her father, Philippe IV, stood apart as the one strong French king in a period of generally weak rule, and it may well be that we should see her career of decimating her family – she is directly or indirectly responsible for the deaths of her husband, his brother and her niece's husband – as a product of his upbringing as much as of her husband's neglect. In these plays, it seems, the principal threat to the institution of the family is, paradoxically, the patriarchal power structure itself; and what Marlowe is showing us, in his analysis of the politics of family, is the inherent self-annihilation which fissures patriarchal ideology. It is, therefore, difficult to tell whether these obsessively repetitive portrayals of families relate to Marlowe's own life or to a political agenda which tilts at the places in which power is currently concentrated; I suspect the latter.

Our uncertainty about the young Marlowe's family life is matched and indeed surpassed by an even greater ignorance about his early education, of which we know nothing. It seems, however, fair to deduce that he must, somehow, have been in a position to demonstrate his promise, because he was fortunate enough to be offered a scholarship at the King's School, Canterbury, something that did not occur until very shortly before he would have been beyond the upper age limit. Once there, he would have been well grounded in classical culture, would have mixed with the sons of those considerably wealthier than he, and would have had early exposure to the theatre;[41] he may perhaps have acted, and later, at Cambridge, he would certainly have had the opportunity to see plays performed. Whether at the King's School or before, he seems to have acquired a genuine love of learning, describing himself in later life not as a playwright but as a scholar, and he must also have been bookish and proud of it: in *Hero and Leander*, we are told that 'Learning, in despite of Fate, / Will mount aloft, and enter heaven gate, / And to the seat of Jove itself advance' – even though, we are told, it will be inevitably attended by poverty: 'to this day is every scholar poor' (Sestiad I, ll.465–7 and 471).

From the King's School, he moved in 1580 to Corpus Christi College, Cambridge, where he would spend half the remaining years of his life. He went there on a scholarship founded by Archbishop Matthew Parker, which meant that he must have been personally selected by the Archbishop's son John, and also that he must have declared an intention to study for holy orders – whether because he actually meant to do so or merely in order to secure a free education, there is no way of knowing, though critics have not been slow to comment on the apparent relevance of his behaviour to the hypocrisy of so many of his characters. At Cambridge, both his bookishness and his familiarity with the classics can only have been confirmed, and he must also have been introduced to other areas of study, many of which are reflected in his plays. Caroline Spurgeon contrasted him strongly with the nature-loving Shakespeare:

> with Marlowe, images drawn from books, especially the classics, and from the sun, moon, planets and heavens far outnumber all

others ... Indeed this imaginative preoccupation with the dazzling heights and vast spaces of the universe is, together with a magnificent surging upward thrust and aspiration, the dominating note of Marlowe's mind. He seems more familiar with the starry courts of heaven than with the green fields of earth, and he loves rather to watch the movements of meteors and planets than to study the faces of men.[42]

All these interests Cambridge was well fitted to nourish.

Marlowe's primary area of study was theology and, as Nina Taunton points out, 'critics rarely fail to make the obvious connection between Marlowe's scholarly habits of mind and the scholastic curriculum at Cambridge in their discussions of *Doctor Faustus* ... the study of postgraduate theology ... was after all the major area of study at this level, and Marlowe spent four years steeped in its debates.' Taunton sees other aspects of the curriculum as equally influential, arguing that '[a] training in Aristotelian logic and rhetoric typically conditioned the framework of Marlowe's plays' and that 'the struggle for Faustus' soul unfolds within the structure of scholastic debate', while the 'defense of Ramus in the core scene of *The Massacre at Paris* illustrates the French logician's contribution to the training of the mind by combining logic with rhetoric in order to make disputation the more effective in the art of practical thinking'.[43] It was not only Marlowe's study of theology that stocked his mind, however. As Irving Ribner noted in 1964, 'Marlowe's relation to the classical studies of his Cambridge years needs to be explored as fully as Cole has explored his relation to the theological, if we are to have any truly balanced perspective'.[44] Geography too would have been part of his curriculum,[45] and he seems to have acquired some knowledge of anatomy and physiology – Carroll Camden remarks that '[h]is psychology is founded upon a firm physiological basis, and he is the first dramatist to show an interest in and a knowledge of the construction of the human body'.[46]

Marlowe, however, was, like so many undergraduates before and since, doing far more at Cambridge than simply studying. He may well already have been at work on one or both of *Dido* and the first part of *Tamburlaine*, as well as on his translations of Lucan and Ovid; interestingly, Roma Gill points to various egregious errors in the translation of the *Elegies* that do not speak well for the degree of his attention to his official studies.[47] Indeed Irving Ribner suggests that *Tamburlaine* springs naturally from this time, for it

> coincided with a turning away from the theological studies to which his Parker Foundation scholarship committed him ... *Tamburlaine* stands in opposition to every religious principle which Anglicans like Matthew Parker revered. Marlowe's turning away from theology must bear some relation to an absorption with classical poetry which he seems to have developed at Cambridge.

In particular, he suggests, *Tamburlaine* exemplifies the 'historical method' and secular perspective of Polybius.[48] And as well as writing, Marlowe was also, it seems, spying.

In 1587, Marlowe's time at Cambridge came to an apparently abrupt and unusual end. Because a considerable amount of documentation has survived, in the shape of the minutes summarising the Privy Council's letter to the University and the Corpus Bursar's books, this has been one of the most copiously discussed episodes of Marlowe's entire career, though several aspects of its precise significances still remain opaque. After his early years at Cambridge, the college records begin to show signs of very considerable absences, far beyond what he would officially have been allowed, and there is no record of his being in residence at Corpus at all after February 1587.[49] Nothing is known of his whereabouts and activities during that period until the Privy Council letter of 29 June 1587, which was minuted in the Council records as being to the following effect:

> Whereas *it was reported that Christopher Morley was determined to have gone beyond the seas to Reames and there to remaine*; their Lordships thought good to certefie that *he had no such intent*, but that in all his accions *he had behaved him selfe orderlie and discreetlie*, wherebie *he had done her Majestie good service* and deserved to be rewarded for his faithfull dealinge: their Lordships request was that *the rumor thereof should be allaied by all possible meanes*, and that he should be furthered in the degree he was to take this next Commencement: Because it was not her Majesties pleasure that *anie one emploid as he had been in matters touching the benefitt of his Countrie* should be *defamed by those that are ignorant in th'affaires he went about.*

The timing of this docment and of Marlowe's absence from the college led Leslie Hotson to conclude that 'the period during which

Marlowe was employed as a government agent lies probably between February and July of 1587', and Austin K. Gray, recording this, further speculates that '[i]nasmuch as his name is never entered on the Bursar's books after February, 1587, we may take it that Marlowe never returned to residence at Corpus after that month'. Gray also spells out the implications of the document and of the evidence from the Bursar's books:

> By leaving Cambridge (apparently suddenly and without permission) in February and remaining away for several months, Marlowe had broken the terms whereby he held his scholarship at Corpus... He was bound by these conditions until Mar. 25th, 1587. Even before 1587, he had been frequently absent from Cambridge after taking his B.A. in 1584, and probably had nowhere near completed nine terms, residence, and had, *ipso facto*, disqualified himself from 'proceeding M.A.,' as he would ordinarily have done in the forthcoming July. In other words, Corpus Christ College refused to present his *supplicat* for an M.A. on the ground of absence without leave. The Privy Council Document somewhat arbitrarily over-rides this objection.

Further evidence that Marlowe's position was seriously irregular comes from the fact that, as Gray points out, 'his scholarship was kept open during his absence for him to complete his terms, and no appointment was made in his place until Nov. 1587. When that appointment was made, his name, as former holder of the scholarship, was ominously omitted.'[50]

The letter from the Privy Council refers in detail to what Marlowe had *allegedly* been doing, but it is not, unfortunately, very specific about what he had *actually* been doing. Gray comments that '[o]n the question whether Marlowe had actually been in Rheims, its language is (I think, studiously) ambiguous', though anyone familiar with Elizabethan documents might well think that it is not so much studiousness as an entirely characteristic casualness which is at work here. Gray is, however, confident that *if* Marlowe had been in Rheims, 'he can only have gone there as a spy on the Seminarists. On no other grounds could he receive an endorsement from Archbishop Whitgift and the Privy Council for a sojourn in that city.' Gray also argues that the intelligence work with which

Marlowe was involved is unlikely to have been, as is often supposed, for Sir Francis Walsingham, even though he was related to Marlowe's friend Thomas Walsingham and was the most usual employer of spies, because Walsingham was not one of the signatories of the Privy Council document, and four of those who were 'were pursuing a policy abroad which ran counter to Walsingham's'. This focused on attempts to negotiate with the Prince of Parma, and Gray, implicitly arguing for or assuming an early date for *Faustus*, suggests that '[a] visit to Antwerp may explain how Marlowe came across the Faust legend so soon after the publication of the *Volksbuch* by Spiess in 1587', and points to the distinctively Dutch context of the play.[51]

We cannot, in the end, know what Marlowe was doing or where he had been during this period, but it seems reasonable to suppose that it did indeed involve espionage. Nor was this the only occasion in his life when he seems to have been involved with what we would now term the 'secret services'; the failure to punish him after his 1592 arrest for coining at Flushing has suggested to many that he was working for the government then too. Charles Nicholl thinks he may have been en route for Brussels, in connection with the traitor Sir William Stanley;[52] and John Michael Archer has recently suggested that he may have been sent as a messenger for Burghley to Utrecht in October 1587 and to France for part of 1591–2.[53] Most notably, of course, his sudden death has often been linked to his government work, and if that is indeed the case, then we would need to think of him as being involved with 'intelligencing', as it would then have been called, throughout his playwriting years.

For a young man interested in geography, travelling under the government aegis probably represented one of the few ways that one *could* travel in the sixteenth century, and would also have provided a welcome supplement to an income which seems otherwise to have been entirely dependent on what he earned from his plays. The reasons for Marlowe's involvement may have been as simple as these, and it is even possible that in the climate of paranoia surrounding the execution in 1587 of Mary, Queen of Scots and the run-up to the 1588 Armada, when spending on 'intelligencing' was running at record levels, getting drawn in was merely taking the path of least resistance. Equally, however, the attraction may have run deeper than this. Marlowe, like many other clever young men at Cambridge after him (particularly, perhaps, homosexual ones, without strong family ties) may have been drawn to the excitement and danger of espionage, the more especially since his record of involvement in street fights and court cases, let alone what we might glean from his plays, suggests that he was by no means averse to violence. At all events, this background of pretence and disguise, of lying and danger, and of ambiguous and perhaps split loyalties provides a suggestive counterpoint to the world of his plays, and it may well be no accident that both his writing and his spying careers seem to have their origins at the same time and in the same place.

3
1587–1589: London and the World

The belief that Marlowe himself is to be found in his heroes is perhaps most prevalent when it comes to the *Tamburlaine* plays, and it is certainly often assumed that Marlowe's attitude towards Tamburlaine was one of uncritical admiration, reflecting his own ambitiousness, which, it is argued, finds expression in his predilection, seen in these plays in particular, for verbs of ascent and for huge numbers (the latter produced from his own head rather than his sources). Irving Ribner, for instance, suggests that

> Marlowe is noteworthy in his age for a peculiar doctrine of kingship ... Tudor political theorists generally held that a king was responsible only to God, but that God would inevitably destroy the king who did not rule for the good of his people and in accord with the natural law of justice. Marlowe's king, however, is completely absolute.

For Ribner, *Tamburlaine* was written to endorse this theory, and glorify its hero;[1] for a critic like Constance Brown Kuriyama, it represents the ultimate wish-fulfilment of the homosexual boy's resentment of his father.[2] For both, Tamburlaine is thus a fantasy-projection of an idealised self.

Not everyone, however, agrees that Marlowe's attitude to his hero is one of simple, or even complex, identification. Michael Hattaway finds a note of comic detachment, rather than one of identification, to be pervasive in Marlovian drama,[3] while Clifford Leech, arguing along similar lines, calls Marlowe 'a man ... who could in his writings make fun of his own propensities'.[4] Lawrence Danson contends that we mistake the situation 'if we assume that the Scythian shepherd is really only the Cantabrigian Marlowe in fancy-dress',[5] and Marjorie Garber suggests that we can see 'a contest between Tamburlaine and Marlowe suggestively similar to those that may be discerned in other plays between Marlowe and Faustus, or Marlowe and Mortimer'.[6] Other critics go even further in seeing a Marlowe genuinely and radically critical of his hero. Roy Battenhouse famously argued at length that a thoroughly orthodox Marlowe condemned all his characters, including and indeed perhaps especially Tamburlaine,[7] and Constance Brown Kuriyama points out that the figure of Calyphas in particular can be seen as offering a powerful critique of Tamburlaine, 'by introducing an antihero who is employed both as an object of ridicule and as a device to ridicule the hero'.[8] Peter Berek, in his survey of imitations of the *Tamburlaine*-effect, reveals his 'private belief, which I will not try to argue in this essay, ... that Marlowe was irretrievably ambivalent about his hero's defiant self-creation: the play is flawed by its brilliant author's own confusions.' He also points out that some at least of the imitations avoid any such ambivalence, and suggests that may mean that the original audiences, while enjoying the spectacle offered by *Tamburlaine*, did not relish the ideological challenge it posed. Indeed, Berek suggests that Marlowe himself may have learned this lesson, allowing Tamburlaine to be judged critically in *Part Two* as he had not done in *Part One*.[9]

So does Marlowe criticise or endorse his hero, and does he indeed display different attitudes in the two different parts? One area of the play as a whole which has been found particularly ambiguous by many recent critics is the question of gender representation. Tamburlaine may initially appear to be the epitome of manliness; but he himself worries about whether his devotion to Zenocrate impairs his manhood, and his marked anxiety about the behaviour of his three sons might perhaps reflect concerns about his own virility. Scythia was, after all, the original haunt of the Amazons,[10] and John Cutts points to various suggestions in the text which work to feminise Tamburlaine: he is compared to Achilles, his arms, in the original 1590 and 1592 octavos, are not 'sinewy' but 'snowy', and, Cutts suggests, '[t]o put Mycetes and Tamburlaine together and alone *off* the battlefield invites scrutiny',[11] especially given Constance Brown Kuriyama's argument that 'Mycetes is discernibly enamored of Meander'.[12] Ann Rosalind Jones and Peter Stallybrass have recently pointed to the classical tradition of regarding Scythians as effeminate and prone to impotence and possibly pederasty; Herodotus recounted how they succumbed to '"the Scythian disease," defined as "the atrophy of the male organs of generation, accompanied by the loss of masculine attributes"'.[13] Perhaps historicising the Renaissance concept of the Scythian may allow us to see a more complex play than the simple wish-fulfilment which earlier generations of critics have found.

Even if the stature of Tamburlaine himself should perhaps be seen as impaired, however, that of *Tamburlaine* – its scale, its sweep, its impressiveness – is unimpeachable, as are its theatrical vigour and inventiveness. In most of the plays which draw on *Tamburlaine*, Berek identifies stage spectacle and exoticism as particular foci of imitation. *Tamburlaine* is clearly intensely interested in the visual, both in terms of display and of emblematic force. Tamburlaine himself is never happier than when he is orchestrating a dramatic self-staging, like his transformation from shepherd to warrior, or a richly emblematic spectacle like the banquet of crowns, and he regards even the pitiful remains of Bajazeth and Zabina as 'sights of power to grace my victory' (*I*, V.i.475). For him, theatre is a fundamental tool of power, and one of the reasons why he was both so revelatory as a hero in his own day and so memorable as one in ours is undoubtedly the fact that he is conceived of as so essentially theatrical a character.

Of particular interest, given what we know of Marlowe's later reputation for impiety, are the ways in which the staged spectacles of both the *Tamburlaine* plays echo, and arguably ape, specifically Christian ceremonies and iconic moments from the history of Christianity. Tamburlaine himself, the shepherd's son attended by three kings who changes his clothes in the manner of the Transfiguration and sacrifices his own son,[14] may well be seen as an impiously inverted type of Christ. Birringer points out the parallel between Tamburlaine's wounding of his arm and Christ's treatment of doubting Thomas,[15] while James Robinson Howe sees this as 'a scene mildly but clearly reminiscent of the Christian communion'.[16] It has also been suggested, as mentioned above, that Tamburlaine's use of Bajazeth as a footstool was prompted by Foxe's picture of Henry VIII and the Pope,[17] and Martha Tuck Rozett considers 'the possibility that Tamburlaine's aspiration is a devilish parody of the behavior of the elect',[18] while John P. Cutts relates the white/red/ black progression of Tamburlaine's tents to the Book of Revelation,[19] and David Bevington sees the whole play as modelled on the moralities with their abstractions of Christian characteristics.[20] Given material of such dangerousness, it is hardly surprising that Marlowe chose to be less than clear-cut about his own tone and attitude.

As well as its density of religious allusiveness, the play is also distinguished both by the breadth of its geographical canvas and by the breadth of the resources on which Marlowe was able to draw for it. The list of the sources he used is extraordinarily impressive[21] – indeed Bakeless observed that 'Marlowe seems to have had access, in some unexplained way, to a group of facts about the historical Timur contained in Oriental works, none of which was translated during his lifetime'[22] – but perhaps even more impressive is the vibrantly contemporary resonance with which the young author managed to imbue both plays, so that the bare boards of a London playhouse do, indeed, become, as in the name of the map from which he worked,[23] a *Theatrum Orbis Terrarum* – a theatre of the world, with infinite riches encapsulated in a little room, and a sense of being in the presence of major world events which is sharply underlined by Marlowe's tendency to introduce significant real-life figures into his plays.

This sense of resonance is evident even as early as *Dido, Queen of Carthage*, even though it is populated not by the figures of history but by those of legend (though Marlowe might perhaps have conceived of both Dido and Aeneas as historical) and is often thought of as virtually a closet drama, rarely resurrected since its putative initial performance by children. Margo Hendricks has recently argued that the play is Marlowe's 'response to the "reinvention" of England' and that '*The Tragedy of Dido, Queen of Carthage* may have been written as a political allegory...Troy and Carthage serve as gendered racial tropes for England and Spain', with the audience being particularly reminded of 'the 1585 conquest and sacking of Cartagena'.[24] For Hendricks, the play thus encodes images of much-debated categories of Englishness, Spanishness and Irishness, sharply topical in the 1580s, and also presents Dido as a figure analogous to Elizabeth I. (This is a point also made by many other critics, and one to which I will return.) Aeneas was the mythical ancestor of the

British royal family; and whatever Marlowe's attitude to Tamburlaine, there seems no question that he critiques rather than celebrates Aeneas, making numerous departures from the Virgilian source which work systematically to reduce the status of the hero.[25] A tragedy which initially seems to be buried in the classical past thus proves to have a powerful relationship to the contemporary English present.

It was not only topicality and breadth of reference which distinguished Marlowe's early dramas, though. Far more immediately striking than either of these things was their astonishing linguistic vitality. Marlowe early became famous for what Ben Jonson termed his 'mighty line', his fondness for a strongly beating iambic pentameter with pronounced, regular stresses, frequently made rich and resonant by mention of exotic, polysyllabic names. Though Marlowe was not technically the first to bring blank verse to the English stage,[26] it had never made such an impact before. He was also innovative in choosing to signal the madness of Zabina by the use of prose. It may be worth remembering here that the father of Marlowe's star actor Edward Alleyn, also called Edward, had been the first City-appointed Keeper of the real Bedlam, London's Bethlehem Hospital,[27] so that Alleyn would have had family connections with madness which might perhaps inform some of the representational choices here. (Though Alleyn senior died when his son was only four, the family also lived in the area and owned an inn there.)[28] The connection seems particularly worthy of note in view of the reference by Drayton to 'bedlam Tamburlaine'.[29]

The presence of Edward Alleyn in the title-role of *Tamburlaine* gives us the first clue to the people Marlowe must have known in London and the circles in which he is likely to have moved there. His other London friends seem to have included Thomas Watson[30] and Matthew Royden, both poets (the former thought in his own day to be so distinguished that Shakespeare was initially acclaimed as his 'heir'),[31] George Chapman, the dramatist and poet,[32] Walter Warner, the mathematician,[33] Thomas Nashe, who may or may not have co-written some of Marlowe's plays, Robert Greene, Thomas Kyd, the dramatist, who said at about the time of Marlowe's death that the two had roomed together, and Edward Blount, who posthumously dedicated *Hero and Leander* to Sir Thomas Walsingham of Scadbury in terms which clearly indicated that all three men were on good terms. Marlowe also may or may not have been part of something called The School of Night, if indeed such a thing existed,[34] and was perhaps linked through it with Giordano Bruno.[35] He seems too to have been associated, though perhaps not until the last months of his life,[36] with Thomas Hariot, an interesting and controversial figure whom some have called an atheist.[37] Anthony à Wood said of Hariot that he 'could never believe that trite position, *Ex nihilo nihil fit*',[38] a remark of some interest in view of Barabas' riddling calculations in *The Jew of Malta* about nothing coming of nothing, and reflections of these men's probable perspectives and interests have often been detected in Marlowe's work.[39] Christopher Devlin suggests that he may have known Robert Southwell,[40] and Marlowe himself, when he was arrested for coining in Flushing in January 1592, told Sir Robert Sidney that he was 'very wel known both to the Earle of Northumberland and my lord Strang[e]'.[41]

In all these cases, he was associating with men who constituted risky and sometimes violent company. In linking himself with them, Marlowe, after a career previously distinguished only by success and luck, was showing the first but crucial signs of what was surely a deliberate and dangerous refusal to conform, which would be manifested in almost every act of his future career – even down to apparently so insignificant a detail as his espousal of tobacco, given that Jeffrey Knapp has recently argued that '[t]o the tobacco hater, tobacco does not complement English values, it inverts them, hell for heaven'.[42] Marlowe's associates were, however, also perhaps the most intellectually adventurous and informed set he could have found. To all these men, knowledge was of supreme importance, and to all of them, as also in Marlowe's own intelligencing career, knowledge always had practical purposes; Sir Francis Walsingham's maxim was 'Knowledge is never too dear'.[43]

What some of those practical purposes may have been may perhaps become clearer if we remember that the first of Marlowe's plays which we know to have been acted in London, *Tamburlaine*, was performed by the Admiral's men, whose patron was responsible for the defence of the sea against invasion (which did in fact materialise, in the shape of the Armada, in the year after the first performance of the play). Marlowe, like the patron of his company, never forgot the interaction of Britain with the rest of the world. *Tamburlaine, Doctor Faustus, The Jew of Malta* and *Dido, Queen of Carthage* are not only set abroad; they all repeatedly dramatise (or, in the case of *Doctor Faustus*, pointedly allude to) that typical Renaissance act: colonisation.[44] And there are two particularly suggestive, and linked, elements of Marlowe's depiction of what it is like to travel 'in another country': the plays' reversal of the processes normally inherent in the possessing colonialist gaze, which makes it crystal clear that the alien object at which we think we stare in fact reflects us back to ourselves, and illuminates the stranger within us; and their perhaps unexpected, and often underrated, emphasis on female as well as male experiences and values. The latter, in particular, makes it clear that Marlowe's exploration of the wider world is not an enterprise which is different and distinct from his exploration of the dynamics of the family, but one which is actually an exension and a complement to it. It is the orientation of the self in relation to both the macroscosm of the world and the microcosm of the family which Marlowe's drama examines, and it does so with a growing subtlety and nuance which will culminate in those final mental journeys along *Edward II*'s waterways of the mind.

If internal voyagings are most profoundly limned in *Edward II*, literal and external ones are at their most sweeping and impressive in *Tamburlaine*, but there, too, evocation of distance is often eerily accompanied by a sense of a dangerous closeness to home. In the prologue to the first part, we are immediately informed of Tamburlaine's racial origin: he is a Scythian. In Elizabethan ideology, the term Scythian demarcated an absolute Otherness, naming a being so sharply inferior to civilised Western man that his very membership of the same species was open to doubt: it is, for instance, partially on the grounds of their supposed descent from the Scythians that Spenser justified the repressive policies which he advocated towards the Irish.[45] It is, therefore, perhaps surprising that the two lines which follow this fixing of Tamburlaine's racial identity proceed to describe him in terms which are by no means automatically negative: 'Threat'ning the world with high astounding terms, / And scourging kingdoms with his conquering sword' (*I*, Prologue, 4–5). In performing these two acts, Tamburlaine is demonstrating excellence in exactly the fields – linguistic and military – most highly privileged in the cultures of those very same classical civilisations which first demonised the Scythians as other. Even more surprisingly, however, we are then expressly invited to 'View but his picture in this tragic glass' (6). What does the glass show – him, or us?[46]

The image of the 'tragic glass' suggests, above all, a mirror, and, as J.S. Cunningham points out, 'effects of mirroring [are] germane to the *Tamburlaine* theatre'.[47] One of the play's sources was George Whetstone's *The English Mirror*,[48] and the play is full of references to mirroring, imaging and reflecting.[49] Tamburlaine instructs Techelles to 'Lay out our golden wedges to the view / That their reflections may amaze the Persians' (*I*, I.ii.139–40), and refers to 'immortal flowers of poesy, / Wherein as in a mirror we perceive / The highest reaches of a human wit' (*I*, V.i.166–7); he also images the corpses of Bajazeth and Zabina as mirrors which reflect his own power (*I*, V.i.477). It is only fitting that the play in its entirety should thus offer itself in its Prologue as glass to its audience, fearful inversion of the customary *Mirror for Magistrates*.

If the play functions as a mirror, then what the audience will see in it is its own reflection; superimposed on the features of the barbarian Scythian will be those of the burghers and apprentices who frequented English playhouses[50] – all the more obviously since, when it comes to the major aspect of his career, the depiction of his prowess in warfare, 'the armies and tactics described in *Tamburlaine* are, except in a few superficial details, neither oriental nor early fifteenth century as historical realism would require',[51] while Paul H. Kocher points to clear 'echoes of English practice at the investiture of a new monarch' in Cosroe's reference to the commons and Tamburlaine's soliciting of his followers' consent,[52] and John Bakeless suggested that Marlowe was 'thinking of English academic dress when he makes Tamburlaine order his generals to don "scarlet roabes" – the traditional dress of Cambridge doctors on great occasions'.[53] Thus begins the astonishing process whereby the play forces us into a radical identification with what, in theory, we most condemn, and at the same time sharply critiques a fundamental aspect of English Renaissance culture, the colonial enterprise, by completely inverting the perspective from which it is habitually viewed.[54]

Marlowe himself would have been well aware of the development and ramifications of imperialist colonialism as practised, or at any rate envisaged, by the English; as Thomas Healy remarks, *Tamburlaine* coincides almost exactly with the first edition of Hakluyt's *Voyages*, and the world the playwright depicts is typically that of the exoticism and abundance figured in travel narratives.[55] Marlowe's cousin, Anthony Marlowe, was the London agent of the Muscovy Company, and partly on the basis of this, Richard Wilson has recently argued eloquently and convincingly for a close relationship between Marlowe's portrayal of Tamburlaine, particularly with regard to his weaponry, and that 'Heliogabalus' and 'right Scythian', Ivan the Terrible.[56] Marlowe, moreover, may well have been a member of the circle of Sir Walter Ralegh, who was deeply involved not only in the attempted practice, but also in the ideological apparatus of colonialism: Ralegh punned on the contemporary pronunciation of his own name as 'Water' to insert himself into the mythology of Elizabeth I as a creature intimately bound up with the sea and with tides, governed by the queen herself, whom he cast as 'Cynthia', the moon goddess, controller of the tides. Ralegh also reveals an unusually acute sense of the inherent gendering of power relations in the act of colonising, revealed not only in his insistent choice of female names for the lands he claimed but also in his use of metaphors such as 'Guiana is a country that hath yet her maidenhead'. Marlowe's own involvement with Elizabethan intelligence-gathering networks, whatever its actual nature may have been, would also have placed him at the forefront of attempts to implement Elizabethan foreign policy, so much of which hinged on relations with the archetypal colonialist power, Spain, which laid claim to large tracts of the New World. Closer to home, Spain was also running various Italian duchies as puppet states, and – as *Doctor Faustus* reminds us, and as Marlowe's own time in Flushing and perhaps in Utrecht would have brought very directly home to him – forcibly occupying the Netherlands. The main thrust of English foreign policy at this time was to frustrate persistent Spanish attempts to overrun or politically subjugate England.

That Marlowe was interested in the questions of colonialism, foreignness and the relation of different nationalities to one another is suggested by the first of the heresies reported against him by Richard Baines, which critics are increasingly inclined to see as genuinely reflective of his thought: that 'the Indians and many authors of antiquity have assuredly written above 16 thousand years agone, whereas Adam is proved to have lived within 6 thousand years'.[57] In this case, we see how encounters with a new world could lead to new suggestions and perceptions which could radically undermine the certainties of the old, in ways which Marlowe the iconoclast would surely have relished. An interest in the foreign and exotic is also apparent throughout his work. All of his plays, except *Edward II*, are set abroad – two, *Doctor Faustus* and *Tamburlaine*, in more than one country; and many of them also involve heroes, or other characters, who are foreign visitors or residents. *The Massacre at Paris* has two English lords and an English agent; *Edward II* ironically pits the foreign Gaveston against the equally foreign queen, and temporarily banishes Gaveston to that perennial site of colonial struggle, Ireland. *The Jew of Malta* boasts a whole complement of invading Turks as well as the inherently exiled Jew himself (even the Knights of Malta are not in fact indigenous inhabitants but of foreign origin, having started life as the Order of St John of Jerusalem and recruiting their ranks primarily from France, Spain and Italy; indeed, nobody in Malta seems to be Maltese, unsurprisingly since the indigenous inhabitants were debarred from admission into the ranks of the Hospitallers). And *Dido, Queen of Carthage* features the man who in many ways can stand for the *ur*-coloniser, Aeneas.

Running through all these works is an insistent concern with alienness, with the viability of normative perspectives and with the problematics of the relationship between personal and national identities. And equally strongly running through all of them is a persistent refusal to maintain the demarcation line between the self and the Other, the foreign and the domestic, in ways that both trouble accepted early modern ideologies and also alert us to the intricate linkages of what I have suggested to be Marlowe's twin projects of examining the family and the world. As Emily Bartels argues, 'what makes Marlowe's plays stand out ... is that their foreign worlds are not only "Englished"; they make a point of that Englishing.'[58] The effect is a vertiginous manipulation of space not dissimilar to the ways in which a map allows us to interpret a small space as standing for a greater, a point well made by Nick de Somogyi, who observes that 'telescoping of space is the very basis upon which Mercator's Atlas was subsequently presented to its potential readership – its counting-house, closet and cabinets containing "the whole world"', and suggests that this is also 'the basis ... upon which Marlowe's theatre represents that world'.[59]

In the case of Tamburlaine, his Scythianness and, concomitantly, his Otherness is the one fixed element of a life during which we see him traverse countless countries and change from shepherd to king to corpse, and from bachelor to husband to widower. Wherever he goes, he is always racially different from those amongst whom he finds himself; his close lieutenant, Theridamas, is a Persian, and his wife, Zenocrate, an Egyptian, and thus even his three sons are only half-Scythian. We never see his parents: only Usumcasane and Techelles have been with him since the beginning and they are dramatic nonentities – the only one of the three lieutenants to achieve a scene to himself is Theridamas, and then only when he features in the Olympia story. Indeed one of the notable elements of Tamburlaine's career is the marked racial prejudice he consistently encounters, which leads both Persians and Turks to despise and prematurely dismiss him. It is perhaps partly in response to this that he embarks on his career of subjecting other lands to his dominion.

The means by which he does so exhibit significant parallels with the English colonial enterprise, as Richard Wilson observes: 'it cannot be chance that Marlowe's epic of "the rogue of Volga" ... should project what Burghley described as "the great end of dealing with the Muscovite: discovery of a passage into Asia"'.[60] There are other similarities. One marked element of Marlowe's plays is the exuberant sprinkling of exotic, alien names – a feature very strongly emphasised by Antony Sher's Tamburlaine in a recent RSC production – supplemented in the case of *Tamburlaine* by copious military terms which are, as Nick de Somogyi points out, almost all of foreign origin.[61] They fill up the mighty line with rolling syllables which convey little but a sense of glamour, and this would be very close to the English linguistic experience of the New World. In the vast majority of locations to which English explorers and traders ventured, they were not the firstcomers: the Spaniards, preceding them, had already exercised the privilege of Adam by allotting names, so that little opportunity remained for the imposition of a coherent English world-view on what they encountered. In *Tamburlaine*, this sense of an inability to order the world through language is pronounced, because the audience's probable inability to recognise or decode the myriad place-names, leading us to perceive them only as random collections of syllables, means that very few of them acquire any real solidity or sense of specific location. They blend into each other, and our sense of Tamburlaine's actual achievements is apt to melt away as we experience repetition rather than movement or progression: 'nomenclature is ceaselessly revised',[62] a process in which Tamburlaine himself will be fully participatory as he calls 'provinces, cities, and towns, / After my name and thine, Zenocrate' (IV.iv.85–6).

There are perhaps more specific links between *Tamburlaine* and Spanish colonialism, in that there seem to be some definite similarities between Tamburlaine and the notorious *conquistador* Lope de Aguirre. Like Tamburlaine, though for different reasons, Lope killed one of his own children: in 1562 he 'murdered his own daughter, Elvira, to prevent her falling into enemy hands' – in which he exactly foreshadows the motives of Olympia in *Tamburlaine Part Two* – and, like Tamburlaine, he signed himself 'Wrath of God'. As Charles Nicholl points out, 'Ralegh tells Aguirre's story in some detail in the *Discoverie*. His account is based partly on printed sources.' Marlowe would, therefore, have had easy access to the story; indeed Nicholl comments on how in the accounts of Ralegh's adventuring '[t]he exotic syllables roll out like some lost line from Marlowe's *Tamburlaine*', and also notes that in 1590 Hariot was given a rutter (a book of sea-charts) by 'Captain Edmund Marlowe, who may or may not be a distant cousin of the dramatist'.[63] Both the New World and the circle of Sir Walter Ralegh may, then, be close indeed to the conception of *Tamburlaine*.

Other links, such as a possible connection between the splendid costumes of Tamburlaine and those for which Ralegh was so distinguished,[64] have also been suggested between Marlowe's play and Ralegh's world of exploration. Nevertheless, though some critics have assumed it,[65] there is no firm evidence that Marlowe actually knew Ralegh; the only real link comes in the accusation that Marlowe had read 'the atheist lecture' to Ralegh and in the form of an apparent overlap between their respective circles, and this is so far from definite proof that a recent Ralegh biographer has flatly asserted that '[i]t is safe to say that Christopher Marlowe was *not* a guest of Sir Walter Ralegh's at Durham House in the 1580s'.[66] More cautiously, Ernest A. Strathmann remarks, 'the circles in which Marlowe and Ralegh moved seem to intersect, but they are not concentric'.[67] One thing which might conceivably be relevant is the often-made link between Marlowe and 'Pauls', as in Gabriel Harvey's 'Weep, Powles, thy Tamburlaine voutsafes to die'. This is usually taken to mean St Paul's Cathedral, in whose churchyard the stationers and booksellers had their stalls, but 'Paul' was also a name often used for Ralegh. Charles Nicholl notes that John Davies's epigram 'In Paulum', which was published in the same volume as Marlowe's translations of Ovid's Elegies, 'tilts at Sir Walter Raleigh [*sic*] ... Harington ... frequently used this name for Ralegh', and plays on Ralegh's identification with the ocean,[68] which may remind us of the water imagery so prevalent in *Edward II*. This is, however, purely speculative, and though it may well seem likely that the overlapping interests of the two men would have led to a personal acquaintanceship, and that the accusations against Marlowe were right in this as, many critics think, they were in other respects, it is not an absolute fact.

Whether or not Tamburlaine recalls features of Ralegh's career, an even more strikingly immediate and much more troubling relationship between the imperialism of Tamburlaine and that practised by Marlowe's contemporaries is their precisely opposed goals. Tamburlaine is not just bent on subduing a few far distant savages and Turks; he is heading, ultimately, towards *us* – and indeed Harry Levin sees the entire trajectory of Marlowe's imagination throughout his career as focusing progressively closer and closer to home, and suggests that '[a]s Marlowe progresses from Tamburlaine and Barabas to Edward and Faustus, the mask seems to fit more closely'.[69] The first scene of the play offers a striking instance of a predatory world in which norms of exploitation and dominance have been suddenly reversed, as Cosroe laments:

> But this it is that doth excruciate
> The very substance of my vexèd soul:
> To see our neighbours that were wont to quake
> And tremble at the Persian monarch's name
> Now sits and laughs our regiment to scorn;
> And that which might resolve me into tears,
> Men from the farthest equinoctial line
> Have swarmed in troops into the Eastern India,
> Loading their ships with gold and precious stones,
> And made their spoils from all our provinces.
>
>   (*I*, I.i.113–22)

The change from quaking to laughter in Persia's neighbours has come close to effecting a similar change in Cosroe himself, who is on the verge of womanish tears at the thought of 'Men from the farthest equinoctial line'. A telling encapsulation of those whom the aliens find alien, this line also introduces a chilling suggestion of relativism into its representation of the colonial experience: the location of 'the farthest equinoctial line' depends, on a round planet, on where one is standing. Since Cosroe's lament is immediately followed by Menaphon's advice that he should undertake the 'curing of this maimèd empery' (*I*, I.i.126) by the invasion of Greece, we may well imagine that, for Cosroe, 'the farthest equinoctial line' is the one which he envisages when he looks towards Europe. We are, indeed, the Other's Other.

The reference to Greece is given added point by Meander's earlier classification of Tamburlaine as advancing on Persia 'with barbarous arms' (*I*, I.i.42). Meander's own possession of an unimpeachably Greek name underscores the original meaning of the word 'barbarian' as one who speaks no Greek (though, ironically, Tamburlaine will very soon prove himself completely at home in deploying the discourse of Greek mythology and culture, while Mycetes will have to consult Meander about the legend of the dragon's teeth [II.ii.51–2]). The classical culture of the Persian court is again evident when Mycetes almost immediately afterwards terms Meander 'a Damon for thy love' (*I*, I.i.50). Soon after, though, Mycetes adjures Meander to return 'smiling home, / As did Sir Paris with the Grecian dame' (*I*, I.i.65–6), thus figuring his friend as a Trojan, and Menaphon's advice to Cosroe to invade Greece is coupled with an invocation of the Persian Cyrus, a subtle reminder that those who are so anxious to label Tamburlaine as a barbarian are in fact the literal descendants of those to whom that term was once most accurately applicable. It is not only the geographical coding of Otherness that is revealed as reversible; the very terms of civility and barbarism are here exposed as culturally relative, and the same game will be played when the Soldan of Egypt enters saying 'Methinks we march as Meleager did' (*I*, IV.iii.1) – one man's Greek is another man's Egyptian. Moreover, the Soldan, like Meander earlier, sees Tamburlaine as 'sturdy' (*I*, IV.iii.12), a word which, as Mark Thornton Burnett points out, encodes, for an Elizabethan audience, specifically English resonances, being habitually used for the description of English beggars.[70] Thus the Greekish Egyptian virtually forces us into a position of identification with Tamburlaine here in national terms (although his language would also work to underline the difference of Tamburlaine's 'class' position).

English adventurers apparently saw themselves as moving from the civilised to the savage, enlightening the natives as they went.

The language used to describe Tamburlaine here may make him briefly reminiscent of a wandering Englishman, but his epic journeys have a reversed teleology, for not only could the advance of a Scythian be read as a self-evident triumph of barbarism, but he also originates in the East – so radically demonised in English Renaissance culture – and advances steadily ever closer to the West: as he says, 'So from the east unto the furthest west / Shall Tamburlaine extend his puissant arm' (*I*, III.iii.246–7), until his imminent death reduces him to mere speculation on 'what a world of ground / Lies westward' (*II*, V.iii.146–7) – as Lawrence Danson has it, '[i]n an interesting variation on the sorrows of Alexander, Tamburlaine weeps because there will always be more to conquer'.[71] Before that, he has threatened to get very close to home indeed, 'Keeping in awe the Bay of Portingale / And all the ocean by the British shore' (*I*, III.iii.258–9). Interestingly, however, this is not presented in the play as a threat. The direct menace to Western civilisation is, as always, embodied by the Turks, and they are disadvantaged by Tamburlaine's expansionism, since he diverts 'the force of Turkish arms / Which lately made all Europe quake for fear' (*I*, III.iii.134–5), and, particularly in Part Two, dramatically relieves the pressure on Christendom's beleaguered frontiers.[72]

As well as his open designs on 'the British shore', Tamburlaine is also metaphorically associated with two crucial figures in the histories both of colonisation and of Britain. At an early point in his career, he directly compares himself with a previous invader of Britain when he says 'My camp is like to Julius Caesar's host' (*I*, III.iii.152). The second figure with whom Tamburlaine is compared is, even more significantly, Aeneas (*I*, V.i.381). Marlowe had almost certainly already depicted the activities of this crucial figure in the westward translation of empire in *Dido, Queen of Carthage*, a play in which it is even more explicitly Europe which is to be colonised, this time by an Asiatic Trojan. *Dido*, which itself performs a sort of act of colonisation on Virgil's *Aeneid*, dramatises many of the archetypal processes of colonisation in general and of English Renaissance colonialism in particular: the coloniser's self-justification and sense of divine mission, the involvement with (and subsequent desertion of) a native woman and the eventual eruption of violence. The traditional pattern of classical epic adventure voyage, on which the *Aeneid* itself is based, has its heroes radically modifying the environments which they encounter, almost always through violence: Polyphemus is blinded, the Harpies caged, the Gorgon beheaded. *Dido, Queen of Carthage* follows this pattern to the extent that a native – as so often, a female one – dies; the ending, however, is slightly unexpected, in that instead of the coloniser triumphing through superior skill and force and subduing the alien culture, he is himself altered by what he finds there, so much so that by the end of the play the apparently daring adventurer turns tail and runs, not even daring to say farewell. Although this is the actual ending of the Dido and Aeneas story, and as such an inevitable given in Marlowe's choice of narrative, nevertheless the episode Marlowe has chosen to dramatise shows the *ur*-coloniser conspicuously failing in his role.

First, Aeneas falls victim to that common fate of Renaissance explorers, landing in the wrong country. He then not only fails to subjugate it, but very nearly becomes subjugated in his turn, as we see him tempted by the most feared of all downfalls of colonisers, the urge to go native. His son – the emblem of his future – is immediately swept away by Dido to be brought up in her entourage; and he himself, in a bizarre and suggestive conceit, is to be dressed in the clothes and ornaments of Dido's late husband Sichaeus, a dramatic drawing of attention to what the woman wants. Aeneas' status as erotic object of Dido's possessing gaze is repeatedly underlined, as she tells her sister Anna 'none shall gaze on him but I' (III.i.73) and affirms that 'His glistering eyes shall be my looking-glass' (III.i.85). It is only divine intervention (again controlled by a female figure, his mother, the goddess Venus) that eventually saves Aeneas and that packs him off to Italy at the end of the play, having gained precisely nothing and having forfeited both time and, I would imagine, the sympathy of the majority of the audience. This first of all colonial enterprises is seen in the most unglamorous of lights.

In the *Tamburlaine* passage that draws on this myth, Philemus, after comparing Tamburlaine with Aeneas, goes on to figures the Arabian king as Turnus, resisting this Asiatic invader with designs on Europe. This doubly encodes a wave of westward invasion, since Aeneas' grandson Brut, celebrated by Layamon, would later arrive in Britain. Aeneas is the founder of Rome and thus, in a major sense, the founder also of Marlowe's Britain – mythically, through Brut, and historically, both through the literal Roman conquest of the island and the metaphorical conquest of its literary allegiances by classical learning. To reveal him as inept is a damning reworking of a potent myth of origins; to cast Tamburlaine as an Aeneas overpowering the King of Arabia's Turnus is, once again, to show us a sharply focused image of the Scythian in the mirror.

To see Tamburlaine as Aeneas also alerts us to the other ways in which, while Tamburlaine himself may be readily branded by many of those he encounters as a savage, he is also seen on many scores as related very closely to Marlowe's audience. Indeed, T.M. Pearce has argued that 'he was Marlowe's conception of the soldier-poet or scholar-warrior in the mold of the Italian courtier described by Castiglione', and suggests that we should read him within the context of Humphrey Gilbert's scheme for 'a military academy designed to provide England with young Tamburlaines'.[73] Additionally, perhaps, Tamburlaine's fondness for Zenocrate would serve to align him with the uxoriousness for which London citizens were soon to become so famous in comedy; and what seems his most fundamentally barbarous act, the stabbing of Calyphas, is, ironically, most easily understood within the cultural context of those arch-colonisers, and ultimate authorisers of Renaissance civilisation, the Romans: 'its source ... may be found ... in the story of the Roman consul, Manlius Torquatus, who slew his own son for disobeying orders'.[74] Even Tamburlaine's appearance would be familiar: not only would he be recognisably Edward Alleyn, but also, instead of the cloak which was normally the trademark of the Scythian, Tamburlaine sported the thoroughly Western garb of 'a coat with copper lace' and 'breeches of crimson velvet'.[75] The very lists of names which apparently serve to signal Tamburlaine's exotic origins can serve equally to position him within the western epic tradition of the list. Moreover, the use of the signature 'Tamburlaine' appended to the Dutch church libel – a virulently anti-immigrant poem found affixed to the wall of the Dutch churchyard which has sometimes been seen as a possible cause of Marlowe's final disgrace and death – paradoxically positions Tamburlaine as an endorsement, indeed an embodiment, of English xenophobia. As suggested in the prologue, he is indeed the Scythian who is us.

The westward trajectory of Tamburlaine's travels, then, is not only not seen as menacing, but can indeed function as an emblem for the narrative trajectory by which the apparently unbridgeable gap between Tamburlaine and his audience gradually shrinks throughout the plays. This is especially so in Part Two, where the Scourge of God is seen as a harassed single parent subject to illness and mortality; and by the end of his story his singularity and Otherness have totally vanished as he falls prey to the most basic common denominator of all: death. The Scythian in the glass is us, and this is brought very clearly home by the speech of Theridamas in Part Two, when he tells Tamburlaine:

> I left the confines and the bounds of Afric
> And made a voyage into Europe,
> Where by the river Tyros I subdued
> Stoka, Padalia, and Codemia.
> Then crossed the sea and came to Oblia,
> And Nigra Silva, where the devils dance.
>
> (*II*, I.iii.207–11)

Of all the curious place-names and exotic descriptions in the plays, I find this the most evocatively suggestive and compelling; and yet this is in Europe (and is also threatened by Theridamas, as the Canaries and Gibraltar have been by Usumcasane). Reversing the direction of the gaze has made Europe strange.

One way in which Europe is indeed strange to most of the characters in the *Tamburlaine* plays lies in their conception of the continent as gendered. The normal gendering processes of the colonialist imagination often proceed on an implied equation between masculinity and subjugation, casting the land as a feminine space to be 'husbanded' by the incoming colonist: not for nothing did Ralegh name his colony Virginia. In *Tamburlaine Part Two*, Orcanes specifically tropes Europe as a woman: she is 'fair Europe, mounted on her bull' (*II*, I.i.42). The bull who husbanded Europa was Jove, with whom Tamburlaine is so often compared, so that the allusion once more underlines the westward trajectory of his conquests; but it also serves to underline the plays' quiet but insistent interest in the intersection between colonialism and gender. Their use of foreign settings serves primarily to point up the similarities between those who are apparently polar opposites of each other, and the principal means by which such similarity is established is to portray both sides as equally bad. There is, however, a group of striking exceptions to this general depiction of all parties as evil, and this is the plays' female characters. It is often suggested that Marlowe cannot create female characters. However, Dido, Zenocrate, Olympia and Abigail are all distinguished by an apparently limitless capacity to love. Dido immediately establishes herself as the kindest of stepmothers in her devotion to young Ascanius; Zenocrate feels not only for Tamburlaine and for all three of her sons but for her father, her neglected suitor and the virgins of Damascus, and Zabina, though haughty, is unshakeably loyal to her husband; Abigail loves Mathias and, even when she has lost all respect for her father, still refuses to betray him. Olympia is in some ways the most interesting of all, for not only is she devoted to her husband and son but, although she is a woman of Soria, her classical name is matched by her adherence to the values of classical civilisation, so highly privileged in the Renaissance, when with stoic fortitude she first kills her son and then unflinchingly engineers her own death. Even Faustus wants a wife, and reserves one of his most disinterested acts for the pregnant Duchess of Vanholt. The plays' ventures into the countries of the Other thus invert familiar norms in two ways: not only is the other fundamentally the same, but foreign women, usually perceived as doubly alien through their twin deviancies of race and gender, are actually presented to us as the true repositories of the dual values of love and honour which are the keynotes of the two major influences on European thought, Christianity and classicism respectively. Just as the westward trajectory of Tamburlaine's conquering march runs counter to the normal logic of east-facing colonialism, so the narrative logic of these three plays finally locates truly civilised modes of behaviour only in the one place where the cultural prejudices of the audience would have made them least likely to look for it: the barbarian woman.

This emphasis on the roles and experiences of women reminds us of the extent to which Marlowe's mapping of the world intersects with his mapping of the family. The story of Tamburlaine's globetrotting is always shadowed by the twin focus on the tiny circle of his immediate family and friends. A particularly troubling and ambiguous figure is his eldest son, Calyphas. Huston Diehl points out that 'the conventional attribute of personified idleness, the deck of cards, contributes to the characterization of Tamburlaine's son Calyphas', and that the whole scene, as so often in Marlovian drama, incorporates emblematic elements which give the events wide-ranging resonances:

> Marlowe gives this scene of moral choice an added realistic dimension which significantly alters the audience's response to it. When the enraged Tamburlaine confronts his card-playing son, accuses him of being an *'Image* of sloth and *picture* of a slave' (IV.i.90; italics mine), curses his 'damned idleness' (IV.i.125), and angrily kills him, Marlowe portrays *both* a symbolic struggle between will and sloth, action and idleness, *and* the ruthless spirit of a driven man infuriated with a son who has rejected his values. In the externalization of an inner struggle, Tamburlaine symbolically kills that part of him given to sloth; in the realistic portrait of a man, Tamburlaine mercilessly kills his own son. The tension which results between these realistic and symbolic possibilities is both disturbing and provocative.[76]

It is this mixture of the external and the internal which is, ultimately, the most powerful effect of *Tamburlaine*, and which, indeed, Marjorie Garber sees as one of the most distinctive features of Marlowe's dramaturgy: 'play after play finds its closure in enclosure; the inner stage, or discovery space, becomes a version of hell, and a place of final entrapment.'[77]

The same intersection of the small and the large, the emblem and the actual, recurs in Marlowe's other plays. Julius Caesar, to whose army Tamburlaine compares his own, recurs, again in the service of destabilising norms, in *Doctor Faustus*, where the beauties of Rome in fact turn out to depend in part at least on the conquered spoils 'Which Julius Caesar brought from Africa' (III.i.43). Indeed, *Doctor Faustus* is a text which is saturated, paradoxically, in both the language of colonialism and the language of resistance to it. William Zunder points out that one of the real Faustus' 'last commissions [was] to prepare a prediction in 1534 for the German explorer Philip von Hutten's expedition to Venezuela',[78] and the initial desire for power of Marlowe's Faustus is characterised precisely as a desire for physical dominion on colonising models – 'All things that move between the quiet poles / Shall be at my command' (I.i.58–9). He wants to 'fly to India for gold' (I.i.84), reminding us of the fabled wealth of the Indies which both fuelled and motivated Spain's colonial expansion. Spanish aggression in the Low Countries, of which Marlowe's time in Flushing and perhaps in Utrecht would have given him direct personal experience, bulks large in the play: Faustus resolves to expel Emperor Charles V's general, the Prince of Parma, from the Low Countries (I.i.95), and the Emperor even makes a personal appearance, though when Faustus summons up for him the ghost of Alexander the Great our principal sense is of the ephemerality of conquest, and this is multipled in the B-text when Alexander is seen defeating the previously victorious Darius.

This sense of a cycle rather than a goal is mirrored in the behaviour of Faustus himself, for we learn that he means to expel Parma not from patriotism, but because he himself plans to 'reign sole king of all our provinces' (I.i.96), and to possess 'the seigniory of Emden' (II.i.23). Faustus will become that which he seeks to defeat, an idea which is repeated in Valdes' enticements to him that he will be treated 'As Indian Moors obey their Spanish lords' (I.i.123). Faustus, like Tamburlaine, dreams of mastering the map as he fantasises that 'I'll join the hills that bind the Afric shore, / And make that land continent to Spain' (I.iii.109–10). But in another inversion, Faustus is himself the unwitting victim of precisely such an act of colonisation, as the ostensible boundaries of the world-map are redrawn indeed and, at the head of his invading army, Mephistopheles can terrifyingly proclaim 'Why this is hell, nor am I out of it' (I.iii.78), and explain that Lucifer too seeks to 'Enlarge his kingdom' (II.i.40). Once again, as hell and earth dissolve and blur, as human motivation is revealed to be the same as diabolical, and as Faustus moves from opposition to the Spanish forces to the performance of conjuring tricks for the Emperor, the most pronounced sense is of a cynical failure to maintain oppositions of difference, and of an inversion of the structuring polarities of civilisation and savagery.

The Prince of Parma, Alessandro Farnese, effectively shares a name with Ferneze, the Governor of Malta who bests Barabas. If Marlowe's first play, *Dido, Queen of Carthage*, staged an originary moment of colonialism, *The Jew of Malta* represents the process as so far advanced that it is barely possible to identify a truly indigenous inhabitant of the much-invaded island of Malta. The Jew is multiply alien: as Barabas, he is the polar opposite of the Christianity which theoretically characterises Marlowe's own audience; as a Jew, he is radically demonised; as a denizen of Malta, he is seen in English eyes as belonging to the furthest fringes of the Christian world, constantly contaminated by contact with the Turk, and in the eyes of the indigenous inhabitants of the island as a suspect resident alien. His behaviour in the play apparently matches well with these stereotypes: he is a monstrous egotist, a mass murderer, crazed by the desire for money and power. Nevertheless, it is starkly apparent not only that his villainy is easily matched by both his Turkish and his Christian opponents, but also that it has been taught to him specifically by a European, Machiavelli. Moreover, his plan for wiping out the convent is a direct parallel to a scheme proposed by another European, the same Richard Baines who was later to accuse Marlowe of atheism, who while a student at the English College at Rheims formed a plan to eliminate the entire seminary by poisoning its well.[79] Once again, the use of an alien environment and an alien protagonist serves only to throw into starker relief the internality rather than the externality of Otherness. The Scythian is in the mirror; however widely Marlowe's explorations of the world may range, they show us, in the end, only ourselves.

4
1589–1592: Daring God out of Heaven

In both *Doctor Faustus* and *The Jew of Malta*, both accomplished and highly metatheatrical pieces of theatre, Marlowe may well be seen as having a more developed sense of himself as a literary figure.[1] The very idea of literariness seems to have interested him; in *Hero and Leander*, he asks, 'And who have hard hearts and obdurate minds, / But vicious, harebrained, and illit'rate hinds?' (Sestiad II, ll.218–19), and A.L. Rowse suggests that 'Marlowe had literary ambitions and meant to be considered as a poet, not only or merely as a playwright. It may be due to this that [*Tamburlaine 1* and *2*] were published…in 1590, in an excellent text…The play[s] must have been printed from Marlowe's own manuscript.'[2] Though the plays did not bear the name of their author, this may well bespeak less an indifference to fame than a supremely confident assurance of it, assuming that *everybody* knew who had written *Tamburlaine*. But while *Tamburlaine* may have become, for Marlowe, a significant written text, it is not itself much concerned with written texts. Tamburlaine may speak poetry, but he does not write it, and in his great soliloquy on the beauties of Zenocrate he is dismissive of poetic achievement, speaking of the description of perfection as something that might have been conditionally possible rather than an actual achievement, and even then 'Yet should there hover in their restless heads / One thought, one grace, one wonder at the least / Which into words no virtue can digest' (*I*, V.i.171–3). Not until the burning of the Koran, very late in *Part Two*, do writing and writtenness come to the forefront. Once there, however, their importance in Marlowe's thought and writing develops rapidly.

By the publication of the *Tamburlaine* plays, Marlowe, then, may well have been trying to define himself specifically as a literary figure, and indeed Graham Hammill has argued that the root of the tragic experience in *Doctor Faustus* lies not in theological debate but in its consciousness of the literary[3]: the Bible is just one book among many, and Faustus' citing of Jerome's version of it in particular reminds us that it has a human author. Michael Keefer similarly suggests that the play 'could be called a tragedy of misreading'.[4] Indeed that much-quoted phrase 'the forme of Faustus' fortunes' could be seen as referring not only to the outcome of the protagonist's career, but also to the forme involved in printing, and at the same time, too, its self-consciously stylish and specifically literary play with sound makes us aware of how hard it is to decode this play when the relentless alliteration and assonance of 'the forme of Faustus' fortunes' fail to echo in either of the two alternatives, 'good' or 'bad', that we are offered, suggesting that neither pat option will fit the complexity of our experience. Nor is the phenomenon confined to *Doctor Faustus*; it is also, suggestively, strongly present in the other play centred on religious issues, *The Jew of Malta*. David H. Thurn remarks that '[e]ach time Barabas's hidden fund of wealth and secrets is betrayed, it is by way of writing... Writing is the instrument by which Barabas loses his control over the plot.'[5] Moreover, as Ian McAdam points out, the text of *The Jew of Malta* is itself steeped in the textual and the metatextual, since '[t]he meaning of the play is largely dependent on the text's web of biblical allusions'.[6]

Of all Marlowe's plays, *Doctor Faustus* has proved the most difficult to interpret confidently. Michael Hattaway, indeed, argues that the play is in some respects deliberately opaque, accessible only to those possessed of considerable extraneous information: he suggests that '[t]he setting recalls countless pictures of St Jerome in his study' and that 'a university man would detect an element of criticism of Faustus'.[7] Even to the educated and sophisticated, however, the meaning of the play is by no means obvious, because throughout it, Marlowe suggests and alludes to so much, and specifies so little: Robert G. Hunter has demonstrated 'how *Dr. Faustus* can be made sense of by semi-Pelagian, "Augustinian" and Calvinist alike',[8] but, widely different though these perspectives are, refuses to allow itself to be pinned down to any of them. This is a play which elevates ambiguity to an artform, which may be one reason why some of the most innovative and provocative of the criticism on it was produced by the high priest of ambiguity, William Empson.

That *Doctor Faustus*, which Charles Masinton calls 'a spiritual biography of Western man in the Renaissance and modern periods',[9] is a play rooted in the experiences and doctrines of Protestantism is perhaps the one thing on which there is genuine critical consensus.[10] Nevertheless, its own religious loyalties are far from clear-cut; indeed G.M. Pinciss asserts that '[b]oth Calvinist and anti-Calvinist views are sustained throughout the action',[11] and John Mebane suggests that we are deliberately meant to be aware of the tug of two balanced and opposing systems of values and feel forced to choose between them.[12] This would, of course, be very close to the experience of a good proportion of the Elizabethan population. At the time of the play's first performances, any man or woman in the audience who had actually achieved the biblical span of three score and ten would have lived through Henry VIII's break with Rome in the 1530s, Edward VI's espousal of Protestantism in 1547, Mary Tudor's return to Rome in 1553 and her subsequent persecution and martyring of Protestants, and all the heady vagaries of the perilous course steered by Elizabeth I as she tried to reconcile conflicting opinions, defuse the effects of her excommunication and bastardisation by the Pope, and deal with the many Catholics who might prefer to see her cousin Mary Stuart on the throne.

Moreover, since almost all Elizabethan espionage activity in the 1580s and early 1590s centred either on the machinations leading up to the death of Mary, Queen of Scots or on the intrigues and invasion plans surrounding its prolonged and complex aftermath, any question of split religious loyalties also brings us very close to what seems to have been Marlowe's other career as an intelligencer. In order to play any such role at all, he would almost certainly have had to be able to pass as either Catholic or Protestant. Perhaps both poses were equally false, or perhaps, as Richard Baines (who himself knew a thing or two about playing the double agent) reported, Marlowe preferred Catholicism to Protestantism on the grounds that at least it had music and ritual, whereas, Baines alleged, he dismissed all Protestants as 'hypocritical asses'. Perhaps, indeed, he had been pretending from the beginning, claiming to intend to take holy orders to be able to benefit from a Parker scholarship, but never feeling a genuine commitment to the idea. In any case, there seems to me to be a suggestive parallel between Marlowe's two worlds here, because just as he must at various times have had to pass amongst those who believed without actually sharing their belief, so a substantial part of the power of *Faustus* derives, I think, from the fact that Marlowe himself seems to stand so far apart from it.

In more than one Elizabethan production, *Doctor Faustus* drove its audience to hysterics, when someone saw, or thought they saw, an extra devil on the stage who was not being played by any of the actors. Alleyn himself is said to have been so scared by the thought of actually conjuring up the Devil that he always wore a cross on stage. In many university departments, *Doctor Faustus* is taught as one of the great western tragedies, often paired with either *Hamlet* or *Macbeth*, which ought to mean that Faustus himself is a tragic hero, someone whose fate inspires us to pity and to fear. And yet it is so easy to feel that, unlike Hamlet or Macbeth, Faustus is not in any sense a great or even a potentially great man, but an idiot, who makes a mistake which ninety-nine out of a hundred people would not be stupid enough to commit, and who unlike other mistaken heroes such as King Lear never has the sense to realise where he went wrong. From this perspective, he looks less like any other Renaissance hero than like a sixteenth-century Willy Loman, inspiring exasperation rather than admiration. Tamburlaine and even Aeneas are successful, Barabas amuses us and Edward can at the very least inspire pathos, but there is nothing that Faustus does or says that need necessarily appeal to our sympathies or even our sense of tolerance. However deaf and cruel the heavens may be in this play, they are no more so than the author, who bestows so few charms on his hero and who steps forward so coolly to assert his own presence, survival and control at the end of the play. Marlowe has painted one of the most powerful of all pictures of religious agony, but it is one that he himself seems to view entirely with detachment.

Apart from the virtually universal recognition of the centrality of the play's interest in religion, one other area of general agreement is that in *Doctor Faustus*, as in *Tamburlaine*, Marlowe drew on an impressive range of materials and sources,[13] and, too, of paradigms: Susan Snyder, for instance, suggests that the play is an 'inverted saint's life',[14] while Nicholas Brooke sees it as a satiric inversion of the Morality form.[15] Marlowe shows himself interested in form in other ways as well in the play: Marjorie Garber points out that '[i]n

Faustus's despairing cry, "O I'll leap up to my God! Who pulls me down?" (5.2.138), we can count not ten but eleven syllables; at the very moment that he aspires most fervently to escape damnation, his language aspires to escape the formal structures of the verse',[16] and Edward Snow suggests that in some sense *Doctor Faustus* is all about the hero's desire never to experience a sense of closure, 'to ensure himself that there will always be some object out there, marking extension in space and time, towards which he will be able to project "his" desire'.[17]

Indeed, in some sense formal experimentation rather than theological controversy may well be seen as the key to *Doctor Faustus* and the problems of interpretation it has posed. Throughout Marlowe's short writing career he was consistently innovative in form and genre, in ways which have perhaps not always been sufficiently appreciated. We are content now to term *Tamburlaine* a tragedy, yet Mark Thornton Burnett suggests that it may originally have been conceived of as a comedy[18]; certainly the printer observed that he had removed some comic material from it, and ending with a marriage, as the first part does, is usually a prime hallmark of Renaissance comedy. Equally, both *Doctor Faustus* and *The Jew of Malta* have been seen to be fundamentally informed by the traditions of vice comedy (with T.S. Eliot famously terming the latter in particular 'a tragic farce'), and William Empson even suggested that in an original, uncensored version of the play, Faustus had escaped damnation or indeed punishment of any kind.[19] *Edward II* and *The Massacre at Paris* may perhaps seem more securely anchored in tragedy, but both are also, and perhaps primarily, history plays, and the latter also comes at least as close as *The Jew of Malta* to comedy or even farce. And what seems almost certain to have been Marlowe's final work is, of course, the most generically puzzling of all: can he really have been proposing to tack a tragic conclusion onto the buoyant comedy of *Hero and Leander*, did he mean to reshape the narrative to allow of a different *telos*, or had he in fact deliberately abandoned it *in medias res*, dispensing with an end altogether?

In *Doctor Faustus*, this habitual generic indeterminacy manifests itself, as Snow so acutely observed, in an obsessive concern with ends and closure. Patrick Cheney points to the 'curiously plural *telos* "fortunes"' and also to the fact that Faustus uses the word 'end' 'five times in the opening monologue alone'[20] (one might well see an interesting parallel here with *The Spanish Tragedy*, by Marlowe's sometime roommate Kyd, which similarly inverts ideas of ending by opening on the hero's ghost and closing with the promise to begin an endless tragedy). This destabilising of the idea of a single, unitary end is of course significantly compounded by the survival of two rather different endings for the play in the A- and B-texts, as well as by the fact that we can in any case never follow Faustus on that final journey beyond the grave – not to mention the added complication that members of different communions would differently envisage the afterlife likely to await him, something which is still further inflected by the invocation of the classical as well as the Christian paradigm, with its quite separate eschatology. Protestants would presumably envisage Faustus as damned, but Catholics might imagine him in Purgatory, and in the classical world-view to which he himself has subscribed hell, as he himself says, is confounded in Elysium. (Again, *The Spanish Tragedy*, where any Christian account of the afterlife has been completely superseded by a thoroughgoing classical schema, seems relevant here.)

Perhaps the primary reason that our sense of closure in *Doctor Faustus* is disturbed, however, is that the protagonist himself has his eye on it so little. One of the most remarkable characteristics of Doctor Faustus is the extent to which he allows himself to be distracted. This is indicated even at the outset as he tries and turns away from each academic discipline in turn, and though it is characteristic of Marlowe to use a short scene to express a longish period of time (as indeed in Faustus' closing soliloquy), I do think we are meant to register here the brevity of his attention span and the short shrift which he accords each one. (Though the fault is not entirely Faustus': we are also, I think, invited to register the irony of the fact that to 'commence' M.A. is to come to the end of the studies which have earned you the title, so that inversion of endings is structurally implicit in the situation.) By line 10 of the opening scene he is confident that he has 'attained the end', though any sense of finality this engenders will be sharply undercut by the fact that he attains it again at line 18, not to mention the devastating irony that, as so many scholars have pointed out, this man who is so eager to get to ends cannot take the time or trouble to finish any of the quotations he cites. This quality is developed still further during the rest of his career: none of the purposes he initially proposes to himself is carried out, and his energy is frittered away on increasingly trivial endeavours (which concomitantly requires Marlowe effectively to invent a new form, a tragedy with frivolous interludes).

Suggestively, this feature of Faustus' career is echoed and paralleled in *Hamlet*, whose hero's Wittenberg education and whose interest in repentance and the afterlife make it in many ways an illuminating companion piece to *Doctor Faustus*. Hamlet too becomes distracted from his purpose, and just as Faustus' grand plans shrivel away to nothing, so the inhabitants of Denmark find that their intentions and actions produce curious and unpredictable results, all structured by an ineluctable logic of perverse displacement: it is Hamlet who goes to sea, but Ophelia who drowns; Fortinbras attempts to invade Poland, but finds himself in Denmark; Hamlet tries to kill his uncle, but it is Polonius who is stabbed. 'Distraction', the word which is in some ways the keynote of Hamlet's character and experiences, is the prevailing deity of *Faustus* too. J.B. Steane cites Greg's objection to a metaphor used by the Old Man: 'the Old Man in the 1604 Quarto speaks of "the gole That shall conduct thee to celestial rest" (1275–6). Greg comments: "a goal cannot conduct to an end" '.[21] But in *Doctor Faustus*, that is just the point: everything that seems to be a goal or an end in itself proves illusory, merely leading on to another end in a process of infinite deferral in ways which, together with the play's overt foregrounding of languages, words and signifying systems, bring Marlowe prophetically close to the concerns of contemporary linguistics and critical theory, but force him by the same token to play some very daring games with the generic practices of the Renaissance. And even when he does seem decisively to assert an ending, with the overt authorial intervention of 'Terminat hora diem; terminat author opus', we surely notice that the word 'terminat' undercuts itself by standing, twice, at the beginning rather than the end of the phrase, and thus conspicuously failing to enact its own meaning.

Other aspects of the play are also twinned and revisited in *Hamlet*, and since one could hardly hope for a more acute or intelligent guide than Shakespeare, one should perhaps pay attention to them. *Hamlet* opens in an atmosphere of war; *Doctor Faustus* is a play greatly concerned with the technologies, language and *matériel* of war. This is another reason why I find it more convincing to see the play as close in time to both *Tamburlaine*, Marlowe's epic of war, and to the

Armada years. One could almost suggest that *Tamburlaine* offers various parallels between the hero and Henry VIII – both are iconoclasts who make iconic images of themselves and their families, with Tamburlaine's bridling of the kings echoing images of Henry toppling the Pope – and thus stages the king who brought about the Reformation, while *Doctor Faustus*, with its world in which any sense of the divine gaze has, until the closing moments, been comprehensively replaced by human eyes, shows us part of the war which was the consequence of that Reformation. (Echoes of Henry are, as I am by no means the first to notice, equally present in *Hamlet*, with its motif of the widow of one royal brother marrying another, just as Catherine of Aragon married first Arthur, Prince of Wales and then Henry himself.)

Faustus, despite the fact that his career so far has been entirely academic, dreams of military success:

> I'll levy soldiers with the coin they bring,
> And chase the Prince of Parma from our land,
> And reign sole king of all our provinces:
> Yea, stranger engines for the brunt of war
> Than was the fiery keel at Antwerp's bridge,
> I'll make my servile spirits to invent.
>
> (I.i.94–9)

It is, moreover, notable that this is an informed fantasy rather than a naïve one. Faustus does not dream of personally performing any glorious and improbable Herculean feats; he knows that war has to be paid for, and that modern warfare further depends on technology, with success most likely to go to those who have the 'stranger engine'. Later, he further demonstrates this practical streak:

> Had I as many souls as there be stars,
> I'd give them all for Mephistophilis.
> By him I'll be great emperor of the world,
> And make a bridge through the moving air
> To pass the ocean with a band of men;
> I'll join the hills that bind the Afric shore,
> And make that land continent to Spain,
> And both contributory to my crown.
>
> (I.iii.104–11)

Once more, Faustus has his eye firmly fixed on agency. Whereas Tamburlaine dreams simply of world domination (and achieves it), Faustus offers the relatively realist proposition 'By him I'll be great emperor of the world'; whereas Tamburlaine on his deathbed prophetically imagines himself personally engineering the Suez canal ('I meant to cut a channel to them both' [*II*, V.iii.135]), Faustus projects an artificial isthmus which will allow his men, rather than himself, to work. That Faustus, unlike Tamburlaine, does *not* succeed in any of these grandiose plans is perhaps most readily attributable that he does not keep his feet thus firmly on the ground, for, with Mephistophilis apparently off in Constantinople (III.ii.33), Faustus goes solo, and not only dissipates his energies but loses all sight of the practicalities to which he had earlier given such prominence:

> I will be Paris, and for love of thee,
> Instead of Troy shall Wittenberg be sacked;
> And I will combat with weak Menelaus,
> And wear thy colours on my plumèd crest:
> Yea, I will wound Achilles in the heel,
> And then return to Helen for a kiss.
>
> (V.i.96–101)

It is, perhaps, not the least part of Faustus' journey to damnation that his sense of practicability diminishes as fast as his goals do. It is true that we are only unevenly and partially aware of this process, but that may well be due not so much to any defect in Marlowe's overall design but to the state of the play as we now have it.

In one sense, however, references to the actualities of war have always taken second place in the play to a sharp awareness that the most effective kind of warfare is waged in the mind, in ways which again rework the interpenetration of exterior and interior so characteristic of Marlowe. Here too it is tempting to relate Marlowe's activities as a writer to his alleged career as a spy, because *Doctor Faustus* does indeed offer a very incisive analysis into the ideological operations that underlie and structure literal conflicts:

> All things that move between the quiet poles
> Shall be at my command. Emperors and kings
> Are but obeyed in their several provinces,
> Nor can they raise the wind or rend the clouds;

> But his dominion that exceeds in this,
> Stretcheth as far as doth the mind of man.
>
> (I.i.58–63)

Here Marlowe sounds strangely like a Foucauldian *avant la lettre*, and so he does too in his emphasis on surveillance, for it is remarkable how often in this play Marlowe stages scenes in which one character is very considerably affected by the actions of another character whom they cannot see: Faustus is sung to by blind Homer (II.iii.26), invisibly torments the Pope, and summons up an Alexander and his paramour, who are apparently quite unaware that they are being surveyed. Perhaps most poignantly – and, in dramatic terms, most frustratingly – Faustus at the end of the play seems to see visible evidences of the tantalisingly absent God which we cannot. 'See, see, where Christ's blood streams in the firmament!' (V.ii.78) he exhorts, before adding 'see where God / Stretcheth out his arm and bends his ireful brows!' (V.ii.83–4) and climaxing in 'My God, my God, look not so fierce on me!' (V.ii.119). Again, this emphasis on invisibility and concealment (with the associated suggestion of both the inscrutability and the inevitability of divine purposes) is echoed in *Hamlet*, where Rosencrantz, Guildenstern, Polonius and the King all, at various times spy on Hamlet, and Ophelia in her madness sings some of the words of the song 'Walsingham', a name resonant in the history of Elizabethan espionage.

The visible as well as the invisible, though, is emphasised in *Doctor Faustus*; indeed this is a play obsessed with sight. Initially, Faustus conceives of himself as living in a world of shadows, with the word 'shadow' itself recurring in his language (I.i.120, I.iii.1) as well as that of Valdes (I.i.130). He first conjures in order to make spirits visible to him (that he has no doubt of their already being present, at least in some sense, is shown by the fact that he speaks to them); when one does in fact manifest itself to him, he shows a surprising concern to control its appearance, instructing it 'I charge thee to return and change thy shape' (I.iii.24). From then on, seeing becomes the governing idea for Faustus. He believes only what he can see, and trusts the evidence of his sight implicitly, remarking with satisfaction 'I see there's virtue in my heavenly words' (I.iii.28), even though 'heavenly' is so obvious a misnomer here that the very words with which he assures the audience of his own powers of sight must

surely serve to convince them of his blindness. Not for nothing does
Faustus conclude 'I'll live in speculation of this art' (I.iii.115), for
that is indeed what he will do, stubbornly refusing to broaden his
perspective to anything beyond it.

Faustus indeed embarks on a career of seeing, which is ironically
shadowed by our awareness of the fact that for Mephistophilis, the
punishment which he must constantly undergo is *not* seeing:

> Think'st thou that I, who saw the face of God,
> And tasted the eternal joys of heaven,
> Am not tormented with ten thousand hells,
> In being deprived of eternal bliss?
>
> (I.iii.79–82)

Careening around Europe sightseeing, Faustus becomes increasingly
driven by the specular impulse. His words 'When I behold the heavens, then I repent' (II.iii.1) mark the extent to which he is geared
almost exclusively to the visual, and it is hardly surprising that when
Lucifer and Mephistophilis want to distract him they promise him
that he shall 'see all the Seven Deadly Sins appear in their proper
shapes', to which Faustus, using the same language, enthusiastically
replies 'That sight will be as pleasing unto me as paradise was to
Adam, the first day of his creation' (II.iii.108–9). Taking a tourist's
curiosity to the ultimate, he even declares, 'O, might I see hell and
return again, how happy were I then!' (II.iii.175–6); later, he longs
to 'see the monuments / And situation of bright splendent Rome'
(III.i.47–8), with Mephistophilis adding 'I know you'd fain see the
Pope' (III.i.50) and promising that 'thou shalt see a troupe of bald-
pate friars / Whose *summum bonum* is in belly cheer' (III.i.52–3).
'When Faustus had with pleasure ta'en the view' (IV.i.1) does indeed
sum up this section of his career.

Though Faustus wants to see, however, he does not want to *be*
seen, instructing Mephistophilis 'Then charm me that I may be
invisible' (III.i.56). (Interestingly, the desire to control seeing and
being seen is one of the many things – including, effectively, a
name, since both are variants of 'fortunate' – which he shares with
Shakespeare's Prospero.) The first condition which he lays down for
selling his soul is that he 'may be a spirit in form and substance'
(II.i.96), which will, as we see, allow him to appear invisible (and in

the B-text also to adopt a deceptive bodily form); the fourth is that Mephistophilis 'shall be in his chamber or house invisible' (II.i.102). There is a notable contrast here with Robin, who rebuffs Wagner's hailing of him as 'boy' with 'How, "boy"? 'Swounds, "boy", I hope you have seen many boys with such pickedevants as I have' (I.iv.2–3). Robin seems to be suggesting here that Wagner has mis-recognised him, failing to register properly what is implied by his appearance almost as much as if he were invisible, and he doesn't like it. Later he makes it explicit that he wants to be seen, and to be talked about in a way which is directly influenced by his appearance: 'Say I should kill one of them, what would folks say? "Do ye see yonder tall fellow in the round slop? He has killed the devil." So I should be called "Kill devil" all the parish over' (I.iv.52–4). Robin does, though, share something of Faustus' scopic fixation when he fantasises about making 'all the maidens in our parish dance at my pleasure stark naked before me and so, by that means, I shall see more than e'er I felt or saw yet' (II.ii.4–6), as does the Emperor when he longs to be shown Alexander the Great because 'It grieves my soul I never saw the man' (IV.i.32), and the scholars when they desire to see Helen. We all, it seems, share an urge to look, but what this play powerfully reminds us is that looking can never be passive or innocent. One of the things on which critics of the play often remark is how very few evil actions Faustus actually performs; but he looks, and that turns out to be enough for Mephistophilis to inform him, 'Thou traitor, Faustus, I arrest thy soul / For disobedience to my sovereign lord' (V.i.65–6). In the dog-eat-dog world of the Elizabethan espionage system, where a man like Robert Poley, as Anthony Babington so painfully observed, might be either one's sweet friend or 'the worst of all two-legged creatures', the idea that someone you trusted might suddenly arrest you as a traitor cannot have been too unfamiliar.

As well as on seeing, Faustus is also fixated on tasting. For all the notably intellectual character of his early preoccupations, Faustus soon reveals himself as also profoundly sensual: he is not just every-doctor, but everyman, and indeed in some sense, given the strategies by which he is so insistently feminised, everywoman too. Moreover, though the frameworks of belief which governed Faustus' world have, in our own day, lost much of their ideological force, his personal predicament retains its power to appal, for Marlowe has cleverly characterised it not only as a choice between salvation and damnation, but as a terrible contrast between being and not being. It is *on kai me on*, rather than any theological issue, which the play actually names and which becomes its watchword, and which raises fears and uncertainties to which a spreading unbelief enables modern audiences to relate perhaps even more urgently than Marlowe's original ones could.

In this sense, it is indeed an atheist's play: Faustus likes life, and death is therefore quite awful enough anyway, even without the prospect of eternal damnation. Moreover, our apprehension of that eternal damnation is only of the vaguest and mistiest: the terrors and punishments which await Faustus are never actually specified. We might well conclude, indeed, that his fate will be no worse than that of Mephistophilis, who still seems to be able to find sources of pleasure in his existence, or we may simply feel uncertain of what will actually happen to him. In one way this is masterly, since it offers such scope for the engagement of the imagination, but in another it could equally well be described as, depending on your point of view, either a failure to convey an othodox theological viewpoint or a brilliantly daring and successful way of insinuating the possibility of an unorthodox one. Perhaps this is why Empson believed that the play in its original form had a happy ending, with Faustus transformed into a spirit rather than damned, but it seems to me equally possible that it always had an unhappy one, with the more discerning members of the audience able to deduce that this was what was in store for them too, because there is nothing after death. *On kai me on*, in this reading, is thus not only the central but the *only* philosophical truth of our being, and the presence of the word 'and' (Greek *kai*) rather than anything meaning 'but' shows us the extent to which being is always configured by non-being. For those for whom this is indeed the play's effect, Marlowe has achieved something truly colossal, for he has made a play grounded firmly in the forms and languages of the past into a prescient and devastatingly accurate image of mankind's spiritual and philosophical future. Just as the twenty-four years promised to Doctor Faustus collapse in the audience's experience into hours, and the hour of the final soliloquy collapses into minutes, so this play which couples *on kai me on* with existential angst strides from its base in the ancient world firmly into the new.

Though its modernity has often been remarked upon, *Doctor Faustus* does, then, in some respects seem to bring us closer than any other play to Marlowe's own world, with its references to academic life and to wars in the Netherlands, and its interest in religious controversy and surveillance. Marjorie Garber even suggests a link between the play and the Corpus Christi cycle, and hence to Marlowe's own college,[22] while Nina Taunton calls it 'a play (in effect a predestinarian tragedy) whose main character is a scholar of theology and whose author was one',[23] and Michael Keefer comments that '[t]he intentions of this would-be god, once he descends to particulars, smell oddly of the study' and that 'academic to the end, the last thing he can think of to abdicate is his necromantic scholarship'.[24]

In some sense, Marlowe seems to invite us to relate the play to his own world, since he 'rejected most of the more extravagant episodes that Johann Spies had included in the *Faustbuch*' and 'brought the legend of Faust down to the level of plausibility'.[25] Faustus' interest in astronomy, too, goes much beyond anything suggested in the sources, and also takes us very near to Marlowe's studies at Cambridge and (despite the notorious absence of any reference to Copernican thought) to urgently contemporary debates in which people who seem to have been members of his own circle were participants. Francis R. Johnson says that

> the playwright has characteristically transformed the ignorant jumble of wholly unscientific astronomical lore of Chapters 18 and 21 of the *Faust Book*. He raises, instead, problems inspired by the disagreement among the astronomical textbooks then current at Cambridge, and has the answers given by Mephistophilis accord with the doctrine expounded by the unconventional rather than the more orthodox authorities.[26]

Nevertheless, Faustus is notably not particularly satisfied with Mephistophilis' responses, reminding us that in this as in every other respect, this play is far more interested in the questions it asks than in any answers to them, which it exposes as always provisional and partial.

The philosophical and interpretative complexities of *Doctor Faustus* are infinitely multiplied by the difficulties of the text, or rather texts,[27] and the uncertainty surrounding their authorship. The comic scenes have often been felt to be so unsatisfactory – Roma Gill cites an undergraduate who adapted the Aristotelian dictum to term it 'a play with "a beginning, a muddle, and an end" '[28] – that critics have often been reluctant to believe they could have been written by Marlowe.[29] Constance Brown Kuriyama is only one of several critics to argue that 'it is not only possible but likely that the two texts of *Doctor Faustus*, in very different ways, are equally bad',[30] a view with which Michael Warren essentially concurs when he argues that 'the compilation or distillation of a single text of any value, let alone authority, from the totality of what is available to us is *not possible*', and that both texts contain non-Marlovian elements.[31] Max Bluestone suggests that the inescapable sense of duality thus engendered is indeed at the heart of the experience of the play: '[j]ust as there seem to be two plays dramatizing different doctrines, there seem to be two Faustuses, the form of his critical fortunes, like his dramatic fortunes, "good or bad" '.[32] Even Michael Keefer, who confidently asserts 'the decisive critical superiority of the A-version of the play', suggests that 'the B-text, in parallel passages, is generally better and more authoritative',[33] a phenomenon which has often been explained as the result of the A-text being a reported text.[34] Disagreement is most heated about the comic scenes, with some critics rejecting them outright and others, like Nicholas Brooke, arguing that even if Marlowe did not write them, 'he planned their existence',[35] while C.L. Barber suggests along rather similar lines that even though Marlowe probably did not write some of the comic scenes, they retain thematic continuity.[36]

I think that it is impossible to read the comic scenes, especially as they currently exist in the B-text, without feeling the presence of a non-Marlovian hand, and Paul Kocher has adduced detailed and painstaking evidence, which I find mostly very weighty, that all the prose scenes in the 1604 quarto were by Thomas Nashe,[37] and were probably written in the summer of 1594 – though he thinks that '[i]n a few places ... the 1616 text better preserves Nashe's prose, just as in some instances it better preserves Marlowe's verse, than does the 1604 text'. Consequently, he feels that these scenes bear the imprint of the anti-Puritan stance already developed by Nashe in the Martin Marprelate tracts.[38] Very often, the differences between the two texts do indeed have doctrinal implications.

Michael Warren, for instance, argues that '[i]f the B-text suggests that Faustus is damned irrevocably after the Helen incident, the A-text maintains by contrast the possibility of his salvation until the moment that the devils take him' (p. 136), and that

> [t]he A-text maintains a consistent Christian context whether the play is characterized by its blasphemy or its orthodoxy; the vigorous and passionate drama is intellectually arresting and challenging, especially in the suspense of its conclusion. The B-text, by contrast, appears to reflect a Christianity which is less intellectual, more homely, more timid, superstitious even. Although its conclusion – that God will withdraw divine grace in anger against a great sinner – is terrible, it reflects a simpler doctrine, a more certain, absolute, and pious confidence in its cautionary morality, in what could be conceived as its homiletic message.
>
> (p. 139)

Nevertheless, significant though the differences may be, and daunting as the task of attempting to unravel the play's textual history undoubtedly is, the effect on prospective critics need not be quite as disabling as Kuriyama's worst-case scenario supposes. One of the profoundest of all criticisms of *Doctor Faustus* is, I think, one of the earliest. It comes from a critic of formidable qualifications, the German author Goethe, who exclaimed of Marlowe's play 'How greatly is it all planned!'.[39] The play is indeed conceived along simple yet colossal lines; and though the details may now be murky, the all-important outlines of that planning still survive.

One thing which those outlines clearly allow us to see is the ways in which *Doctor Faustus* both develops and nuances concerns visible elsewhere in Marlowe's literary career. Ascribing the prose scenes to Nashe, Kocher also suggestively points to Nashe's independent description of the play as 'Faustus: studie in indian silke', which implies a perception of the play as situated very much within the discourses of the New World, and indeed Peter Holland calls it 'the greatest of all Elizabethan plays of travel', and argues that the understanding of space is at its heart: '[t]he court of the Duke of Vanholt can be shown, the heavens cannot. Marlowe's play is the object-lesson in the limitations of representation of place'.[40] There may be other reasons to connect parts of *Doctor Faustus* with the Elizabethan concern with exploration and colonisation: Christopher

Highley notes that the Irish rebel Tyrone was given 'assorted labels ... by Lord Deputy Burgh – the Running Beast, the Great Bear, the Northern Lucifer, and Beelzebub'.[41]

A concern with colonisation not only links *Doctor Faustus* with *Tamburlaine*, it also affords us new ways to understand the text's own more distinctive features. Colonisation, in the experience of Tamburlaine, is a process of infinite journeying which never produces a definite arrival; even at the very end of his life he laments the fact that there were places left for him still to visit. This idea of an effectively endless deferral returns us squarely to that multiplying of ends which so disables any idea of an ending in *Doctor Faustus*, and prompts us to notice the ways in which Faustus, too, is geared always towards the future at the expense of any meaningful participation in the present: as C.L. Barber remarks, in *Doctor Faustus*

> [t]he verbs are typically future and imperative, not present indicative ... When finally he takes up the necromantic works, there is a temporary consummation, a present-indicative simultaneity of words and gestures: 'Ay, these are those that Faustus most desires'.[42]

Inevitably, however, that consummation is *only* temporary.

Another concern of *Tamburlaine* can also be detected in both *Faustus* and *The Jew of Malta*, and this time it is one which was merely sketched before but is now developed more fully. If Scythians sometimes considered prone to effeminacy, Faustus is repeatedly and emphatically feminised. He compares himself with Eve; his pact with the Devil makes him, technically, a witch, a role so much more often associated with women[43]; and Max Bluestone points out that '[i]n the Prologue ... there is the sexual confusion of a Muse which vaunts "*his* heavenly verse" (6), thus anticipating Helen's later assimilation to Jupiter and Apollo, and Faustus' to Semele and Arethusa, and to Diana, too'.[44] C.L. Barber links this marked emphasis on the female with the play's insistent images of orality and breastfeeding,[45] and the food motif also ties in with the play's interest in theology: Masinton and Leech both see an inverted last supper in the play,[46] and Masinton also links spiritual and physical starvation, in ways which suggestively return us to *Hamlet* and its punning play with the Diet of Worms in Hamlet's disposal of Polonius' body.

The same pattern of gender inversion is also visible in *The Jew of Malta*. Several critics have pointed out that Barabas' reference to 'Infinite riches in a little room' draws on the iconography of the Virgin Mary,[47] and Ian McAdam argues that Barabas too is feminised by being conceived of as exhibiting maternal behaviour. McAdam suggests that this is to do with 'Marlowe's increasing anxiety over his own thoughts "effeminate and faint"',[48] and it may well be worth noting that in the original versions of the story, which Marlowe would certainly have known, Dr Faustus is a sodomite. 'In May 1532 the city council of Nuremberg refused a safe-conduct to "Doctor Faustus, the great sodomite and necromancer"',[49] and Empson saw the devils in the play as sodomites.[50] Just as *Faustus* recapitulates the major concerns of *Tamburlaine*, then, it also echoes (or, if one accepts the early date, foreshadows) those of *Edward II* and *The Massacre at Paris*.

To remember that the historical Faustus was a sodomite may well seem to take us even closer to the world of Marlowe himself, and to that central, if ultimately unanswerable, question of the dramatist's attitude to his protagonist. If they seem startlingly to coincide in the matter of academic leanings and sexual preferences, did Marlowe also, as many have assumed, share Faustus's unbelief? The question seems especially pertinent given that Marlowe appears to have regarded the issues of sexuality and Christianity as linked, if Kyd was quoting him correctly when he reported that 'Marlowe told him that to write in imitation of St. Paul could only lead to bad poetry ... "He would report St. John to be our savior Christes *Alexis* ... that is that Christ did love him with an extraordinary love"'.[51]

Some critics have been very reluctant to believe in an atheist Marlowe.[52] Michael Keefer sums up an earlier stage of *Faustus* criticism by deploring the fact that 'the moralists insisted, with New Critical obstinacy, that even if both Faustus and his creator died swearing, no connection could be admitted between the meanings generated by the "forme of *Faustus* fortunes" ... and what other texts might suggest about the poet's opinions',[53] and Leo Kirschbaum certainly exemplifies this stance when he demands, '[w]hat has biography to do with a play which we are presumably watching in the theatre? Whatever Marlowe was himself, there is no more obvious Christian document in all Elizabethan drama than *Doctor Faustus*.'[54]

Nicholas Brooke declares,

> [i]t seems to me clear that Marlowe was not strictly an atheist at
> all … The 'atheism' for which he should have stood his trial, and
> which he hints throughout his plays, was not atheism at all, but
> blasphemy, a repeated protest against the nature of God implied
> in His treatment of Man, a protest whose bitterness implies
> acceptance of the *existence* of God.[55]

And writing from a very different perspective, Lawrence Danson
declares that '[o]bviously it is not an atheist's play in any sense
beyond what an Elizabethan Privy Council might construe', and adds
'that Marlowe shares Faustus' desperate theology cannot be proven'.[56]

As John Mebane remarks, however, 'an interpretation which comes
to terms with the biographical record is more convincing than one
which ignores it',[57] and others have been more willing to allow of a
correspondence. A.L. Rowse declares sweepingly 'Faustus *is* Marlowe',
even suggesting that Marlowe himself dabbled in witchcraft,[58] Una
Ellis-Fermor referred unhesitatingly to 'Marlowe's Satanism',[59] and
Paul Kocher was sure that the Baines note did indeed represent an
accurate transcript of Marlowe's opinions (and indeed of a specific
articulation of them).[60] Constance Brown Kuriyama interestingly
points out that '[t]he only common oaths in Marlowe are the mild,
omnipresent "marry" and "i'faith." Perhaps Marlowe, like some
modern free thinkers, had decided that it would be inconsistent to
swear by what he did not believe in',[61] while Robert Ornstein wonders pertinently 'whether the legend of Marlowe's atheism could
have flourished well into the seventeenth century, if *Dr. Faustus*, his
one play that held the Jacobean stage and reading public, had
seemed as obviously orthodox to viewers then as it does to scholars
today'.[62] Finally, George T. Buckley sees him as 'one of the best
examples of what is well called Renaissance paganism. His atheism,
if such it was, seems not to have been an organized philosophical
system, but a temper of mind that expressed itself in life and
action', influenced largely by Machiavellianism.[63]

The religious opinions endorsed by the play itself – or, given its
textual state, selves – are no clearer than those of its creator. For Lily
Campbell, the crucial question is whether or not we believe in a

continuing possibility of repentance – '[s]urely the suspense which every witness of the play has felt could not be maintained if there were not a continuous uncertainty as to the final outcome of the play' – but 'it is not the initial sin and its consequences that hold us in suspense as we read or behold Marlowe's *Doctor Faustus*. Rather it is the continuing struggle of conscience, the conflict between hope and despair', and she thinks that Marlowe may have been influenced in this respect by the case of Francis Spira, who fell prey to religious despair.[64] Greg famously ascribed Faustus' damnation to demoniality, but T.W. Craik argues against that,[65] while Empson went so far as to doubt whether Faustus was indeed damned at all. It is thus simply not clear whether Faustus might have been saved if he had espoused Catholicism, or had been a better Protestant, or had repented more genuinely, or whether he was, as Calvinists would believe, damned from the outset. It is not even absolutely clear that God exists, only that the Devil does.

In one way, though, it is profoundly appropriate that we should be left in so much doubt about *Doctor Faustus*, because this duplicates and enacts the hero's, and indeed arguably the entire culture's, own experience of choice between inscrutable spiritual alternatives. (In an irony which Marlowe cannot have planned but which does not work entirely to the play's disadvantage, we cannot even choose securely which text to read it in.) Michael Keefer points out that Faustus' 'habitual, his characteristic, mode of speech is second-person self-address',[66] which may well increase the audience's sense of being part of a dialogue. The questions raised by Faustus are thus made frighteningly real and close to us, and all the more so because Marlowe presents them as both unanswered and, ultimately, unanswerable.

Just as *The Jew of Malta* echoes *Doctor Faustus* in indeterminacy of both gender and genre, so too it continues to put theology and religious practice at the forefront of its concerns. The play is often said to be hopelessly uneven: Tucker Brooke, for instance, remarks that '[i]t is not to be supposed that the extant text represents very faithfully the play of Marlowe', and doubts especially the authenticity of the third and fourth acts,[67] where the mighty line does indeed seem to sound only sporadically.[68] Howard S. Babb, however, has argued for its unity in at least one respect:

> For one thing, however the qualities of its action may vary, *The Jew of Malta* explores a single set of issues: religious hypocrisy and

governmental expedience as they are informed by a pervasive lust for wealth. For another, a recurrent pun on *policy*, a term appearing thirteen times in all, makes the play something like a running critique on these attitudes.

He later points out that the term *'profession'*, too, runs through the play. For Babb, indeed, the play is not fragmented at all: it merely 'demands that we respond seriously to caricatures presented as such. Its dramatic standard of reality is completely fluid.' He argues that it 'creates a realm of dramatic experience for which we have no name', but that in order to appreciate it we must first concede its artistic wholeness.[69] Here too, it seems, the unconventionality of the ideas is matched by the innovativeness of the form.

Another area of hot debate about *The Jew of Malta* concerns its representation of Machiavellianism. Irving Ribner, though conceding that 'we find in Marlowe's serious political thought, particularly in *Tamburlaine*, about as close an approximation of Machiavelli's central premises and conclusions as anywhere in Elizabethan writings', nevertheless concludes that '*The Jew of Malta*, although it is a classic example of Elizabethan "Machiavellianism", contains absolutely no reflection of Machiavelli's own ideas. There is no evidence, furthermore, that Marlowe in writing the play had any political purposes whatsoever.'[70] Elsewhere, he even suggests that the play is essentially *anti*-Machiavellian in spirit: 'the Machiavellian view of the world so proudly asserted in *Tamburlaine*, is in *The Jew of Malta* subjected to some ridicule.'[71] Other critics, though, have seen Marlowe as well versed in the doctrines of the historical Machiavelli: Margaret Scott, for instance, points out that '[m]aterial such as the Cambridge letters of Gabriel Harvey ... indicates that Machiavelli was widely read, much debated, and quoted at length in literary circles and at the universities',[72] while Michel Poirier observes that one of the surviving manuscript copies of an English translation of *The Prince* appears to have been in the hand of Marlowe's sometime roommate Kyd.[73] *The Jew of Malta* is often dated to 1589 or 1590, and it has been argued that 'in France in 1589 there occurred a sudden enlargement of knowledge of Machiavelli, though usually at a very superficial level', and that Marlowe had a good knowledge of French thought about the civil wars.[74]

Most ingenious is Catherine Minshull's argument that Marlowe may have been deliberately presenting Barabas as a stage Machiavel while the really Machiavellian villain is Ferneze all along; this, she thinks, would be a typically Marlovian approach, since 'irony was a habitual mode of communication for him'. (It is certainly noticeable how often Marlovian characters mean the precise opposite of what they say.) She also suggests, though, that there is more than just a joke at stake here: '[t]he legend which Marlowe dramatizes shows the trend of the new Protestant thought on the Continent, in which, contrary to Christ's promises, salvation is not available to everyone...in writing such a play Marlowe shows himself to be true to Bacon's definition of an atheist as one cauterized by holy things.'[75] What he shows even more directly, though, is that Machiavellianism disturbingly parallels Christianity: both are systems of thought whose truth we may not be able to know but whose influence we will be unable to escape. The sinister difference is that, while we may be gullible if we allow ourselves to be 'kept in awe' of Christianity, since God and the afterlife might not actually exist, we would be foolish if we were not in awe of Machiavellianism, since it is so ever-present and potent a political force and feature of human behaviour.

The Jew himself, that putative but unsuccessful Machiavel, presents not the least of the interpretative problems of the play. Discriminated against and insulted by the Christians,[76] he first invites the sympathy of at least a modern audience and then seems to spit it back in our faces by the growing outrageousness of his behaviour. As many critics have noted, however, every excess of Barabas' behaviour, however monstrous, is either learned from a member of another creed or culture which his society finds more acceptable than his own (he can even cite the classical precedent of Agamemnon for his infanticide) or equalled, and in the end, surpassed, by the actions such a member. Barabas can, then, be understood only in the context of the society which has created and conditioned him, and to bring this powerfully home to us Marlowe, as Shakespeare was to do in *The Tempest*, imprisons his characters on a small island on which their influence on each other is all-pervasive, and subjects their social interactions to a wry and acute observation.

Marlowe also adds a further dimension with which Shakespeare dispensed. The island of *The Tempest* is teasingly unidentifiable, an everywhere and nowhere which, for all its imbrication in the discourses of colonialism, can thus equally be read as a transhistorical dreamscape; but Marlowe's Malta is sharply and, on the whole, accurately characterised as strategic commodity and trading station, a stopping-post where Moslem, Jew and Christian meet and, as in a Sartrean vision of hell, proceed each to demonstrate either, according to your perspective, the inadequacy of their religious system or their own inability to live up to it. Historicising Marlowe's play allows us to see that *The Jew of Malta* is radically informed by a very precise set of perceptions of the island of Malta and its rôle in the history of Europe and of Christendom, and where it does actually deviate from historical truth it does so in the service of a very specifically formulated aesthetic, representational and political agenda.

The island of Malta is a small (it measures nine miles at its widest point, and is eighteen miles long) but strategically vital rocky outcrop in the Mediterranean. The indigenous inhabitants speak a language suggestive of Arabic origins, but by the sixteenth century they were very much playing second fiddle to the hospitaller order of the Knights of St John of Jerusalem. The Knights had been driven out of their previous fortress at Rhodes by the Turks in 1522, and had then suffered eight years of exile, during which Grand Master Villiers de l'Isle Adam visited the rulers of Europe (including Henry VIII) in turn before finally persuading the Emperor Charles V (the emperor whom Marlowe stages in *Doctor Faustus*) to make the Knights a gift of the Maltese Islands, which he had done on the condition that the Knights should defend them against the Turks. The Knights were an international order under the leadership of a Grand Master, of whom the most famous is Jean de la Valette, after whom Valletta, the present capital of Malta, is named. By the sixteenth century, their nominally hospitaller function was taking a back seat to the more pressing need to act as a bulwark of militant Christianity against Turkish incursions, and in 1565, during the Grand Mastership of La Valette, a Turkish fleet laid siege to Malta. The Great Siege, as it became known, is one of the most famous episodes in the island's history, and was followed with avid interest throughout Europe, since if Malta fell Sicily and Italy would then be in immediate danger of Turkish invasion. Prayers were said in England for the deliverance of the island, and two centuries later Voltaire could still say, 'Rien n'est plus connu que le siège de Malte' (nothing is better known than the siege of Malta).

If the Siege itself was famous, the most famous episode within it was undoubtedly the separate sub-siege of Fort St Elmo, a small, poorly defended, star-shaped subsidiary fort a short distance from the Knights' main headquarters, and the key to the strategically vital harbour of Marsamxett. La Valette's policy was to give Fort St Elmo up for lost but to allow the Turks to waste as much time, energy and ammunition as they liked on assaulting it, and he consequently refused to relieve it or, initially, to allow reinforcements to join the existing defenders. The Knights and the other defenders in the fort held out for considerably longer than had initially seemed possible; the Turks had expectated that it would fall in five days, but instead, with desperate gallantry, it resisted for almost a month. Inevitably, though, it fell in the end, and the garrison was shown no mercy. La Valette's plan had, however, succeeded: the Turks had dissipated their energies, and as summer began to draw to a close they turned tail and sailed away, leaving Malta untaken and with its reputation for impregnability magnificently enhanced. The whole episode thus became a byword for the triumph of Christian heroism and resolution against wicked infidels, and was celebrated as far away as England, where Matthew Parker, Archbishop of Canterbury, and founder of the scholarship which later took Marlowe to Cambridge, laid down a Form of Thanksgiving for six weeks.

It is usually supposed that all of this has very little to do with Marlowe.[77] The real-life Siege was not at all like the siege shown in the play, the most striking difference being that historically the Knights never capitulated, and consequently very few critics have ever troubled to explore the relationship between the events of the Siege as they actually happened and the events as Marlowe depicted them. Doing so, however, yields some surprising and illuminating results.

In her history of the Order of St John, Claire-Eliane Engel comments that during the Great Siege, 'les juifs de Malte avaient été d'une loyauté au-dessus de tout éloge' [the Jews of Malta had behaved with a loyalty above all praise].[78] When Fort St Elmo was conducting its gallant but doomed defence against the Turks, the Grand Master allowed one final volunteer force to attempt to force their way from the Knights' main stronghold at Fort St Angelo to its relief. Anyone who went on such a mission faced certain death, but nevertheless two Jews of the island chose to join the relief expedition, although in the event the boats carrying the would-be volunteers were unable to get past the Turkish cannon and were forced to turn back to the town of Birgu. However, relations between Jews and

Maltese had not always been so happy. Since the islands were dependencies of the Aragonese crown, Jews had been officially expelled from them in 1492, and their property confiscated:

> It appears from a notarial deed of 2 June 1496, that the monastery of St Scolastica had just been founded ... The monastery was then occupying what had once been the synagogue of the Jews that had been expelled from the island only four years earlier. The monastery of St Scolastica eventually moved to Birgu. Their short stay at Mdina is fairly well documented. On several occasions they sought help from the *Università*, as in 1516 when the city wall had collapsed, pulling down part of the monastery with it.[79]

The convent installed in the literal remains of a Jewish residence seems strongly suggestive of the confiscation of Barabas' house for a nunnery. Originally situated in the old capital of Mdina, the convent is later moved to Birgu, which, if there is any pretence at topographical accuracy at all, would logically be the principal setting of *The Jew of Malta*, since it was the only major town involved in the Siege of 1565. The collapsing wall, too, is reminiscent of Barabas' blowing up of the house with the Turkish soldiers in, though there is also a parallel with two other significant acts of undermining which had a telling effect on the course of Maltese history: the virtual destruction of the bastion of Castile by the Turks during the Great Siege,[80] and, after it, Grand Master La Valette's attempt to forestall a second invasion planned by the Turks for the year after the Great Siege by having his spies in Constantinople set the arsenal on fire by blowing up magazines.[81]

Jews, however – or, at least, one Jew in particular – had featured far more prominently than this in the history of Malta. Malta owes much of its fame, some of its place-names, its distinguished Christian ancestry and, legend avers, its freedom from snakes, all to one very famous Jew: St Paul. 'Paul could as yet perhaps still be reckoned as a Jew,' comments Cecil Roth, referring to the future saint and his party as 'the first Hebrew visitors of whom we have record'.[82] This particular Jew of Malta, in whom, according to both the Baines note and Kyd, Marlowe took a particular interest, is, however, far more famous for his status as perhaps the most celebrated convert in recorded history from ultra-orthodox Judaism to Christianity. As such, he might well serve as an interesting comparator for the analogous conversion of Abigail; moreover, anyone familiar with accounts of the Siege of 1565 would be aware that the final engagement was fought in St Paul's Bay, legendary scene of the saint's shipwreck, where the Turks suffered a decisive defeat and left the beach and waters clogged with their dead.

It fits well with the ironic, ambiguous tone of Marlowe's play to remember this story of a Jew distinguished by adherence to Christianity, and the same kinds of complexities of association play over the name of the patron saint of the Knights of Malta. As Knights Hospitaller of the Order of St John of Jerusalem, they brought the island, argues Cecil Roth, 'into a sort of sentimental dependence upon the Holy Land', even though, by a particularly savage irony, 'it was expressly forbidden for any person of Jewish blood to be received into the Maltese Order' (p. 213), a prohibition which automatically excluded all indigenous Maltese on the grounds of allegedly Semitic ancestry. To be aware of these two associations would work to remind Marlowe's readers of what they might very often tend to forget: all Christianity has its origins in Judaism; the original Barabas was Christ's contemporary, and indeed his co-religionist; and Abigail's status as convert from Judaism to Christianity is thus no more than emblematic of the spiritual history of the faith itself. Even as it excludes Jews from its ranks, the Order of St John of Jerusalem proclaims its own Hebraic affinities. Rather than seeing the Jew as the Other, in short, this network of associations forces us instead to see him as essentially the Self.

Indeed the play in one sense at least engineers precisely such an identity of viewpoint; as David Farley-Hills points out, 'Marlowe's use of the term "City of Malta" is incidentally paralleled in contemporary Jewish references'.[83] Moreover, since the rich prehistoric legacy of Malta was, until the twentieth century, wrongly attributed to the Phoenicians, with Maltese as a language lyrically described in a modern historical novel as 'the soft, slurring dialect that Dido and Hannibal spoke',[84] we are once again in the territory of not only Christian but also classical myths of origins, especially since Barabas may well remind us of Aeneas both in his predilection for carpentry,[85] and in his famous admission of 'Fornication? / But that was in another country: / And besides, the wench is dead' (IV.i.40–2). There is no other reference to this episode in the play, and it squares with nothing else that we know of the character and behaviour of Barabas. But it is, above all, the sin of the roving Aeneas, loving and leaving behind him the suicidal Dido. The echo is hardly a strong one, but it may perhaps serve to remind us of the ways in which Mediterranean settings with Phoenician connections had already proved of interest to Marlowe the dramatist.

As well as Paul, another Jew associated with the history of the Maltese islands would have been a figure of considerable interest to Marlowe. Abraham Abulafia of Saragossa, born in 1240 and 'founder of the practical Cabbala',[86] was exiled to neighbouring Comino in around 1288, and composed one of his works there. Giordano Bruno, who may well have been a member of Marlowe's circle, showed much interest in occult writing and wrote a work called *Cabala del cavallo pegaseo*; John Dee, who may also have had links with Marlowe, was 'a practical cabalist'.[87] (Dee, too, seems a likely comparator for Faustus.)

Despite their official departure in 1492, there were Jews on the island during the Siege – indeed Roma Gill sees a possible parallel between the circumstances of their continued residence and the offer put to Barabas: 'could Marlowe have known that after the expulsion of the Jews from Malta in 1492 some were allowed to stay on the island on condition that they purchased the privilege of baptism by forfeiture of 45% of all their possessions?'[88] – and there were rumours of collusion between them and the enemy:

> [t]he repulsed siege of Malta was not only known as a Christian victory over Islam, but it was also the subject of contemporary rumours about financial complicity between the Jews and the Turks, who were said to have joined forces because the aggressive raids of Malta's Knights had turned it into an infamous market for enslaved captives.[89]

Cecil Roth comments that

> the Knights on their side professed to regard the Jew as more dangerous enemies even than the Turks, accusing them of espionage and worse ... The great Turkish attempt on the island in 1565 (which, according to contemporary rumour, the Jews actually financed) was certainly watched by them with eager eyes, and their disappointment at its failure must have been extreme.

'The monks of Malta are still to-day a snare and trap for the Jews', records the chronicler sadly, at the end of his account of the siege.

The reason for this, as Roth observes, lay not only in the Jews' earlier dispossession from the island, but specifically in the nature of the sufferings at the hands of the Knights, who took considerable quantity of Jews prisoner, so that

> the island continued to occupy in Jewish eyes a disproportionate importance, becoming a symbol for all that was cruel and hateful in the Christian world. Jewish scholars referred to it with an unwonted maledictory formula. A Messianic prophecy current at the beginning of the seventeenth century detailed how the Redemption would begin with the fall of the four kingdoms of unrightreousness, first among which would be Malta.

Roth further suggests that by far the greater part of the Jews expelled from the island in 1492 found refuge in Turkey,[90] which would further have inclined the Jewish populations of the Mediterranean to support the attackers rather than the defenders.

There were, then, essentially three basic patterns of Jewish behaviour on Malta that might have been available for Marlowe to draw on: the Jew as treacherous collaborator with the Turk, the Jew as dispossessed landowner and victim, maltreated by Christians, and the Jew as selfless hero, prepared to die alongside the Christian defenders of St Elmo. He makes use of elements of all of them, although, in typically Marlovian manner, with additional twists and complications. The most obvious correlation is between Barabas' expulsion from his house and the requisitioning of the former synagogue for a convent in Mdina. There is a more or less direct parallel here, to the extent that one might even regard the historical episode as a possible source for this aspect of the play – the irony of Christians inhabiting a building already sacred to another faith would have been of rich appeal to Marlowe. However, he has also used the episode in a very different way from that in which its historical analogue functioned. The actual nunnery of St Scolastica was founded in or shortly before 1496, 60 years before the Siege and 30 before even the loss of Rhodes. It stands as an isolated incident, with no motivational or structural connections with the successive engagements with the Turks; it represents merely a clash between Christianity and Judaism. Marlowe, however, has turned his account of a similar event into a three-cornered affair, focusing not binary oppositions but a complex and shifting pattern of racial and religious allegiances, personal qualities and political implications. His chronological dislocation of the event makes it into the immediate stimulus for Barabas' vengeance as well as an apt symbol for the Christians' opportunism and rapacity.

Similar subtle alterations reconfigure the relationships between other events in the play and their historical analogues. The Jewish moneylenders alleged to have collaborated with the Turkish besiegers do so, in the historical accounts, out of mere malice. This is a stereotypical reading of Jewish behaviour which Barabas in fact invokes in his extravagantly virtuoso introduction of himself to Ithamore:

> As for myself, I walk abroad o' nights,
> And kill sick people groaning under walls:
> Sometimes I go about and poison wells
> (II.iii.179–81)

Ironically, however, any member of the audience familiar with the events of the Siege of Malta would have an alternative framework available within which to read this confession. Poisoning of water was a repeated feature of the Knights' defence – a very wise precaution on so barren and hot an island. Before the Turkish invaders arrived, Grand Master La Valette gave orders for the poisoning of all the wells in the Marsa, the area of low-lying ground at the head of Grand Harbour[91]; when the Knights defending St Elmo unsuccessfully begged permission to make a final sally, the contemporary observer Balbi records that they wrote in their letter to the Grand Master that 'should they fail, they would at least die happy, and they would leave instructions that, in case of disaster, the water in the fort should be poisoned and the guns spiked'.[92]

To present Barabas as a poisoner of water, then, could be used to invoke the twin perspectives of the irrationally malevolent Jew and the rational action of heroic, Christian resistance. And it is of course doubly ironic that Barabas' very evil is, in one sense, an essential element for the proper functioning of the contrasting charitable activity of the Knights. 'In Marlowe's black humor, Barabas's cruelty is even shown to act as a necessary prop to the Church, enriching "the priests with burials" ' (II.iii.185)[93]; similarly, his claim that he 'with young orphans planted hospitals' (II.iii.96) can suggest an equally symbiotic relationship with the Knights if we read it in the light of their primary function as hospitallers, and recall in particular that 'the Hospital of *Santo Spirito* at Rabat, near Mdina, besides treating the sick also received unwanted babies or foundlings and catered for their upbringing and well being'.[94] If read with close attention to the history of Malta, there are few actions of Barabas' which cannot be seen at least to have a place in the overall functioning of the internal economy and social order. And even his most gratuitous act of cruelty, the poisoning of the entire convent of nuns, was actually a scheme proposed in the name of true belief and statecraft, when a plan was drawn up to eliminate all the students of the English College at Rheims by poisoning their well – a plan of which Marlowe would have had good reason to know, since the man responsible for it was his eventual accuser, Richard Baines.

A similar duality plays over Barabas' actual role in the Siege. Whatever his intentions, the effect of his actions is to work towards the Knights' complete victory. Of course, this is not the immediate result of his interference in events: in Marlowe's single biggest divergence from the events of recorded history, Barabas initially triggers a defeat for the Knights and an apparently unequivocal triumph for the Turks. With extraordinary abruptness, however, Barabas performs a complete volte-face:

> I now am Governor of Malta. True,
> But Malta hates me, and in hating me
> My life's in danger; and what boots it thee,
> Poor Barabas, to be the Governor,
> Whenas thy life shall be at their command?
> No, Barabas, this must be looked into;
> And since by wrong thou got'st authority,
> Maintain it bravely by firm policy,
> At least unprofitably lose it not ...
>
> (V.ii.29–37)

This may seem an improbable and poorly motivated transition, but it is in fact perfectly in line with the principles of Machiavelli, who has appeared at the outset of the play as Barabas' sponsor. Speaking of 'new principalities acquired with the help of fortune and foreign arms', Machiavelli recommends the example of Cesare Borgia:

> a new prince cannot find more recent examples than those set by the duke, if he thinks it necessary to secure himself against his enemies, win friends, conquer either by force or by stratagem, make himself both loved and feared by his subjects, followed and respected by his soldiers, if he determines to destroy those who can and will injure him, to reform ancient institutions, be severe yet loved, magnanimous and generous, and if he decides to destroy disloyal troops and create a new standing army, maintaining such relations with kings and princes that they have either to help him graciously or go carefully in doing him harm.[95]

Machiavelli's precepts – which, Luc Borot has recently argued, have been very thoroughly absorbed by Marlowe in this play[96] – serve effectively as a blueprint for Barabas' actions. There is also, however, another possible model for Barabas' thought processes here, if not for his actions. It might well be profitable to compare his pinnpointing of the weak spot in the defences with a parallel action by two captured Knights, and pehaps even to relate his psychologising approach to that of Grand Master La Valette himself. Accounts of the Siege unfailingly stress the heroism and indomitability of La Valette, who, at the age of 70, untiringly directed operations. Equally, however, they stress the fact that he was not engaged in physical warfare alone, but in an unremitting psychological battle both with the Turks and also, especially in the earlier stages of the Siege, with his own men.

La Valette's advanced age meant that he was one of the few Knights to have had personal experience of the loss of Rhodes and the peregrinations thereafter; he had also served as a galley slave, and so was accustomed to appalling hardship. At the outset of the Siege, he experienced some difficulty in holding in check the younger Knights, who, with little direct experience of combat, were spoiling for a fight rather than being prepared to husband their resources and endure the prolonged attrition of siege warfare. Knowing that pitched battle against the vast numerical superiority of the Turkish troops was simply not a viable option, La Valette had his work cut out to restrain them. His task became even more difficult during the dreadful last days of St Elmo, when the Knights in the doomed fort clamoured insistently to be allowed an open sally against the enemy rather than being slowly picked off. Faced with what amounted effectively to a revolt, the Grand Master lashed the dissenters with scorn:

> A volunteer force has been raised under the command of Chevalier Costantino Castriota.[97] Your petition to leave St Elmo for the safety of Birgu is now granted. This evening, as soon as the relieving force has landed, you may take the boats back. Return, my Brethren, to the Convent and to Birgu, where you will be in more security. For my part, I shall feel more confident when I know that the fort – upon which the safety of the island so greatly depends – is held by men whom I can trust implicitly.[98]

Later, the Grand Master's unshakeable resolve was to refuse to bow to sentiment when he determined that St Elmo should not be evacuated, since every day it could hold out bought invaluable time for the further fortification of Birgu, St Angelo and neighbouring Senglea.

The Grand Master has been universally acclaimed as heroic, but it is still possible to argue that there are pronounced similarities between his reliance on psychology rather than force in the enforcement of his authority, and Barabas' decision to opt for a power based on placing the island in his debt. The Grand Master was, moreover, capable of ruthlessness. His action of poisoning wells, so closely parallel to Barabas' alleged activities, was of course fully justified by the necessities of war, but he has also been much criticised for his retaliation to the Turks' mutilation of those who had defended St Elmo: as one commentator scathingly remarks, 'he commanded the heads of his Turkish prisoners to be struck off and shot from the large guns into the enemy lines – by way of teaching the Moslem a lesson in humanity'.[99]

Far more suspect than those of La Valette, however, were the actions of other Knights and Christians connected with the Siege and its immediate aftermath. The Viceroy of Sicily, Don Garcia de Toledo, came in for particular criticism, and Marlowe may well, as Emily Bartels suggests, have known better than his editors when he implied considerable tension between the Knights and the Spanish, who go so far as to threaten them with expulsion.[100] Since the Maltese islands had been the gift of Spain, and since Don Garcia's own territory of

Sicily would be so directly threatened if Malta was lost, the Knights looked repeatedly to him for support, but the help he provided was minimal. He hedged around every offer of assistance with impossible conditions, and when he finally allowed the small relief force known as the Piccolo Siccorso (the 'Small Succour') to leave Sicily it was only with express orders that it was not to land unless St Elmo were still in the Knights' hands; if it were not, they were to be abandoned to their fate. He did, however, leave his son, Frederic, as a pledge of his goodwill; the boy fought gallantly and was eventually killed in action during the siege of Birgu.

The stark contrast between the heroism of young Frederic and the dilatoriness of his father – the English agent in Spain commented that Toledo 's'était complètement déshonoré' [had completely dishonoured himself][101] – may well seem quite closely analogous to the distance which separates the loving commitment of Abigail, dying alongside the nuns in the community which her father has destroyed, and Barabas' opportunism. The latter is a quality he shares with Don Garcia, who, despite the pitifully small part he had played in events, was not slow to be publicly associated with the Grand Master after the Turks' eventual withdrawal. Don Garcia arrived on the island with the final Sicilian relief force, and shared in a celebration banquet. Since provisions were naturally scarce, however, he brought his own food to it.[102] Again there is a parallel here with *The Jew of Malta*, this time with the rather unexpected reaction of Calymath to Barabas' invitation to a similar occasion:

> To banquet with him in his citadel?
> I fear me, messenger, to feast my train
> Within a town of war so lately pillaged,
> Will be too costly and too troublesome
>   (V.iii.20–3)

This seems an odd detail to include; but it, like the mining of the monastry, does offer a very close echo of the events of the later part of the Siege, after the theatre of war moved from St Elmo to Birgu. And perhaps there is a reason for the closeness of the echo.

When the Chevalier Robles brought the Piccolo Siccorso to the aid of his beleaguered brethren in June 1565, there were two Englishmen in it. One of them, Sir Edward Stanley, is almost certainly identifiable with the uncle of Ferdinando Stanley, Lord Strange – by whose acting company *The Jew of Malta* was performed – who had been implicated in a plot to rescue Mary, Queen of Scots in 1571 and was 'listed as a recusant and a "dangerous person" in 1592'.[103] The Piccolo Siccorso arrived on the island at a crucial stage in the siege, immediately after the fall of Fort St Elmo. The loss of St Elmo triggered a complete change in the strategic situation and the conduct of the siege, which was now directed entirely at the peninsula towns of Senglea and Birgu and at Fort St Angelo, all on the other side of Grand Harbour. The Piccolo Siccorso was, as remarked above, transported in Sicilian galleys which actually had orders not to land if Fort St Elmo was not still in Maltese hands, since possession of it was considered so vital that the island was to be written off as lost if it was gone; but the Knight of St John who was sent ashore to learn the situation lied to the Sicilian commander, and the force was landed anyway. In fact, Turkish brutality to the captured defenders of St Elmo had been so monstrous that the loss of the fort had, if anything, stiffened the backbone of Maltese resistance; determined to avenge their dead brethren, and heartened by the fact that this, their smallest fortress, had put up so lengthy a resistance (which had bought time for strengthening the fortifications of Senglea, Birgu and St Angelo), the Knights were grimly resolved to defend their position to the last man, and the indigenous Maltese gave them complete support.

Sir Edward Stanley, then, arrived at a vital turning-point of the Siege. Spared the lingering horrors suffered by the indomitable defenders of St Elmo, spared too the discussions attendant on the Grand Master's agonised decision to leave them to their fate, spared the sight of the decapitated bodies, their hearts gouged out of their chests, which the current wafted across to St Angelo, Sir Edward served not in the living hell of the tiny, ruined fort but in a large, well-supplied garrison fired by furious determination and, thanks to the length of the resistance offered by St Elmo, a reasonable chance of survival, which improved significantly with every extra day they could hold out. When the Turks finally did abandon the Siege in September, two and a half months after he arrived, Sir Edward also witnessed the withdrawal of their humiliated army, in poor morale and devastated by the loss of some of their ablest commanders, and the ensuing jubilation and thanksgiving of the

Knights, the Maltese and the Sicilians who had brought the final relief force. There is no indication of when he left the island, but he would surely have been aware that Grand Master La Valette had immediately begun making plans for its regeneration and for the foundation of the new capital, to bear his own name of Valletta. Since Sir Edward did not die until 1609, he would presumably have been well able to give evidence of his experiences.

When Marlowe wrote his play, then, he did so in the service of a patron whose own immediate family had almost certainly had significant experience of both the island of Malta in general and the Great Siege in particular, and for an audience who were likely to be well aware of the strategic and historic role that Malta had played. I have dwelt at some length on the probable experiences of Sir Edward Stanley because they seem to me to overlap in some significant respects with Marlowe's dramatisations of the siege, which, intriguingly, is represented in greater particularity towards its closing stages – precisely those which Sir Edward witnessed.

One further aspect of the Maltese reality also deserves to be compared with Marlowe's representation of it. At III.v.7, Ferneze assures the Turks, in response to the Basso's assertion that what has brought him to Malta is 'Desire of gold', that 'In Malta are no golden minerals' (III.v.4 and 6). The song that rapidly spread as a commemoration of the Siege offers a direct contradiction of this:

> *Malta of gold, Malta of silver, Malta of precious metal,*
> *We shall never take you!*[104]

Quite apart from this unequivocal assertion, anyone with the slightest knowledge of the island would be aware of its tradition of jewellery manufacture and the abundant supply of gold and silver; gold was among the items whose export was expressly forbidden to the Jews expelled in 1492.[105] If, as seems highly likely, Marlowe too had access to this commonplace information, then he is representing Ferneze as telling a deliberate, barefaced lie. Such an action would certainly be well in accord with Marlowe's overall characterisation of Ferneze, and in that sense an uncovering of it may seem to add little to a conventional reading of the play, though it would certainly sit well with Coburn Freer's brilliant exploration of the significance of lying in general in the play;[106] but knowledge of such a dynamic nevertheless subtly shifts our understanding of the politics of the scene, and implies decisively that the key to decoding such exchanges must lie in understated irony rather than in any overt authorial guideline.

If Marlowe is indeed not only echoing the various uses of deception by the Knights themselves, but also effectively mimicking their deceptiveness by himself functioning as a slyly non-directive authorial presence, then presumably part of the point he is making is that deception in the name of religion seems always to be accepted by those who believe in that religion, which in Western society allows Christians to lie with impunity but forbids Jews or Muslims to do so. Marlowe, however, refuses to allow us to dismiss Judaism so contemptuously, taking the religion seriously both as the forerunner of Christianity and in its own right. Not the least remarkable feature of Marlowe's representation of Barabas is the strength of his attachment to his Jewishness. Roma Gill comments that 'Marlowe has thoroughly researched a Jewish identity for Barabas, creating from the Old Testament a character far richer than any of the stereotypes that he could have inherited from popular tradition (which would only have given him the features that Ithimore can describe)';[107] even Stephen Greenblatt, who sees Barabas' identity as 'to a great extent the product of the Christian conception of a Jew's identity', nevertheless notes that 'Marlowe invokes an "indigenous" Judaism'.[108] Barabas is aware of Jewish history, referring to the conquest of Judaea by Titus and Vespasian (II.iii.10), and is scornful of Christians:

> Rather had I, a Jew, be hated thus,
> Than pitied in a Christian poverty:
> For I can see no fruits in all their faith,
> But malice, falsehood and excessive pride,
> Which methinks fits not their profession.
> Haply some hapless man hath conscience,
> And for his conscience lives in beggary.
> They say we are a scatterèd nation:
> I cannot tell, but we have scrambled up
> More wealth by far than those that brag of faith.
>
> (I.i.113–22)

The underlying assumptions that pattern the logic and progression of this speech are revealing ones. Barabas seems to take the term

'Jew' as synonymous with 'wealthy', and to have little sense of other possible connotations of Jewishness, since he denies knowledge of the very diaspora which has, presumably, brought him to Malta, and associates the concept of 'faith' with Christianity alone. He also uses the term 'profession' of Christianity, and this word recurs when, like Tamburlaine the destroyer musing on beauty, Barabas the faithless contemplates faith:

> As good dissemble that thou never mean'st
> As first mean truth and then dissemble it;
> A counterfeit profession is better
> Than unseen hypocrisy.
>
> (I.ii.292–5)

Whatever the precise meaning of this extraordinarily difficult passage, it clearly invites us to consider the complexities of the relationship between external avowals, interiorised belief and action – a network of factors which structure so much of the action of this play, with its cast of Christians, Jews, Turks and Jewess-turned-Christian convert, and where a war is won and lost by first the prowess and then the destruction of the Janissaries (mentioned at V.ii.16), the feared Turkish troops who were originally the children of Christian parents. If Marlowe came across the story of the Jews who volunteered to die in St Elmo for a faith not their own, or considered the indomitable gallantry of the defence of the tiny fortress, he must surely have felt that Malta and its history afforded a spectacularly suitable setting for an exploration of the psychology of faith, and the ways, too, in which faith is always vulnerable to exploitation by those with more pragmatic agendas.

5
1592–1593: Tobacco and Boys

> As in my boat I did by water wander
> Repeating lines of Hero and Leander.

Marlowe's last year of life seems to have been a troubled one. In May 1592, two constables of Shoreditch appealed for protection from him, and in September he was involved in a fight in Canterbury, apparently attacking one William Corkine with a sword and dagger, though the matter was patched up before it came to trial. In the same month his friend Thomas Watson died (Marlowe was probably responsible for the Latin dedication of Watson's posthumously published *Amintae Gaudia* to the Countess of Pembroke). He also parted company from Lord Strange's Men, perhaps, if Kyd was right, because their patron objected to him as a blasphemer, and thus from Edward Alleyn, who had played so large a part in his success. Conceivably, he may have received some compensation for his losses and difficulties in the shape of a relationship which was something more than friendship with Thomas Walsingham, nephew of Francis, at whose country house at Scadbury he was staying when the Privy Council put out their order for him in May 1593. We cannot know, however, whether there was an emotional or physical involvement with Walsingham. Even if there was, the fact that it was Walsingham's personal servant who not only stabbed him, but conspicuously failed to suffer for it, suggests that Walsingham found Marlowe's death at least excusable, and perhaps even expedient.

Whatever the difficulties of his personal situation, however, Marlowe's literary career during this period went from strength to strength, producing in *Edward II* the one play of his which we can feel confident has survived as he left it (even *Tamburlaine* had had comic parts expunged, but there seems no reason to suspect the integrity of *Edward II* in any respect) and in *Hero and Leander* the work which, incomplete though it may be, was nevertheless to cement his literary reputation. Once again, as Marlowe moved from one stage to the next of his career, interests that were latent in the previous stage are developed, and concerns that were previously at the forefront of the his mind remain to inform his thinking. *Edward II*, too, is a play which has been carefully researched[1] and which is interested in the idea of writing – the King is, after all, destroyed by an ambiguous letter[2] – and the concern with literariness continues to inform *Hero and Leander*, of which Harry Levin has said '[t]hat men should need the authority of books to celebrate, if not to recover, the enjoyment of their senses is a paradox of the Renaissance which has nowhere been more vividly set forth'.[3] Moreover, there is a similar absence of any demonstration by heaven: while in *Doctor Faustus* an empty throne descends from heaven, in *Edward II* Charles R. Forker notes 'the absence of any action ... that requires the use of the upper stage ... the apparently missing "above" ... implies ... a ... profound skepticism about inherited religious categories'.[4]

If *Doctor Faustus* appears to offer us a glimpse of Marlowe's own religious beliefs, *Edward II* may well appear to be openly based on his own sexual preferences, and indeed to reflect his life in other respects too – Harry Levin thinks that the play reflects some personal sorrow, that 'Marlowe must have felt a hell of grief, like Edward', Dennis Kay proposes that 'Spencer's advice to Baldock about how he should turn himself from a scholar into a courtier has some relevance to Marlowe's own situation' (with perhaps a malicious sideswipe at Spenser, who claimed to be related to the Despensers), and Stephen Orgel suggests:

> For Marlowe to translate the whole range of power politics into sodomy certainly says something about his interests and that of Elizabethan audiences, but it also has to be added that it was probably safer to represent the power structure in that way than it would have been to play it, so to speak, straight ... Maybe Edward's sexuality is a way of protecting the play, a way of keeping what it says about power intact. This is the work of Marlowe

the government spy, at once an agent of the establishment and deeply subversive.[5]

The play cannot, though, be read as simply a reflection of Marlowe's own life and concerns. For one thing, it is clear that Marlowe is not simply drawing on personal experiences of passion, but is also acutely aware of how passion has previously been represented in literature – particularly, as Robert A. Logan points out, in Ovid.[6] Previous generations of critics have too often found the play so offensive that they have even tried to gloss over its obvious meanings – thus, for L.J. Mills, it is nothing more than 'a friendship play' – but though we are now much more willing to see it as a play which explores homosexuality, it is not axiomatic that Marlowe endorses his troubled hero.[7] Derek Jarman had to do a lot of rewriting and rearranging to turn it into a celebration of a gay counter-culture, and Sidney Homan suggests that 'Edward II may indeed stand as the playwright's tragic parody of the earlier Tamburlaine, as the manly world conqueror is reduced to a pathetic, effeminate ruler, opposed, for the play's first half at least, by men clearly his moral superiors'.[8]

Marlowe's hero may, then, share his creator's sexuality, but he does not seem to receive an unequivocal endorsement any more than Faustus does. David Thurn argues that

> it would be a mistake to ignore the way in which the play, even as it refuses to stigmatize Edward's desire for Gaveston in the terms of Christian teaching, allows the spectator to recognize the effects of an insidious, because partially concealed, entanglement of sexual and political properties. Drawing a structural parallel between Edward's love for Gaveston and Mortimer's dangerous alliance with Isabella, Marlowe undermines any attempt to distinguish homosexual from heterosexual desire on moral grounds. Still, the play asks us to witness and to recognize as familiar the sometimes barely perceptible slippage from the political to the sexual spheres in the representation of transgression.[9]

And Kathleen Anderson sounds a similar note of caution, observing that

> blindness to artistic ability is one of the most consistent characteristics of Marlowe criticism. Critics have always seen Faustus,

Edward II, Tamburlaine, and the Jew as simple variations of Marlowe's own personality. Some critics even go so far as to see these characters as the spokesman for the playwright. (This is particularly true of critics who see Edward II as Marlowe's spokesman for homosexuality.)

Anderson advocates a concentration less on Edward than on what she sees as the unusually well-developed characterisation of Isabella,[10] while Michael Manheim suggests that uncertainty of response is part of the point: 'the play seems built around a sudden and unexpected shift in appeal to audience sympathy following the murder of Gaveston in Act III, scene i.'[11]

Perhaps, though, *any* attitude that treats all Marlowe's heroes as eliciting a similar response is inherently problematic. Undoubtedly we are invited to be acutely aware of the folly of Faustus, but we may also register the fact that he is not actually wicked. In the case of Tamburlaine this balance may well seem to be inverted, especially if we imagine *Part One* as having been originally envisaged as free-standing and the story as thus concluding with unalloyed triumph for its hero, and while we may not admire Aeneas at all we can hardly fail to observe that he too triumphs. Even if we dwell on Tamburlaine's cruelty and Aeneas' lack of initiative, we must surely notice that they are at least luckier than Faustus, Barabas and the Guise, not to mention the hapless Edward. Whatever Marlowe's project in these plays is, it does not seem that it is in their attitudes towards their heroes that we may find it most consistently expressed.

I think a better guide than the personal would be the political. All drama is, of course, about the interaction of individual humans in social groupings, but because some of Marlowe's individuals are so towering this has tended to be lost sight of in his case. The fact that Edward himself is noticeably less towering than his great predecessors has tended to be written off as an historical accident, the result of an unfortunate breach with Lord Strange's Men which meant that Marlowe could no longer call on the services of Edward Alleyn and felt he had better turn to writing for ensemble playing instead. (John Berdan, for instance, argues that the layout of the title-page proves that '[t]he editor of the quarto was not clear in his own mind who is the protagonist'.)[12] But this assumes, of course, that he knew about the likely difficulties with Strange's troupe from the outset of composition, and that is purely speculation. It seems to me at least as likely that we can read Edward as interacting in a different way with his society because of the type of *character* Marlowe had conceived as because of the type of *actor* he was writing for. (In any case, if Alleyn, as seems likely, played Henry VI, it was by no means the case that he was associated exclusively with dominating, overbearing characters.) Perhaps Tamburlaine towers above the rest of his play because that is what conquerors do, and because Marlowe in this play is exploring the idea that social roles cannot inhibit those who are born to rise and command. Nor, however, can being born to high rank protect those whose tendency is not to dominate. Perhaps society is more tolerant of exceptional achievers, however brutal and ruthless, than it is of those whose sexuality does not conform to accepted norms. To some extent, indeed, all of Marlowe's theatre can be seen as probing and testing what society will or will not tolerate, particularly in the specific arenas of religious dissidence, lack of conformity to the norms of heterosexuality, and unwillingness to accept constituted authority. Given the increasing frequency of his brushes with the law in 1592/3 it is not being merely romantic to see him, whether consciously or not, engaged in a roughly parallel enterprise in his own life too.

Perhaps, however, *Edward II* is political in a specific as well as a general sense, and deals with authority as well as sexuality. It has often been seen as offering a covert representation of James VI of Scotland,[13] the man who, as Marlowe's involvement in government work would doubtless have made him sharply aware, was the probable successor to the throne of England in the event of the Queen's demise (which in 1592 could realistically have been expected to be not far off) and to whom Kyd claimed that Marlowe himself had thought of fleeing, as his friend Royden was said to have done. But it is surely Elizabeth herself, as much as or perhaps even more than James, who is reflected in this play's tragic glass, and to no very flattering effect. Marlowe's plays strike at many targets: morality, organised religion, norms of sexual behaviour, foreigners, women, politicians and even himself have all, at various times, been read as the victims of his wrath. His apparent dislike of the Queen has, however, been less clearly identified,[14] even though it is possible to see it hinted at in several of his plays. It has, for instance, often been suggested that *Tamburlaine* inscribes various aspects of the career of

Sir Walter Ralegh. Equally, it seems to me to make repeated and unmistakable allusion to Elizabeth, the Cynthia to Ralegh's adopted persona of the Ocean – and to do so, suitably enough in the light of Ralegh's preferred iconography of her, in the form of references to the moon. But whereas the moon in Ralegh's praises, and in other instances of Elizabethan allegory focused on the Queen, is glorious and beautiful,[15] in Marlowe it, and other emblems of the Queen herself or of queenship in general, are characterised in very different and far more derogatory terms. Marlowe, who is alleged to have personally made light of the power of Elizabeth when he supposedly said that he himself had as good a right to coin as the Queen of England, offers her no compliments in his plays.

Margo Hendricks has recently argued that what seems likely to have been the earliest of Marlowe's plays, *Dido, Queen of Carthage*, is Marlowe's 'response to the "reinvention" of England' under Elizabeth. For Hendricks, the play presents Dido as a figure analogous to Elizabeth I[16] – a parallel made very visible to the Renaissance consciousness by the fact that Dido's other name was Elissa, as in Ovid's Elegy 'Ad Macrum', which Marlowe translated.[17] Marlowe further stresses the relevance of the play to Renaissance Britain by highlighting the ancestry of Aeneas, whose grandson Brutus was the legendary ancestor of the British royal family. Despite this stress on Aeneas' putative position in the Tudor family tree, however, it is notable that Marlowe vigorously critiques him. Moreover, Dido dies in flames, like the phoenix which was one of the favourite emblems of Elizabeth I, but unlike the phoenix, she is not reborn; royalty, it seems, is not mythic or immortal after all, but perishable and sublunary, with that resonant name 'Eliza' presented as 'a hideous echo' (IV.ii.9) rather than a glorious paean. And the play's great emphasis on children – indeed, the very fact of its performance by the Children of the Queen's Chapel – surely served to underline and highlight Elizabeth's childlessness, and the resulting precariousness of the succession.

Similar processes can be seen at work in other plays. At a very early stage of *Tamburlaine*, Cosroe laments, 'Unhappy Persia ... / Now to be ruled and governed by a man, / At whose birthday Cynthia with Saturn joined' (I, I.i.6, 13–14). The kingdom, it seems, has been made unhappy by the influence of Cynthia, an inference which runs directly counter to every tenet of the cult of Elizabeth by imaging her as a malign power rather than a gloriously benign and inspiring one. Soon afterwards, Theridamas begins a speech with the words 'Before the moon renew her borrowed light / Doubt not, my lord and gracious sovereign ...' (*I*, I.i.69–70). Here the moon is a sovereign whose authority is only borrowed, in marked opposition to the undoubted legitimacy Theridamas concedes to the male ruler. In similar vein, Bajazeth ominously invokes the moon and its power immediately before his defeat:

> You know our army is invincible;
> As many circumcisèd Turks we have
> And warlike bands of Christians renied
> As hath the ocean or the Terrene sea
> Small drops of water when the moon begins
> To join in one her semicircled horns
> (*I*, III.i.7–12)

Tamburlaine repeats the 'borrowed light' figure when he contrasts the ineffectual radiance of the moon with his own:

> Smile, stars that reigned at my nativity
> And dim the brightness of their neighbour lamps!
> Disdain to borrow light of Cynthia,
> For I, the chiefest lamp of all the earth,
> First rising in the east with mild aspect
> But fixèd now in the meridian line,
> Will send up fire to your turning spheres
> And cause the sun to borrow light of you.
> (*I*, IV.ii.33–40)

Tamburlaine, moreover, tilts again at the 'theology' of the cult of Elizabeth when he slaughters the Virgins, implicitly deriding any mystification of virginity; and when Zabina cries piteously 'Make ready my coach, my chair, my jewels' (*I*, V.i.317–18) she both invokes the principal, and treasured, personal trappings of Elizabeth I – who was figured in the 1575 Kenilworth festivities as Zabeta, a name close to 'Zabina' – and shows their utter inefficacy at a time of crisis. Finally, when we hear that the Arabian king 'Comes now as Turnus 'gainst Aeneas did' (*I*, V.i.381), the simile silently co-opts for

Tamburlaine himself the authority of Aeneas, descent from whom allegedly boosted the prestige of Elizabeth's family tree, and thus concomitantly leaches it away from those who oppose him. Moreover, the extent to which *Tamburlaine* does *not* pay court to Elizabeth may be further emphasised by contrasting it with a moment in Marston's *Antonio and Mellida*, in which 'Mount tufty Tamburlaine' has already been specifically mentioned in the Induction: Antonio, disguised as an Amazon, claims that 'After long travel through the Asian main, / I shipped my hopeful thoughts for Brittainy, / Longing to view great nature's miracle, / The glory of our sex'.[18] It is notable that Tamburlaine's desire to visit Britain is driven by no such gallant imperative.

This process of subtle denigration of the moon continues and indeed gathers pace in Part Two. Tamburlaine says he will stop 'When heaven shall cease to move on both the poles, / And when the ground whereon my soldiers march / Shall rise aloft and touch the hornèd moon' (*II*, I.iii.12–14). This suggestion that the moon may not be able to retain her pre-eminence and distance is followed by a direct avowal that Tamburlaine does not intend to be bound by the laws of primogeniture, the authorising principle of the Elizabethan succession:

> If thou exceed thy elder brothers' worth
> And shine in complete virtue more than they,
> Thou shalt be king before them
>
> (*II*, I.iii.50–2)

Even Orcanes, who plays things much more by the book, has an interesting reference to the power of the moon:

> Open, thou shining veil of Cynthia,
> And make a passage from th'empyreal heaven,
> That He that sits on high and never sleeps
> Nor in one place is circumscriptible,
> But everywhere fills every continent
> With strange infusion of His sacred vigour,
> May in His endless power and purity
> Behold and venge this traitor's perjury!
>
> (*II*, II.ii.47–54)

For Orcanes, it seems, Cynthia is merely something that gets in the way of proper justice by the male power of godhead, and her role is even less flatteringly envisaged when he crows over the dead body of Sigismund, gloatingly mocking 'His power, which here appears as full / As rays of Cynthia to the clearest sight' (*II*, II.iii.29–30): in a typical piece of Marlovian irony, Cynthia, effectively, is as powerless as a dead man. Tamburlaine threatens to demote her even further when he orders,

> Apollo, Cynthia, and the ceaseless lamps
> That gently looked upon this loathsome earth,
> Shine downwards now no more, but deck the heavens
> To entertain divine Zenocrate
>
> (*II*, II.iv.18–21)

The limitations of the queen's power are hinted at even more strongly in Zenocrate's speech on her deathbed:

> I fare, my lord, as other empresses,
> That, when this frail and transitory flesh
> Hath sucked the measure of that vital air
> That feeds the body with his dated health,
> Wanes with enforced and necessary change.
>
> (*II*, II.iv.42–6)

In a play fundamentally concerned with the acquisition of land, Elizabeth, whose attitude to the English colonial enterprise was, Karen Newman suggests, at best ambivalent,[19] does not come off well.

Only once, towards the end of the play, does the figure of Cynthia seem to rally and fight back against Tamburlaine. Orcanes decrees,

> Our battle, then, in martial manner pitched,
> According to our ancient use shall bear
> The figure of the semicircled moon,
> Whose horns shall sprinkle through the tainted air
> The poisoned brains of this proud Scythian.
>
> (*II*, III.i.64–8)

The moon, here, becomes an emblem to be deployed against Tamburlaine, a counter-image of authority. It functions thus too in

Theridamas' speech to Olympia, though his evaluation of the respective strengths of the two figures is very different:

> But lady, go with us to Tamburlaine,
> And thou shalt see a man greater than Mahomet,
> In whose high looks is much more majesty
> Than from the concave superficies
> Of Jove's vast palace, th'empyreal orb,
> Unto the shining bower where Cynthia sits,
> Like lovely Thetis in a crystal robe
>   (*II*, III.iv.45–51)

Cynthia is even further disempowered in Theridamas' next appeal:

> Olympia, pity him in whom thy looks
> Have greater operation and more force
> Than Cynthia's in the watery wilderness,
> For with thy view my joys are at the full,
> And ebb again as thou depart'st from me.
>   (*II*, IV.ii.28–32)

Not only less powerful than Tamburlaine, she is even less powerful than Olympia.

Queenship in other guises is also given short shrift in the play. Tamburlaine puns on queens / queans as he distributes the concubines to the common soldiers (*II*, IV.iii.70–1), and there is a reference to the notorious Semiramis (*II*, V.i.73), infamous for her lust and incest. Finally comes what is perhaps the cruellest blow of all: Callapine, hoping that Tamburlaine will soon meet his end, says, 'when the pride of Cynthia is at full, / She wanes again, and so shall his, I hope' (*II*, V.ii.46–7). The ultimate enfeeblement of Tamburlaine can, it seems, be suggested most aptly by imaging him as reduced to the level of Cynthia. Throughout both plays, he has been repeatedly imagined as a figure of opposition to her; but *Tamburlaine* is, as the Prologue tells us, a 'tragic glass', and as Tamburlaine and Cynthia wane together, the barbarous Scythian is suddenly revealed as that most terrifying of all monsters, the one that is seen in the mirror.

Doctor Faustus, too, dismantles some of the most prized layers of Elizabethan iconography, repeatedly evoking, for instance, the myth of Actaeon, who spied on Diana, and thus 'figure[s] ... the abject ...

consequences of gazing upon the queen'.[20] Like the Queen, Faustus proposes military involvement in the Netherlands, and has designs on the riches of the New World (I.i.81–99 and I.i.121–35). His rivalry is made even more direct and obvious when he orders Mephistophilis,

> I charge thee wait upon me whilst I live,
> To do whatever Faustus shall command,
> Be it to make the moon drop from her sphere,
> Or the ocean to overwhelm the world.
>
> (I.iii.37–40)

Faustus does not actually order the ousting of the moon from her sphere, but he contemplates it, and does so, moreover, in terms which pointedly refer to the politics of the Elizabethan court, if the 'ocean' is seen as referring to her pet name for Ralegh. Distinctively Elizabethan uses and pronunciations also make sinister Faustus' claim of himself that 'This word damnation terrifies not him, / For he confounds hell in Elysium' (I.iii.59–60): 'Elizium', the home of Eliza, here becomes indistinguishable from hell. And here, as in *Tamburlaine*, chastity, so clearly identified as the Queen's distinguishing virtue, goes by the board when Mephistophilis promises Faustus,

> She whom thine eye shall like, thy heart shall have,
> Be she as chaste as was Penelope,
> As wise as Saba, or as beautiful
> As was bright Lucifer before his fall
>
> (II.i.158–61)

Moreover, Michael Hattaway points out that in fetishising Helen, Faustus celebrates 'the destroyer of the home of the mythical ancestor of Elizabeth', and that his desire to 'make a bridge through the moouing ayre' also treads on the iconographical purlieus of Elizabeth, since this, and the proposed accompanying acts, 'are parodies of … the powers of Fidelia in *The Faerie Queene*'.[21]

Chastity is also tilted at in *Hero and Leander*. In the first Sestiad, Mercury pursues a country maid who, like the Queen, is associated with pearls and roses (ll.389 and 391). Mercury 'would needs discover / The way to new Elysium' (ll.410–11), and, because 'All women are ambitious naturally' (l.428), she is not entirely unwilling. The mystique of virginity is, in this poem, comprehensively mocked; and, as Harry Levin observes, '[i]n attacking Hero's virginity as an "idoll" (I, 269), Leander is committing *lèse-majesté* as well as undermining the constraints of monasticism'.[22] Moreover, Marlowe also translated Ovid's strictures on queens (Book II, Elegy XII, ll.17–26).

As Dennis Kay has most recently observed, *Edward II* too fits very well into this model:

> I ... relate *Edward II* to the cult of Elizabeth, suggesting that it participates fully in the discursive procedures that surrounded the Tudor monarchy ... I propose that in Marlowe's play the image of the king may be construed as a negative exemplum, being defined negatively in terms of the well established cult of Queen Elizabeth.[23]

However, though I agree completely with both Kay and Dympna Callaghan, who also says that 'there is an undeniable resemblance between Edward and Elizabeth's sovereignty',[24] that the play does indeed relate to the cult of Elizabeth, I am much less sure that Marlowe's Edward is designed as a figure who can be condemned because he is unlike Elizabeth. Rather, the parallels between the two seem to me to be dangerously pointed.

The contemporary resonances are hinted at early. Gaveston, like Faustus, seems to gesture at the standard Elysium / Elizium pun when he says,

> The sight of London to my exiled eyes
> Is as Elysium to a new-come soul –
> Not that I love the city or the men,
> But that it harbours him I hold so dear,
> The King, upon whose bosom let me die
> And with the world be still at enmity.
>
> (I.i.10–15)

Again as in *Faustus*, however, Elysium/London has nothing to recommend it except a king – a commodity strikingly absent from Elizabethan England. Moreover, we are immediately introduced to the darker and more frustrating aspects of court culture when we hear Gaveston proposing to work the clientage system operated by so many noblemen at court, frequently to the despair of their dependants:

> [*aside*] Ay, ay. These words of his move me as much
> As if a goose should play the porcupine
> And dart her plumes, thinking to pierce my breast.
> But yet it is no pain to speak men fair;
> I'll flatter these and make them live in hope.
> [*To them*] You know that I came lately out of France,
> And yet I have not viewed my lord the King.
> If I speed well, I'll entertain you all.
>
> (I.i.38–45)

Moreover, Gaveston proposes to ape the sights of power of Elizabethan court culture, but to very different effect:

> Music and poetry is his delight;
> Therefore I'll have Italian masques by night,
> Sweet speeches, comedies, and pleasing shows;
> And in the day, when he shall walk abroad,
> Like sylvan nymphs my pages shall be clad;
> My men, like satyrs grazing on the lawns,
> Shall with their goat feet dance an antic hay.
> Sometime a lovely boy in Dian's shape,
> With hair that gilds the water as it glides,
> Crownets of pearl about his naked arms,
> And in his sportful hands an olive tree
> To hide those parts which men delight to see,
> Shall bathe him in a spring; and there, hard by,
> One like Actaeon, peeping through the grove,
> Shall by the angry goddess be transformed,
> And running in the likeness of an hart
> By yelping hounds pulled down and seem to die.
> Such things as these best please his majesty
>
> (I.i.52–70)

This is designed to celebrate not the moon, but, again, a male figure who vies for her majesty; and the threat to Elizabeth is even more obvious in the words of Lancaster, with their clear echo of sixteenth-century events in Ireland shadowing their ostensible description of fourteenth-century ones:

> Look for rebellion; look to be deposed.
> Thy garrisons are beaten out of France,
> And lame and poor lie groaning at the gates.
> The wild O'Neill, with swarms of Irish kerns,
> Lives uncontrolled within the English pale.
>
> (II.ii.160–4)

The Elizabethan nightmare in Ireland, presided over once again by an O'Neill, and the recent and still painful loss of Calais both seem to loom here. Moreover, J.B. Steane has suggested that Mortimer's 'Nay madam, if you be a warrior / Ye must not grow so passionate in speeches' represents a cruel undercutting of Elizabeth's famous appearance at Tilbury in Armada year,[25] which would thus work still further to underline the suggestion that the queen is at a disadvantage in war.

Still another reference in *Edward II* not only points us in the direction of Elizabethan rather than mediaeval England, but also suggests an additional reason for Marlowe's representation of the Queen in this way. In the fourth act, Leicester tells the king, 'Your majesty must go to Killingworth', to which Edward replies, '"Must"! 'Tis somewhat hard when kings "must" go' (IV.vii.81–2). 'Little man, little man,' Elizabeth I was to say to Robert Cecil on her deathbed, 'the word "must" is not to be used to princes'; she might almost have been remembering Marlowe, and perhaps it would not be so strange if she were, since the play takes us so close to her own concerns. As Dennis Kay points out, '[t]he mythological entertainments he imagines, with Italian masques and water pageants (1.1.60–9) – are wholly characteristic of Elizabethan shows'; and they are particularly reminiscent of the 1575 entertainments hosted by the Earl of Leicester at Kenilworth. It is, therefore, striking that not only does Kenilworth (as indeed history dictated) feature here too, though its name has been more ominously remembered as Killingworth, but that, as Kay observes, '[t]he play's Earl of Leicester is given a markedly gentle ride'.[26]

A number of references to Elizabeth's favourite, Robert Dudley, Earl of Leicester, may be detected in Marlowe's plays. Faustus proposes that he will

> chase the Prince of Parma from our land,
> And reign sole king of all our provinces:
> Yea, stranger engines for the brunt of war
> Than was the fiery keel at Antwerp's bridge
> I'll make my servile spirits to invent.
>
> (I.i.95–9)

This takes us very close to the experiences of Leicester's governorship of the Netherlands. It may, therefore, be worth noting that Sir Francis Walsingham, with whom either Marlowe's intelligence work or his friendship with Walsingham's nephew Thomas is likely to have involved him, was a follower and intimate of Leicester (the Spanish ambassador wrote of 'Leicester, whose spirit is Walsingham') that Roger Manwood, for whom Marlowe may have written an epitaph, was involved in a masque fêting Leicester, and that 'in conjunction with his nephew [Philip Sidney]... Leicester probably sponsored the famous visit to Oxford by Bruno'.[27] All these names take us very close to what seems to have been Marlowe's own circle, and even the decision to have Baldock in *Edward II* fetch his gentry from Oxford, rather than Marlowe's own alma mater Cambridge, might look like a compliment to Leicester, who was Chancellor of Oxford, while Leicester's particular interest in coastal fortifications might perhaps be reflected in *Tamburlaine*'s expatiation on them (*II*, III.ii.85–90).

Leicester was still alive at the time of *Tamburlaine Part Two*, but he was dead by the time *Edward II* seems almost certainly to have been written. The play's apparent compliments to his memory can have only two likely causes. In the first place, *Edward II*, unlike Marlowe's other plays, was written for the Earl of Pembroke's Men, as we are reminded when Warwick orders 'My Lord of Pembroke's men, Strive you no longer' (II.vi.6–7), and Pembroke had been Leicester's nephew-in-law and brother-in-law of both his heir presumptive, Sir Philip Sidney, and of his actual heir and successor in the Leicester title, Sir Robert Sidney. The name of Leicester, therefore, would be virtually sacred in a performance by Pembroke's Men, just as the play's Pembroke, as Dennis Kay points out, is also represented in a very favourable light (with a marked reference to the beauty and desirability of the fourteenth-century countess which provides an interesting parallel to Marlowe's probable dedication of *Amintae Gaudia* to the sixteenth-century one). As well as Pembroke, however, there was another powerful figure who might have been pleased by a flattering picture of Leicester – the late earl's stepson and political heir, the Earl of Essex, whose star was rising rapidly. Moreover, although Essex, like all other courtiers, had perforce to pay lip-service to the Queen, his agenda and values were both very different from hers, and indeed come much closer to the warrior ethos of Tamburlaine. Perhaps, then, in the distinctive tone of Marlowe's denigration of the moon, we hear an ominous foreshadowing of the shift in court culture which was, within seven years of the play-wright's death, to see a serious attempt at armed rebellion against the Queen on the streets of London, since 'dissing' the Queen, as a recent collection of essays terms it, seems not only to occur in these plays, but perhaps even to do so in ways that openly support the concerns and agendas of some of those she thought closest to her.

To be aware of this apparent political dimension of *Edward II* may alert us to the manner in which it presents personal relationships not as the product of free affective choice, but as structured and config-ured by social groupings, in ways that develop to its most nuanced and sustained point the interest in the family group inherent throughout Marlowe's career. The play also draws on that other pre-ferred Marlovian motif, the journey; and this time it does so with both enhanced psychological insight and power, and with a newly insistent awareness of the extent to which the manoeuvrings of both the body natural and the body politic are informed and under-pinned by the journeys of the mind. Consequently, although this is the only one of Marlowe's plays not set abroad, it nevertheless offers a fascinating development of his earlier uses of colonialist and impe-rialist motifs, suggesting that, as so often to a homosexual sensibil-ity, the home to which one is born is the strangest and most alien place of all – Derek Jarman, in his film of the play, eliminates the nobles from all the earlier scenes, suggesting that the only thing you really need to make you unhappy is a family – and also suggesting that all journeys are essentially internal ones. Moreover, not only does the acuteness of Marlowe's analysis seem to have increased, but the fact that the text of this play has survived in a better state of preservation than that of any other means that we can watch the workings of that analysing mind with unparalleled closeness.

Throughout *Edward II*, land and water imagery is prominent.[28] Water imagery is indeed to be found in much of Marlowe's life and career; it is implicit in both the name of 'Water' Ralegh and in the poetic persona he invented, and Marlowe himself was characterised by Chapman as one who stood '"vp to the chin in the Pyerean flood"'[29] – a fitting enough description of a writer who had, after all, produced that *locus classicus* of 'soft pastoral', 'The Passionate Shepherd to his Love', with its lush evocation of an idealised waterside landscape. There was, of course, a strong tradition of emphasis on water in pastoral writing, as in Sannazaro's *Piscatory Eclogues*; it is perhaps one of *Tamburlaine*'s many ironic inversions of the pastoral that its ex-shepherd hero often orients himself in relation to the cities he wants to conquer by means of establishing which river, lake or sea they are near.

In *Edward II*, where the presence of the Mower reminds us that pastoral is indeed an appropriate and indeed necessary context within which to read the play, the note is sounded early, in Gaveston's first speech:

> Sweet prince, I come; these, these thy amorous lines
> Might have enforced me to have swum from France
> And, like Leander, gasped upon the sand,
> So thou wouldst smile and take me in thine arms.
>
> (I.i.6–9)

Gaveston's imagery brings the play close to the world of *Hero and Leander*, in which water is again dominant (indeed, Alan Haynes observes that it 'is the commanding element of many epyllia'),[30] and foreshadowings of the poem seem present also in Lancaster's 'Madam, he comes not back, / Unless the sea cast up his shipwreck body' (I.iv.204–5), which, as the Revels editor's note points out, parallels *Hero and Leander*'s 'shipwreck treasure'. The passage also suggests, though, that Gaveston – unlike Leander, who is nearly drowned by Neptune's passion – is at home in the sea: 'gasp[ing] upon the sand' makes him seem almost like a fish out of water. As the play unfolds, water comes more and more to seem Gaveston's natural element: as David H. Thurn comments,

> Frequently associated with water … Gaveston is linked with a thematic pattern of language that suggests precisely the loss of

stability and order, the destruction of the forms of identity. The sites of subversion seem frequently to have a fluid aspect. The civil wars bring 'lakes of gore,' … [and] channel water is a real or imagined instrument of humiliation.[31]

Philip Edwards also remarks on the extent to which in this play 'the sea plays a vital role' despite the fact that it is 'land-locked … apart from one French scene [it] is firmly located on English soil'.[32] Interestingly, Derek Jarman's 1991 film of *Edward II* picks up on this emphasis, opening with the sound of dripping water and punctuating Gaveston's first speech with the cries of seagulls; later Edward looks at himself in the water in which he will finally be tortured.

Water is a central feature of the entertainment that Gaveston plans for Edward, which are worth quoting again to make the point:

> Sometime a lovely boy in Dian's shape,
> With hair that gilds the water as it glides,
> Crownets of pearl about his naked arms,
> And in his sportful hands an olive tree
> To hide those parts which men delight to see,
> Shall bathe him in a spring.
>
> (I.i.60–5)

There is, moreover, a suggestive inversion here: though Dennis Kay sees a clear allusion to Actaeon, and argues that '[f]or Gaveston, Spencer and Mortimer, the opening allegory of Actaeon is actualised in their experience as a salutary warning to future ages',[33] Gaveston's emphasis on the male gender of the performer makes the homoerotically charged male, rather than the female object of the heterosexual gaze, the inhabitant of the water.

Most obviously, Mortimer tells Isabella,

> Fair Queen, forbear to angle for the fish
> Which, being caught, strikes him that takes it dead –
> I mean that vile torpedo, Gaveston,
> That now, I hope, floats on the Irish seas
>
> (I.iv.221–4)

Moreover, Mortimer images Gaveston not only as a fish, but also as a ship:

> when he shall know it lies in us
> To banish him, and then to call him home,
> 'Twill make him vail the topflag of his pride
> And fear to offend the meanest nobleman
>
> (I.iv.274–7)

Flying his 'topflag', Gaveston becomes an overweening galleon lording it on the seas. Finally, Mortimer associates him with yet another marine figure when he says that the costumes of Gaveston and his followers are as fantastic 'As if that Proteus, god of shapes, appeared' (I.iv.410).

Mortimer is not the only one to make the association. Lancaster says,

> Pliny reports there is a flying fish,
> Which all the other fishes deadly hate,
> And threfore, being pursued, it takes the air;
> No sooner is it up, but there's a fowl
> That seizeth it. This fish, my lord, I bear;
> The motto this: *Undique mors est*
>
> (II.ii.23–8)

'Undique' here suggests not merely 'on all sides' but also a pun on waves, and Edward is quick to see the point of the emblem:

> Though thou compar'st him to a flying fish,
> And threat'nest death whether he rise or fall,
> 'Tis not the hugest monster of the sea
> Nor foulest harpy that shall swallow him
>
> (II.ii.43–6)

For Edward, the entire court has here become an ominously threatening seascape.

In marked contrast to this, there is a clear tendency in the play for the barons who are opposed to Edward and Gaveston to be identified with the land. Edward tells Lancaster, 'The sword shall plane the furrows of thy brows / And hew those knees that now are grown so stiff' (I.i.93–4). Lancaster seems here to be virtually rooted in the ground: in the first line, the description of him as a thing with furrows figures him as a field to be ploughed, while in the second, the imagery approximates to that of a tree being felled. It is richly appropriate that Lancaster should vow that 'This ground, which is corrupted with their steps, / Shall be their timeless sepulchre or mine' (I.ii.5–6), while a different kind of preference for the ground is implied in Warwick's rebuke to Gaveston, 'Ignoble vassal, that like Phaethon / Aspir'st unto the guidance of the sun' (I.iv.16–17). For them, indeed, land becomes almost fetishised, as we see in the outrage charging Mortimer's rebuke to Edward that 'You have matters of more weight to think upon; / The King of France sets foot in Normandy', which is sharply contrasted with the flippancy of Edward's reply: 'A trifle. We'll expel him when we please' (II.ii.8–10). Indeed, land in this play is, as historically, the very essence of the nobles' power: as Mortimer reminds the King, 'My lord, the family of the Mortimers / Are not so poor but, would they sell their land, / Would levy men enough to anger you' (II.ii.149–51), and later he resolves that 'Wigmore shall fly, to set my uncle free' (II.ii.195), though their territorial holding seems ultimately to be increased rather than diminished, since Edward notes that 'we hear Lord Bruce doth sell his land, / And that the Mortimers are in hand withal' (III.i.53–4). Moreover, it is in the name of land that Kent finally deserts his brother to side with the barons: 'My lords, of love to this our native land / I come to join with you and leave the King' (II.iii.1–2).

Mortimer, however, is not identified only with the land. After Mortimer's first speech, Gaveston says aside '*Mort Dieu!*' (I.i.89), and that there is a pun on the etymology of Mortimer's name here (to which it is of course deeply appropriate that the watery Gaveston should be particularly sensitive) is made clear when Mortimer himself says,

> This tattered ensign of my ancestors,
> Which swept the desert shore of that Dead Sea
> Whereof we got the name of Mortimer,
> Will I advance upon these castle walls
>
> (II.iii.21–4)

Indeed Edward seems almost to recognise this dual allegiance when he says,

> But wherefore walks young Mortimer aside?
> Be thou commander of our royal fleet,
> Or if that lofty office like thee not,
> I make thee here Lord Marshal of the realm.
>   (I.iv.352–5)

Mortimer, it seems, can be associated with either land or sea, and indeed his final speech offers images of a kind of amphibious exploration as he says that he 'scorns the world and as a traveller / Goes to discover countries yet unknown' (V.vi.64–5): discovering countries always, from the perspective of an island like England, involved sea travel, but his actual destination is radically chthonic, under six feet of earth. Just as the sea with which he is associated is pointedly a dead one, so, in this last speech, his sea journey is literally towards death. It makes a striking contrast with the characteristic imagination of Gaveston as a fish, and one, moreover, distinguished by attributes of unusual power and flexibility, and the very different charge of the two images is underlined if we remember the customary use of fish as an erotic symbol in pastoral, and the importance of running water in 'The Passionate Shepherd to his Love'.

The other character who is ambivalently poised between sea and land is Edward himself. At one point, Marlowe makes a significant, and fairly uncharacteristic, departure from his source. In Holinshed, as the Revels editor points out, Edward, 'leauing the queene behind him, tooke shipping'; in Marlowe's play, however, the King tells Gaveston, 'Take shipping and away to Scarborough; / Spencer and I will post away by land' (II.iv.5–6). It is only a tiny alteration, but it seems to me a significant one, for Marlowe's Edward is indeed a character who has a fear of fully committing himself to the sea. (It is, moreover, a change not prompted by the plot, since it is, appropriately enough, on land that Gaveston is eventually caught [II.v.8], and therefore seems the likelier to be due to some sense of the reversal being more fitting to the character of the King.) Edward fears the sea, and images it accordingly, as when he tells Gaveston, 'sooner shall the sea o'erwhelm my land / Than bear the ship that shall transport thee hence' (I.i.151–2): though he seems here to recognise

its association with his lover – Philip Edwards comments suggestively that 'Dido and Edward II wait by the edge of the sea; what lies
beyond is utterly mysterious, a region of danger and threat, yet the
sea is also the route by which love comes and by which it departs'[34] –
he regards it as something fundamentally dangerous and menacing,
as also when he exclaims: 'The wind is good. I wonder why he stays; /
I fear me he is wracked upon the sea' (II.ii.1–2).

Edward's unease with the sea is, of course, not out of place in a
culture which, as Gareth Roberts reminds us, produced 'standard
Renaissance images of subversive disordering and collapse into watery
chaos, which reverse God's divine ordering in his separation of
the created world from the waters in Genesis',[35] but it may also be
inflected by more immediate fears, as is suggested by Mortimer's
observation that 'The haughty Dane commands the narrow seas, /
While in the harbour ride thy ships unrigged' (II.ii.167–8). As the
Revels editor's note on these lines observes, '[t]he notion of Denmark's
controlling the English Channel ("the narrow seas") in Edward II's
reign is totally unhistorical'; but so too is the idea that England
ought to have been a significant naval power in the reign of Edward II.
The lines are surely designed to make a point about character rather
than about history, and contribute to the impression of the King as
a man who shuns the sea, and who feels himself secure only when
matters can be confined to land – 'Spencer, as true as death, / He is
in England's ground; our port-masters / Are not so careless of their
King's command' (IV.iii.21–3). He even images his enemies as waves
when he says, 'Do what they can, we'll live in Tynemouth here, /
And, so I walk with him about the walls, / What care I though the
earls begirt us round?' (II.ii.220–2). Indeed, at times Edward seems
positively chthonic, praying, 'By earth, the common mother of us
all' (III.i.128). At the end, earth is all he wants: 'all places are alike, /
And every earth is fit for burial' (V.i.145–6). If *Edward II* thus shares
with *Hero and Leander* a structuring opposition between land and
sea, in which the land is linked with stagnation and conventionality
and the sea with fluidity and innovation, Edward himself is poised
uneasily between the two, fearing the sea and failing to realise the
extent of his own association with it.

If Edward clings to the land, though, it is increasingly to water
that he is subjected. There is a repeated image in the play of people
being punished by water. Early on, Lancaster warns him, 'look to see

the throne where you should sit / To float in blood' (I.i.130–1). The
note is sounded very clearly in Edward's and Gaveston's ill-treatment
of the Bishop of Coventry:

Edward.	Throw off his golden mitre, rend his stole,
	And in the channel christen him anew.
Kent.	Ah brother, lay not violent hands on him,
	For he'll complain unto the See of Rome.
Gaveston.	Let him complain unto the See of hell

(I.i.186–90)

The reference to 'the channel' here may make us willing to hear a
pun on 'see / sea' as well, and perhaps there is another pun when
Edward proposes to Gaveston to send the Bishop to 'the Tower, the
Fleet, or where thou wilt' (I.i.197), where the original etymology of
the Fleet prison from the Fleet Ditch may be in play. It is perhaps
worth pointing out that the word is used elsewhere in the play in a
distinctly maritime context – 'Ere my sweet Gaveston shall part
from me, / This isle shall fleet upon the ocean / And wander to the
unfrequented Inde' (I.iv.48–50) – and certainly Edward is thinking
of streams when he threatens that he will 'With slaughtered priests
make Tiber's channel swell' (I.iv.102). In similar vein, he threatens,
'Treacherous Warwick, traitorous Mortimer! / If I be England's King,
in lakes of gore / Your headless trunks, your bodies will I trail'
(III.i.134–6).

It is not they, however, but he himself who eventually suffers by
water. What is to come is perhaps hinted at when Isabella apos-
trophises Edward as one 'Whose looseness hath betrayed thy land to
spoil / And made the channels overflow with blood' (IV.iv.11–12).
Her imagery is hideously actualised in his prison:

Edward.	… O water, gentle friends, to cool my thirst
	And clear my body from foul excrements.
Matrevis.	Here's channel water, as our charge is given.
	Sit down, for we'll be barbers to your grace.
Edward.	Traitors, away! What, will you murder me,
	Or choke your sovereign with puddle water?
Gurney.	No, but wash your face and shave away your beard,
	Lest you be known and so be rescuèd.

(V.iii.25–32)

As Matrevis says to his companion,

> Gurney, I wonder the King dies not,
> Being in a vault up to the knees in water
> To which the channels of the castle run,
> From whence a damp continually ariseth
> That were enough to poison any man,
> Much more a king brought up so tenderly.
>
> (V.v.1–6)

Finally, the body of Lightborn is thrown in the moat (V.v.117); his fire, appropriately enough, is put out by water.

One reason for the emphasis on death by water may be the extent to which the play is structured as a revisiting of one of the most famous of all ordeals by water, the *Odyssey*.[36] We should be alerted to this parallel by the remarkable number of the epic's personnel whom we encounter in the play. Isabella wishes, 'Would, when I left sweet France and was embarked, / That charming Circe, walking on the waves, / Had changed my shape' (I.iv.171–3);[37] she also exclaims that 'Like frantic Juno will I fill the earth / With ghastly murmur of my sighs and cries' (I.iv.178–9), and she herself seems almost like a mythical sea-peril when she wishes 'that mine arms could close this isle about, / That I might pull him to me where I would' (II.iv. 17–18). Edward declares, 'My heart is as an anvil unto sorrow, / Which beats upon it like the Cyclops' hammers' (I.iv.311–12),[38] and Gaveston is like 'the Greekish strumpet' (II.v.15) who was the cause of the war and whom Telemachus encounters on his voyage in search of news. Finally, Edward, believing himself preparing to die, thinks not of the Christian pantheon but of the classical one: 'Let Pluto's bells ring out my fatal knell / And hags howl for my death at Charon's shore' (IV.vii.89–90), and the extent to which his sufferings represent the visit to Hell which is also the traditional lot of the epic hero is made clear in the resonant name of 'Lightborn', an Anglicised version of 'Lucifer'. Edward, who started the play safely at home with his wife and son, has inverted the teleology of the *Odyssey* by undergoing a series of terrifying watery journeys, strewn with shipwrecks and forced landings, which have taken him, inexorably, ever further away from them.

If Edward is envisaged as on a journey which will take him far away from the familiar, however, Marlowe himself, in his last writings, inverts that teleology. While the barons' agitation at the presence of Gaveston may seem to take us close to the 1593 anti-stranger riots in which the name of Tamburlaine was to be tossed about, *The Massacre at Paris*, which Henslowe recorded as new in January 1593, brings us still closer to home, though it is, ironically, set abroad. Andrew Kirk wonders whether the English agent in the play is 'perhaps a reflection of Marlowe's own service as an agent on the Continent in Walsingham's intelligence network', which would provide a neat reflection of the riddling of identity he sees elsewhere in the play – 'personal identity is masked by inexplicable malevolence or destabilized by shifting exteriors' – and, as in *Doctor Faustus*, there does indeed seem to be a note of personal interest discernible throughout.[39] Paul Kocher, for instance, points out that 'Marlowe is particularly profuse with the blood of scholars and preachers, all five of the persons he chooses for extinction being one or the other',[40] and Ramus in particular surely constitutes a direct memory of his Cambridge years. The Admiral Coligny of the play, moreover, had been buried in Canterbury Cathedral, and indeed David Potter argues that '[t]he intertwining of the literary career of Christopher Marlowe and Henri III's life is in some ways arresting', while John Michael Archer points to the fact that Marlowe himself might have 'attended Guise's seminary at Rheims sometime before 1587'.[41]

The Massacre at Paris is another play which is interested in writing. The Duchess of Guise is having a love affair with Mugeroun, but she does not *meet* him, she *writes* to him – as Cheney remarks, 'the play's most intimate scene – and one of the most remarkable – stages the act of writing itself' – and her husband resents her actions by demanding 'hath my love been so obscured in thee / That others need to comment on my text?' (Scene Fifteen, ll.25–6).[42] Moreover, the Guise's self-inscriptions of himself as Caesar further underline the sense of action and self-image in this play as things essentially literary. It is just a shame that its current state of textual preservation allows us few glimpses of such subtleties.

One thing that is obvious, however (and that might even perhaps be thought to account for some of the deficiencies in the surviving text), is how dangerous and risk-taking a play *The Massacre at Paris* must originally have been. At every turn, it outrages conventions governing both what is fit to be represented on stage and the ways in which it should be represented. Violence in Marlowe is often emblematic and ritualised to the point of stylisation, significantly attenuating its emotional impact, but never more so than here. To the Queen Mother's brilliantly deadpan question 'What order will you set down for the massacre?', the Duke of Guise replies:

> Thus, madam.
> They that shall be actors in this massacre
> Shall wear white crosses on their burgonets,
> And tie white linen scarfs about their arms;
> He that wants these, and is suspect of heresy,
> Shall die, be he king or emperor. Then I'll have
> A peal of ordinance shot from the tower,
> At which they all shall issue out and set the streets;
> And then, the watchword being given, a bell shall ring,
> Which when they hear, they shall begin to kill,
> And never cease until that bell shall cease;
> Then breathe a while.
>
> (Scene Four, ll.28–39)

Quite apart from the breathtaking effrontery of the idea of an order in a massacre, there is the separate, daring paradox that this will be an 'order' which consists of overturning all established norms of rank. It is, indeed, an order fundamentally dependent not on customary ideas of order at all, but on 'ordinance', or cannon, which represents the Guise's ultimate authority: might is right. There is also the dreadful inversion of the fact that bells and crosses, which normally summon Christians to prayer, will here incite them to kill. Marlowe may or may not have had any religious faith himself, but he has sufficient grasp of what it ought to mean to make scathing mock of the monstrous shortcomings he sees in the ideal.

Equally risky, though in a different way, is the fact that violence in this play is strongly physical as well as strongly emblematic. Marlowe had always been prepared to make his theatre one of bodies as well as words: the kings of *Tamburlaine, Part Two* are not only lashed by the force of Tamburlaine's tongue but also have to kneel down and actually pull his chariot, and there is a terrifying account of an early performance in which the Governor of Baghdad's death-scene went hideously wrong and a child and a pregnant woman were killed in the audience. Here, the body of the Admiral is first thrown down (Scene Five, l.32) and then hanged on a tree, placing real demands on the actor unless, as in the 1984 Royal Shakespeare Company production at The Other Place, a dummy is used – and even then that needs to be manipulated by at least two of the other actors.

Even more basically physical is Epernoun's reply to the Guise's query about the King's whereabouts: he has, we are told, '[m]ounted his royal cabinet' (Scene Twenty-One, l.30). Although I have never seen it commented upon, this can mean only one thing: the King is answering the call of nature. Though it was a common feature of court life in both France and England for kings to be attended in such circumstances (in Sir Thomas More's life of Richard III, Tyrrell is suggested to the King as the murderer of the princes at precisely such a moment), it is *not* something normally seen on stage. Unless we are to suppose that Epernoun is lying, presumably in order to insult the Guise, we must take it that this is what we are watching Henry do during this scene. And a risk of a different sort is taken when King Henry demands of the Guise, 'Did he not draw a sort of English priests / From Douai to the seminary at Rheims'? (Scene Twenty-One, ll.105–6). Yes, he did; how many people in the audience knew more about that than they ought to have done, and is Marlowe not bringing his two worlds dangerously close together at this point? When one reads what remains of *The Massacre at Paris* and speculates as to what else there may once have been in the play, one may well be tempted to think that it is not particularly surprising that Marlowe seems not to have survived it very long.

The other work which seems clearly datable to the last year of Marlowe's life is his great epyllion, *Hero and Leander*. There has generally been broad agreement with Tucker Brooke's view that

> [t]he poem is clearly mature work, and is evidently incomplete in the form in which Marlowe left it. Therefore, it is reasonable to assume, as has commonly been done, that it is one of Marlowe's latest works, left unfinished at his death. We may infer that the author was impelled to take up non-dramatic writing by the fact that the Privy Council recommended the closing of the playhouses (on account of plague) on January 28, 1593.[43]

In an age which valued the art of poetry above that of drama, much of Marlowe's Elizabethan and Jacobean reputation rested on this poem, and many contemporary allusions to him are couched in terms of it: Tucker Brooke notes that '[e]ven before the appearance of the first known edition in 1598, *Hero and Leander* seems to be referred to as Marlowe's most characteristic work'.[44] Like *Edward II*, this is a work overwhelmingly concerned with sexuality, but with a highly complex view of the subject, as William Keach shows when he argues against the idea that the Venus of the poem is some other, chaster goddess and suggests that the poem is fully aware of its erotic ambiguities, even down to invoking the other meaning of 'nun' as 'prostitute'.[45] M. Morgan Holmes argues that all of Marlowe's homo-erotic works share

> an opposition to the definition of individual identity through the discourse of an exclusive and immutable sexual desire … the deployment of homoerotic desire in *Hero and Leander* undermines the production of sexualized personal and textual identities, thereby making nonsense out of so-called 'sensible' orthodoxies.

For Holmes, 'the poem's strategic deployment of the discourse of homoeroticism interrogates and destabilizes early modern society's burgeoning penchant to establish "sexuality" as a principal root of subjective identity',[46] and indeed much recent comment on Marlowe's own sexuality and on his representations of sexuality has focused on differences in the structuring perceptions of sexuality between the sixteenth century and our own. Moreover, it may be another facet of what Holmes sees as the carnivalesque inversions of the poem that it fails to go on to the end of the received story, with its traditionally tragic ending.

Whatever the criteria used, few have failed to agree on the great-ness of Marlowe's achievement in *Hero and Leander*, and that it offered rich promise for the future development of his art. Robert Speaight suggests that '[i]f *Hero and Leander* is the last of Marlowe's works, as many critics believe, it shows a development in the understanding of human nature. Where this would have led him is anybody's guess; I think myself that even in the golden age of playwriting it would have led him away from the theatre'. Holmes declares that '[o]ne of two scenes invented wholly anew by Marlowe, Neptune's seduction of Leander ranks as one of the aesthetically richest homoerotic pas-sages in all of early modern English literature', and Clifford Leech remarks on Marlowe's clever use in the poem 'of dissyllabic rhyme, which he manages in such a way as to achieve a familar tone and a sense of human hesitation'.[47] What is much less clear, however, is whether the poem as we have it is all Marlowe intended to write, or whether its composition was interrupted by his untimely death. It has been variously argued that he meant it to be complete as it stood, and that he would ultimately have reverted to the traditional tragic ending.[48] Chapman implies that Marlowe asked him to finish the poem, and though this has largely been dismissed on the grounds that Marlowe's death was too sudden and too unexpected to have prompted such a request, we might well remember that there was plague raging – perhaps the reason why Marlowe was in Deptford in the first place, perhaps the reason why he was writing poetry rather than plays – and *everyone* had thus some reason to fear an imminent death.

Perhaps there is one faint clue within the poem itself which may conceivably deserve more exploration than it has received. Towards the beginning of what Chapman would later constitute as the second Sestiad, the poem's overall pattern of rhyming couplets is suddenly and slyly suspended in favour of a subtly different effect:

> She, fearing on the rushes to be flung,
> Strived with redoubled strength; the more she strivèd,
> The more a gentle pleasing heat revivèd,
> Which taught him all that elder lovers know.
> And now the same 'gan so to scorch and glow,
> As in plain terms (yet cunningly) he craved it;
> Love always makes those eloquent that have it.
> She, with a kind of granting, put him by it,
> And ever as he thought himself most nigh it,
> Like to the tree of Tantalus she fled,
> And seeming lavish, saved her maidenhead.
>
> (Sestiad II, 66–77)

Fred B. Tromly has recently remarked of this passage that

> [p]articularly brilliant is the extended play on the plain but cunning word with which four consecutive lines end: 'it.' As often happens in Marlowe, the most suggestive pronouns have the most unclear antecedents, and the anatomical possibilities of 'it' shift with every inflection.[49]

In fact, the trick is even cleverer than that, because even the nominal antecedent is unclear, being merely given as 'the same' – technically, perhaps, referring to the 'heat' which has previously been the subject of the sentence, but inevitably suggesting something rather more immediate and solid than that.

This passage is central to both the poem's meaning and its method. Both Hero and Leander are virgins at the start of the narrative. Leander has only the sketchiest of ideas of what would actually constitute consummation of their relationship, and if Hero knows any better, decorum forbids her from saying so. A considerable part of the playfully erotic effect of the poem derives from the fact that, as in *Doctor Faustus*, the sense of a *telos* or climax is constantly, flirtatiously, snatched away from us. At the outset of the poem, Marlowe repeatedly reminds us of the fact that the course of events is known and predetermined: the opening line refers to 'Hellespont, guilty of true love's blood', and the very first mention of Leander is immediately followed by the ominous 'Whose tragedy divine Musaeus sung' (Sestiad I, 52). Thus foreknowing that events will have a tragic outcome, and quite likely also to be ourselves familiar with the usual course of courtship, we surely think that we know what will happen in the poem. Astonishingly, however, we soon find ourselves confronted with the very real possibility that we actually don't know what is going to happen at all, because the lovers don't. Leander cannot escape the foregone conclusion of dying, but is he, with devastating irony, going to escape enjoying the foregoing consummation which every previous version of the story had allowed him – and, even more ironically, not even know what he has missed? In one sense, that would be extraordinarily frustrating for the reader; and yet, in another, it is perhaps even more exciting to be thus plunged back into sharing a perspective in which the end is uncertain. It is always assumed that experience can never again give place to innocence, but *Hero and Leander* very nearly achieves that.

Given the state of uncertainty which Marlowe deliberately creates here, it is hardly surprising that our sense of what would constitute appropriate closure for the poem, and thus of when or whether its end has been achieved, is so disrupted. The rhyming quadruplet formed by those four uses of 'it' further draws attention to the ways in which Marlowe's adoption and deployment of a rhyme scheme here, as opposed to his usual blank verse, also militates against the sense of an ending. So far from not possessing an ending at all, the poem, like all verse written in rhyming couplets, actually multiplies them, and mini-closures proliferate so much that they may well distract our attention from the thought of any ultimate one. Potentially, this process could go on indefinitely. In sonnets, the introduction of a rhyming couplet signals the end of the poem, but when all couplets already rhyme there is no formal reason why any individual one should constitute the conclusion. In practice, however, there must eventually be an end, and though the presence of a rhyming couplet cannot signify that end, I do wonder whether the sudden disruption of the pattern by the introduction of a rhyming quadruplet might not have been intended to signify a middle. Five hundred and fifty-four lines of the poem lead up to that triumphant, multiple play on 'it'. Only 259 follow it, and the narrative does not seem to me, as it did not to its original publisher, to Petowe, or to Chapman, to be complete. Might this conceivably, in Marlowe's original schema, have been the structural as well as the narrative heart of the poem?

If so, or even if this suggestion is found unconvincing but the poem is nevertheless conceded to be incomplete, how would it have ended? Marlowe has given us plenty of clues that Leander will die, and in the passion of Neptune he has given us a reason for that to happen. Paradoxically, I agree both with those who have believed that Marlowe would have retained the original tragic structure and with those who have commented on the poem's increasingly comic tone. In this last year of his life Marlowe, as we have seen, was taking risks, and the fact of his death may well suggest that he wasn't stopping until the limit had been reached. I would not at all put it past him to have planned to preserve the traditional ending of the poem, but to make it funny by having Leander (who after all shows no great aptitude for heterosexuality) finding that he actually likes what Neptune has to offer, and, like Edward II of England and Henry III of France in what seem to have been the other works of this period, deliberately espousing a homosexual identity. This is, of course, purely speculation, but in any case, whether Marlowe intended to finish it or not, the perfection of the verse of *Hero and Leander* can only make us regret that the fate which, in its present state, was averted from the poem's Leander was so soon to fall on its creator.

6
A Great Reckoning:
From 1593 to Immortality

Marloe, still admir'd Marlo's gon
To live with beautie in Elyzium.[1]

Many explanations have been advanced for the series of events that led up to Marlowe's death in the house (not, as used to be thought, an inn, but possibly a kind of safe house for government intelligencers) of Eleanor Bull, a widow with connections at court, at Deptford, on 30 May 1593. Thanks to dedicated archival work, we can now reconstruct the sequence of events in the preceding weeks.[2] Marlowe's erstwhile roommate Kyd was arrested on or before 12 May; on 18 May the Privy Council issued a warrant to seek for Marlowe at Scadbury, presumably but not certainly in connection with the same affair; on 30 May Marlowe was fatally stabbed by Ingram Frizer's dagger; and on 2 June Richard Baines submitted a memorandum detailing Marlowe's 'monstrous opinions'. Kyd, who had been tortured and dismissed from the service of his patron (who was probably Ferdinando Stanley, Lord Strange), was equally busy incriminating his dead friend, though it is of course possible that he, and conceivably Baines too, were simply using Marlowe as a scapegoat because no further harm could now befall him.

What caused these events is much less easy to pin down. If Marlowe's death was murder, he outraged so many norms that possible suspects proliferate. Smoker, coiner, homosexual, atheist, spy – which one of these did society or its government finally find unacceptable? Was he silenced before he could reveal something compromising about someone – Ralegh, Essex, Walsingham – with whom he had been associating? Or was it, as the three other men in the room unanimously averred, an accident which occurred during a scuffle of precisely the kind which we know Marlowe to have been involved in on other occasions, and of which the immediate cause on this occasion was that he could not afford to pay the bill? And why was he in Deptford in the first place – because it was free of plague, because he had a cousin there, or because it was a port – with departures for Scotland being particularly common – and he was about to take ship for somewhere?

Jonathan Goldberg points out that '[w]e do not know why the Privy Council ordered Marlowe's arrest – it may as easily have been to secure his testimony against someone else as to charge him with criminal activity'.[3] J.M. Robertson suggests that '[t]he inquiry which elicited the testimony of Baines and the prosecution and torture of Kyd was probably directed in a spirit of hostility to Raleigh [*sic*], whose name had been dragged to the front by Parsons'. He points out that Ralegh 'had spoken in the House of Commons in support of the expulsion of foreigners' and was himself investigated on the grounds of suspected atheism in the following year.[4] Austin K. Gray agreed: asserting rather boldly that 'Baines is obviously one of Lord Keeper Puckering's spies, set to keep an eye upon Raleigh, Harriott and their "Schola Atheismi"', he goes on:

> [i]t is obvious from the Baines Report that the Privy Council were going to use Marlowe (almost certainly, a former spy) as a stalking-horse for attacking Raleigh. Marlowe forestalled them by breaking his bail (which confined him to Middlesex) and escaping to Deptford, in Kent, probably with a view to sailing for Scotland.

Poley, he thinks, may have been tailing Marlowe, and thus followed him to Deptford, and he speculates on Marlowe's 'desperation when these two worlds clashed, when he realised that he was going to be revealed to Raleigh and Northumberland as a common spy and probably forced to give information against them'.[5]

Another theory is that the events surrounding Marlowe's death were prompted less by politics than by religion (in so far as the two were separable during the sixteenth century). William Urry thought that 'Marlowe was probably arrested for reasons of religion during Archbishop Whitgift's fierce campaign to eradicate religious dissidents', and Nicholas Davidson, noting that 'Baines's and Kyd's documents on [Marlowe's] religious opinions were delivered to Sir John Puckering, who was responsible at the time for collecting information about Protestant and Catholic dissenters and recusants', similarly suggests that 'Marlowe's case became involved in a much wider official campaign against religious dissent', of which the next year's investigation of Ralegh on suspicion of atheism also formed part. Ethel Seaton points out that 'not only Poley, but almost all characters mentioned in the Kyd–Marlowe–Cholmley documents, were engaged on one side or the other in recusant plot and counterplot, and had especial connection first with the Babington Plot of 1586, and secondly with Sir William Stanley's plot to kill the Queen in 1593, which was thwarted by the measures taken immediately after Marlowe's death', and she therefore wonders whether 'in this play of mine and countermine there was some urgent reason why Marlowe should be prevented in May 1593 from telling tales'.[6]

The question has been most comprehensively explored in Charles Nicholl's *The Reckoning*, which situates Marlowe's death squarely within the context of his espionage work and ultimately points the finger at Essex. Others have related Marlowe's death to the same concerns and same groups of people but have identified different suspects: for Curtis Breight, it is Cecil, in the course of a power struggle with Essex, who is the likely culprit; for others it has been Audrey, Lady Walsingham (though there is in fact no evidence that she was married to Thomas Walsingham, or in any way connected with Marlowe's circle, until some years later).[7]

It certainly seems as if the rivalry between Essex and Ralegh may well have played a part in Marlowe's death, even if we cannot now determine how. Since Essex's meteoric rise to favour in the summer of 1587, the year of *Tamburlaine*, they had been persistent competitors, in a rivalry which Roy Strong has seen as best exemplified in the twin images of them dressed in black and white, the Queen's colours, and thus openly aspiring for her favour.[8] And since Nicholl's monumental work, other discoveries have been made. One concerns Nicholas Skeres, one of the three other men in the room when Marlowe died, and a known conman. Paul E.J. Hammer points to 'a fact which Nicholl did not know: that Skeres looked to Gelly Meyrick for any chance of favor by the Earl [of Essex]. It suggests that Skeres should be viewed in a financial rather than intelligence context. This raises interesting implications for the whole question of

Marlowe's death.' Indeed, Hammer takes issue with Nicholl's account as a whole, arguing that after his own reinterpretation of the evidence '[e]ach of the key planks in Nicholl's "frame" now appears questionable or straightforwardly improbable', and that it is more likely that Marlowe owed money to Skeres and Frizer, set up a meeting with them to which he invited Poley as 'a mutually-acceptable observer', and was stabbed more by accident than design.[9] To me, though, Poley's presence seems rather more significant than this scenario, which virtually dismisses him, would suggest. Neverthless, money may well have played a part in events; it is certainly noticeable that the inquest was concerned to record both the value of the dagger and their consternation that they did not know the extent of Ingram Frizer's possessions, and there may well have been some truth to Frizer's, Skeres' and Poley's naming of money as the cause of the quarrel.

Amidst all the uncertainties, some things, mercifully, do seem clear. Marlowe's summons before the Privy Council may not have been directly prompted by concern about his alleged religious opinions, but they certainly became an issue with remarkable rapidity, and Marlowe's name soon became implicated in accusations of atheism. Kyd was found in possession of a document which he alleged originally to have been Marlowe's and which was considered suspect, though, as W.D. Briggs among others has argued, '[h]eretical the doctrine therein expounded unquestionably was, but, of course, in no sense atheistical', while Boas comments that 'the fact that Kyd was charged with "Atheism," owing to the discovery of this Theistic pamphlet among his papers is the strongest possible proof of the lax way in which the term was used'.[10]

The other document which was used as evidence of Marlowe's religious belief was the so-called Baines note. For Paul Kocher, this was the 'master key' to the mind of Marlowe, though Roy Kendall has recently argued that 'great caution must be used when turning this "master key"', both because it was fashioned to fit a lock made by Thomas Drury, of whose involvement Kocher … was not aware, and because Richard Baines, who fashioned the key, was not the man Kocher took him to be'. Indeed, for Kendall, it is Baines' own mind to which the note is the 'key': he argues that 'the portrait Baines painted of Marlowe in 1593 was remarkably similar to the dark self-portrait(s) which Baines had painted ten years before when in prison in Rheims', and also highlights the evidence in Sir Robert

Sidney's letter from Flushing that 'Marlowe was the "chamber fellow" of Richard Baines in early 1592 – and in all likelihood in late 1591 as well'. Kendall even goes so far as to invert the normal process whereby the mind and personality of Marlowe are detected in his characters, and detects those of Baines instead, whom he compares to Edward II, Faustus, Barabas and King Henry in *The Massacre at Paris*. Arguing that Baines was a Cambridge man, not an Oxford one as previously supposed, and a Walsingham spy, Kendall posits a Marlowe who 'might have looked up to [Baines] in his formative years'.[11] Boas interestingly points out that Ralegh's name was omitted from the version of the Baines note sent to Elizabeth, which might certainly bear out the suggestion that Ralegh was involved in some way, though Kendall points out a possible kinship between Poley and Sir Christopher Blount, who was Essex's stepfather and actively involved in his cause.[12]

Other things can also be deduced about Marlowe's death. If the three men with him had been determined from the outset to kill him, they were a very long time about it, for they had spent the whole day together. This seems to me to argue very powerfully against deliberate murder. It looks much more as though the death was indeed an accident (though perhaps one waiting to happen in such company), or, conceivably, that a proposition needed to be put to him and that he would only be killed if he declined it, which duly occurred. The story told by Poley, Frizer and Skeres is highly unlikely to be factually accurate. The wound simply could not have caused instant death if it was where they said it was; quite recently, a young woman who was attacked on a train and stabbed in the head survived the assault, although a five-inch combat knife with a serrated edge was driven into her head up to its hilt. (This was a point made with particular force in Samuel Tannenbaum's provocatively titled *The Assassination of Christopher Marlowe*, which argues that Marlowe was most likely asleep or drunk at the time and that the dagger penetrated further than stated, and that Marlowe was killed on the orders of Ralegh to prevent him from making any compromising revelations.)[13] One would also very much like to know what Poley and Skeres were doing while the man sitting in between them on the bench supposedly fought for his life.

It is unsurprising that no one has ever believed this narrative, and indeed so much doubt has at various times been cast on the official story that even schoolchildren are encouraged to disbelieve it: *The Terrible Tudors*, which is in the *Horrible Histories* series, stages a mock-up playlet and sketch of the scene of the crime and the conversation afterwards between Eleanor Bull, Frizer, Poley and Skeres, and invites its readers to choose between the 'execution' and 'escape' theories.[14] However, anyone who has been in a totally unexpected and very dangerous situation may well find that they have only a frustratingly partial memory of events, and even if the three men were lying deliberately, what they were concealing need not necessarily have been premeditated murder, but might have been merely provocation or aggression on their parts, to admit to which might have compromised their chances of acquittal. In any event, it does not seem very likely that we are, at this distance, going to be able to reconstruct with anything like certainty what really happened, or why.

Marlowe was said to have died blaspheming. Whether his soul went to hell, heaven or oblivion, or, in the kindly fate Henry Petowe envisaged for it, 'To live with beautie in Elyzium', his plays and poems were safely launched on a career of immortality. Competition over the meaning of his life and works has lasted late (including the bizarre phenomenon of the McCarthy hearings asking if he was a Communist), and began early. M. Morgan Holmes suggests, for instance, that 'Hero and Leander's tragedy had become, among the "smart set" of 1590s London, a site of conflict between competing philosophical and social visions of how desire ought to be inscribed in order to shape individual and collective destinies'; he sees Chapman and Petowe's continuations as attempts to reassert orthodoxy, countered by the fact that '[i]n 1599 ... Thomas Nashe's *Lenten Stuff* and William Shakespeare's *As You Like It* joined the fray and showed that "all men" did not, in fact, expect or even desire the same things'.[15] Other critics, though, have seen Chapman, who seems indeed to have conceived of himself as Marlowe's literary executor, as much closer than this to the spirit of his predecessor, commenting, for instance, on similarities between Tamburlaine and Chapman's own Herculean heroes, while Sidney Homan argues that '[t]he playwrights' affinity was even closer than a mutual interest in the Herculean hero'.[16]

As well as Chapman and Petowe, other Renaissance writers clearly signalled responses to Marlowe, including Marston, Middleton, Ben Jonson, Beaumont, Elizabeth Cary, Barnabe Barnes, whose *The Divils Charter* (1607) is clearly indebted in its devil-raising scenes to *Doctor*

Faustus, and, of course, his exact contemporary Shakespeare, who refers to him in *As You Like It*, quotes him in *The Merry Wives of Windsor*, may have collaborated with him on the three parts of *Henry VI*, and is clearly influenced by him in a host of plays including *Richard III, Richard II, The Merchant of Venice* and *The Tempest*, together with the narrative poem *Venus and Adonis*, often taken to be a response to *Hero and Leander*. (There is also, of course, a view that Marlowe is the rival poet of the sonnets.)[17]

Marlowe's reputation endured well into the century after his death. In 1633, Thomas Heywood oversaw the publication of *The Jew of Malta* with a dedication to 'Mr Thomas Hammon, of Greyes Inn', who had been Marlowe's classmate at the King's School, Canterbury, and had later followed him to Corpus Christi.[18] Heywood's own play, *The Captives*, shows clear signs of indebtedness to Marlowe: Godfrey quotes 'Who ever loved, that loved not at first sight', and a friar who is in fact already dead is 'killed' by another.[19] One of those who seems to have been particularly affected by this 1630s revival of interest in Marlowe was John Ford, who in *Love's Sacrifice* parodies both *Tamburlaine* and, it has been suggested, Edward Alleyn's acting style; indeed Marlowe is a powerful presence throughout Ford's work.[20] Sharing an interest in the socially displaced, whom they typically term 'mushrumps', they both create characters who, as Lawrence Danson says of Marlowe's heroes, 'amaze or dismay us by the sheer tenacity of their will to be always themselves', and Richard McCabe has commented suggestively that '*Perkin Warbeck* might well be regarded as *Tamburlaine* rewritten by Ford'.[21] Marlowe's presence is felt in *Tis Pity She's a Whore* in particular, where the opening lines, with their reference to atheism, seem overtly to evoke his legend, while when Bergetto's belly 'seethes like a porridge-pot' (III.viii.18) he reminds one of Barabas' poisoned porridge, and there are marked parallels between Giovanni and both Doctor Faustus and Tamburlaine – indeed there is a suggestive switch from one mode to another of Marlovian excess in Giovanni's progression from the doomed but essentially harmless scholar Faustus to the atrocities of Tamburlaine.[22]

After this period appreciation of the distinctive qualities of Marlowe's *oeuvre* seems noticeably to have waned; arguably his greatest work, *Doctor Faustus*, was debased into farcical and harlequin versions, and indeed deafness to his voice was such that some critics even asserted that he had not written *Tamburlaine*, an ascription which no one now doubts. As Irving Ribner notes, 'Marlowe's reputation was gradually revived by Romantic critics of the nineteenth century'.[23] *Hero and Leander* was an obvious influence on Byron, and after the early death of that other celebrated atheist Shelley, comparisons were often made between the two; there were even two operas by Berlioz which covered Marlovian ground, while a passion for *Hero and Leander* got the young Edmund Gosse into trouble with his puritanical father. Indeed so intense was late nineteenth-century interest that Thomas Dabbs has recently proposed that 'Marlowe was originally invented by Victorian scholars, critics, and educators and then handed on to us'.[24]

In the twentieth century, Marlowe became the subject of many novelisations and some dramatisations of his life, not to mention a small but crucial cameo in *Shakespeare in Love*, in which Rupert Everett's benevolent and more successful Marlowe acts as role model to the young Shakespeare, buying him drinks and helping him think of a better plot for his projected play *Romeo and Ethel, the Pirate's Daughter* before dying in a brawl in a Deptford pub for which Shakespeare, who has given his name as Marlowe to get out of trouble, initially fears he may be responsible. Though the film makes no pretensions to historical accuracy, it does include some interesting suggestions: *Doctor Faustus*, we are told, is an early work, while Marlowe has just finished writing *The Massacre at Paris* on the day of his death. Shakespeare acknowledges a debt to him in *Henry VI* and *Titus Andronicus*, and we also may notice that though the fictional Lord Wessex proves not in fact to have ordered Marlowe's murder, there is nevertheless a discrepancy between the Marlowe who is so ready to buy Shakespeare a beaker of the best brandy and the Marlowe who apparently quarrels over the bill. Marlowe's work, though not himself, also has a bit part in another Shakespearean film, Richard Loncraine's *Richard III*, in which the first words we hear are a chanteuse at the victory ball singing a setting of 'The Passionate Shepherd', and there are at least three films centring on Marlowe's own life which are rumoured to be in pre-production as I write. Natural Nylon is said to be producing *Marlowe*, with Johnny Depp as the hero and Jude Law as Thomas Walsingham, in which Marlowe survives Deptford and starts a new life on the continent with – of all people – Ingram Frizer, while the company Stranger

Than Fiction is apparently preparing *Dead Man in Deptford*, perhaps with Rufus Sewell, and Bronco Films plans *Vainglory*, stressing Marlowe's homosexuality. Whether all or any of these will see the light of day remains to be seen.

In general, these modern retellings portray very much the Marlowe of legend, often with particular emphasis on fidelity to the picture of him offered by the Baines note. Stephanie Cowell's *Nicholas Cooke: Actor, Soldier, Physician, Priest* is centred on the London theatrical scene of the 1590s and has its adolescent hero meet Marlowe, here called Morley, who gets him apprenticed to John Heminges. Cowell's Marlowe endorses the speculations of Giordano Bruno, hobnobs with Hariot and flirts with atheism and homosexuality. Liam Maguire's *Icarus Flying* has Marlowe dying not in a brawl at Deptford – it is a Christopher Morley who is killed there instead – but from a combination of pox and exhaustion. He is both atheist and homosexual, though guilty and confused about the latter, being made to say 'He's a boy or a fool who does not like tobacco' rather than the received version. He joins the School of Night – an organisation which is here considerably larger than it is generally envisaged as being, and of more conservative ends – to prove that he is not a Catholic. But despite all these attempts to conform, his plays get him into trouble: the School of Night believe their rituals have been parodied in *Doctor Faustus*, Essex is offended by the portrait of Gaveston, and Marlowe appears to crack under the pressure. Finally, Anthony Burgess's *A Dead Man in Deptford*, stylishly postmodern, has a Marlowe much happier with his own homosexuality, though he is eventually killed for motives which are obscure, but which seem to centre on his relationship with Ralegh, while Chris Hunt's *Mignon*, which is very sexually explicit, positively revels in its hero's sexuality, and has him dedicating 'Come live with me and be my love' to a young French boy before disappearing from the novel.[25]

Perhaps the most interesting of the novelisations is Robin Chapman's *Christoferus or Tom Kyd's Revenge*, because it strays into the realm of interpretation. After the nice touch of observing that Chapman's 'adjectives came in cow-like droves mooing at the subject noun', and suggesting that Bates and Frizer committed the murder in the service of Rome, the novel first offers close reading – in *Hero and Leander* '[o]nce again Christofer wins a doubtful argument with a feline rhythm and the pounce of rhyme' – and then a full-blown and not uninteresting reading of *Doctor Faustus*:

> first we have Faustus as an unseen presence in the Vatican, a spy in other words. Next comes Mephostophilis, a fellow agent from Hell, who can grant Faustus anything – at a price. Call Faustus Christofer and Mephostophilis Baines, who then serves whom and who, come to that, i[s] the Archbishop? Answer: an important papal authority from the very seminary Christofer attended. The Archbishop refers to a ghost – the Cockney name for a spy or informer is *ghost* – and says Christofer comes from Purgatory. On the face of it an unexceptional provenance entirely suited to such a relentless spirit except Christofer once told me there were three courtyards at the seminary of Rheims which were commonly known as Heaven, Purgatory and Hell. And the English students took their air and exercised themselves at football in Purgatory.

Doctor Faustus, in this account, is thus Marlowe writing his own literary life.[26]

Peter Whelan's *The School of Night*, set at Scadbury, where Marlowe is preparing to stage *Dido, Queen of Carthage* for a visit from Ralegh, sees Marlowe as foreshadowing the literary dissident, and also as fundamentally dependent on the fortunes of Ralegh. Whelan's Marlowe, who plays Venus himself, is homosexual, prays to 'Dog' rather than 'God', and wants to continue the School of Night's inquiries into truth, which both Ralegh and Thomas Walsingham now wish to abandon as too politically risky. Walsingham proposes instead to have Marlowe escape to Venice with the aid of 'Tom Stone', the pseudonym of Shakespeare, who wittily compares with Marlowe ideas for a possible *dénouement* for *Othello*. Walsingham's wife, however, has other ideas, and arranges for Frizer to murder Marlowe.[27]

In one way, the modern world which produces these adaptations can be seen as Marlowe's natural home. *Edward II*, in particular, has spoken very powerfully to the more open homosexual identities of our own time; as well as Derek Jarman's film version of it, there is also a recent ballet, with music by John McCabe, choreography by David Bintlev, and costumes by Jasper Conran, and accompanied, when performed by the Birmingham Royal Ballet in 1997, by a mock

Daily Herald for 19 October 1330 which compared Isabella with Princess Diana. Howard Felperin titles his discussion of him 'Marlowe our Contemporary', Nicholas Brooke compares his work to Brecht, Ionesco and the *Marat/Sade*, and Robert B. Heilman remarks of *Doctor Faustus* that 'in the century of world wars it will seem suitable enough that the master scientist's climactic feat will be in the invention of "stranger engines for the brunt of war"', while Kenneth Golden calls the same play 'a visionary work speaking significantly to the modern condition'. In similar vein, Michael Keefer asks, 'does Marlowe's *Doctor Faustus* not also answer to a cerain apocalyptic mood in late twentieth-century culture?', and Philip Edwards suggests that '[t]he tragic paradigm of Marlowe's plays, like that of Shakespeare's *Macbeth*, is the conversion of fantasy into reality ... It was not the destiny of Marlowe's heroes to end up in a play. Their role was to be prophets of the twentieth century, which is as real as can be.'[28] Indeed Marlowe narrowly avoided experiencing one of the oddest of reincarnations in the twentieth century: the stage name originally proposed by Columbia Pictures for the actress eventually known as Kim Novak was 'Kit Marlowe'.

Perhaps the ultimate fascination of Marlowe, however, is the ways in which he defies easy assimilation into the modern world and retains his mystery. Dying in odd circumstances, which we will perhaps never fully understand, he was buried hugger-mugger in a location we can no longer precisely identify. With him died attitudes towards religion, sexuality and society which we are unlikely ever to be able to reconstruct in their original complexity, and he went to the grave leaving his greatest works in a hopeless textual muddle, with one of them probably incomplete. Perhaps all we can ever be sure of, from the fragments we have left, is that he was indeed, as Nashe termed him, 'a diviner Muse'.[29]

Notes

1 Introduction

1 Irving Ribner, 'Marlowe and the Critics', *Tulane Drama Review* 8 (1964), pp. 211–24, pp. 213 and 214. For the assumption that Marlowe's plays are autobiographical, see, for instance, A.L. Rowse, *Christopher Marlowe: A Biography* (London: Macmillan, 1964), Matthew Proser, *The Gift of Fire: Aggression and the Plays of Christopher Marlowe* (New York: Peter Lang, 1995), and A.W. Verity, *The Influence of Christopher Marlowe on Shakespeare's Earlier Style* (Cambridge: Macmillan and Bowes, 1886).

2 A. Bartlett Giammatti, 'Marlowe and the Arts of Illusion', *Yale Review* 2:62 (summer 1972), pp. 530–43, p. 535. Michael Goldman, in his interesting study of Marlowe's heroes as 'ravished', similarly sees them as all sharing an essential characteristic ('Marlowe and the Histrionics of Ravishment', in *Two Renaissance Mythmakers*, edited by Alvin Kernan [Baltimore and London: The Johns Hopkins University Press, 1977], pp. 22–40, p. 23).

3 Don Cameron Allen, 'Marlowe's *Dido* and the Tradition', in *Essays on Shakespeare and Elizabethan Drama in Honour of Hardin Craig*, edited by Richard Hosley (London: Routledge and Kegan Paul, 1963), pp. 55–69, p. 65. Much the same sort of argument is advanced by Charles G. Masinton in *Christopher Marlowe's Tragic Vision: A Study in Damnation* (Athens, Ohio: Ohio University Press, 1972), p. 4.

4 Ribner, pp. 224, 222 and 217; Paul H. Kocher, 'Christopher Marlowe, Individualist', *University of Toronto Quarterly* 17 (1947–8), pp. 111–20, p. 115. Kocher argues that both Marlowe's plays and his life are fundamentally structured around ideas of religion (p. 113), as do Claude J. Summers, *Christopher Marlowe and the Politics of Power* (Salzburg: Salzburg Studies, 1974), p. 20, and James Robinson Howe, *Marlowe, Tamburlaine, and Magic* (Athens, Ohio: Ohio University Press, 1976), p. 84.

5 Harry Levin, *Christopher Marlowe: The Overreacher* (London: Faber & Faber, 1961), p. 133.

6 Eugene Waith, *The Herculean Hero in Marlowe, Chapman, Shakespeare and Dryden* (London: Chatto & Windus, 1962), p. 60.

7 J.M. Robertson, *Marlowe: A Conspectus* (London: Routledge, 1931), pp. 7 and 181–2.

8 David Bevington, 'Marlowe and God', *Explorations in Renaissance Culture* 17 (1991), pp. 1–38, p. 14.

9 *Marlowe: A Conspectus*, pp. 28–9, 76, 42, 45, 85–108, 145, 112–15, 126-9, 136-7, 144–5, 152–5 and 176. A.W. Verity also believed in Marlowe's authorship of part of *Titus* (*Influence of Marlowe*, p. 104), as did Coleridge and Isaac Disraeli (see introduction, pp. 14–15).

10   For some of the more egregious efforts in this direction, see, for instance, Roberta Ballantine, 'The Shakespeare Epitaphs', *Shakespeare Bulletin* 14:3 (summer 1996), pp. 25–6.

11   Calvin Hoffman, *The Man Who Was Shakespeare* (London: Max Parrish, 1955), pp. 59 and 142. Della Hilton also thinks that Marlowe survived Deptford, though for reasons which are not entirely clear to me she asserts that he was definitely dead by 1598 (*Second Unto None* [Durham: Durham Academic Press, 1997], p. 170). A more sober and more recent attempt to claim *Edward III* for Marlowe is Thomas Merriam's 'Influence Alone? Reflections on the Newly Canonized *Edward III*', *Notes and Queries* 244 / 46:2 (June 1999), pp. 200–6.

12   I have found a surprising degree of correlation between people who think Marlowe wrote Shakespeare and people who think Marlowe cannot possibly have been homosexual, though the reasoning on the latter point is often so hedged about with coyness and euphemism as to be virtually impossible to understand (see for instance Hilton, *Second Unto None*, p. 34, and, more circumspectly, A.D. Wraight and Virginia F. Stern, *In Search of Christopher Marlowe*, 2nd edition (Chichester: Adam Hart, 1993), pp. 303 and 337–9).

13   C.F. Tucker Brooke, *The Life of Marlowe and the Tragedy of Dido, Queen of Carthage* (London: Methuen, 1930), pp. 402–4, 412 and 416. Jonathan Hope's linguistic analysis of *Arden* yields results which leave Marlowe's authorship of it open as a possibility (*The Authorship of Shakespeare's Plays: A Socio-linguistic Study* [Cambridge: University of Cambridge Press, 1994], p. 131).

14   On parallels between these plays and *Edward II* and *The Massacre at Paris* in particular, see, for instance, Rupert Taylor, 'A Tentative Chronology of Marlowe's and Some Other Elizabethan Plays', *PMLA* 51 (1936), pp. 643–88, p. 643; U.M. Ellis-Fermor, *Christopher Marlowe* (Hamden, Connecticut: Archon Books, 1967), p. 5; Roy T. Eriksen, 'Construction in Marlowe's *The Massacre at Paris*', *Papers from the First Nordic Conference for English Studies*, edited by Stig Johansson and Bjørn Tysdahl (Oslo: Institute of English Studies, 1981), pp. 41–54, p. 42; and F.S. Boas, *Christopher Marlowe: A Biographical and Critical Study* (Oxford: The Clarendon Press, 1940), p. 197.

15   For a particularly sustained argument to this effect, which entirely discounts the possibility of Marlovian authorship, see Yashdip S. Bains, *The Contention and the True Tragedy: William Shakespeare's First Versions of 2 and 3 Henry VI* (Shimla: Indian Institute of Advanced Study, 1996), especially p. 34.

16   Thomas Merriam's computer-assisted analyses have found distinctly Marlovian features in these three plays. See his 'Tamburlaine Stalks in Henry VI', *Computers and the Humanities* 30:3 (1996), pp. 267–80, p. 276. Tucker Brooke also assigned these plays to Marlowe ('The Marlowe Canon', *Publications of the Modern Language Association of America* 37:3 [September 1922], pp. 367–417, p. 368, and *The Life of Marlowe*, pp. 38–9), as did Swinburne in 1908 (cited in Millar MacLure, ed.,

Marlowe: The Critical Heritage, 1588–1896 [London: Routledge, 1979], p. 181). On parallels between the *Henry VI* plays and *The Massacre at Paris*, see David Potter, 'Marlowe's *Massacre at Paris* and the Reputation of Henri III of France', in *Christopher Marlowe and English Renaissance Culture*, edited by Darryll Grantley and Peter Roberts (Aldershot: Scolar Press, 1996), pp. 70–95, p. 71.

17 As I write, B.J. Sokol is proposing a definitive date for *1 Henry VI* of between November 1591 and April 1592, but his work is still unpublished.

18 See, for instance, William Shakespeare, *The First Part of King Henry VI*, edited by Michael Hattaway (Cambridge: Cambridge University Press, 1990), p. 43.

19 Margaret E. Owens, 'The Many-Headed Monster in *Henry VI, Part 2*', *Criticism* 38:3 (summer 1996), pp. 367–82, p. 379. See also David H. Thurn, 'Sovereignty, Disorder, and Fetishism in Marlowe's *Edward II*', *Renaissance Drama* 21 (1990), pp. 115–41, pp. 122–3, and Constance Brown Kuriyama, *Hammer or Anvil: Psychological Patterns in Marlowe's Plays* (Brunswick, NJ: Rutgers University Press, 1980), p. 190.

20 J.B. Steane, *Marlowe: A Critical Study* (Cambridge: Cambridge University Press, 1964), p. 231.

21 William Shakespeare, *Henry VI, Part 1*, edited by John Dover Wilson [1952] (Cambridge: Cambridge University Press, 1968), I.I.5. My quotations from Parts 2 and 3 will also come from the Dover Wilson editions.

22 For comment on this treatment of Pucelle, see for instance Jean E. Howard and Phyllis Rackin, *Engendering a Nation* (London: Routledge, 1997), pp. 44–5; Leah Marcus, *Puzzling Shakespeare: Local Reading and its Discontents* (Berkeley: University of California Press, 1988), pp. 52 and 66–71; and Nina S. Levine, *Women's Matters: Politics, Gender, and Nation in Shakespeare's Early History Plays* (Newark: University of Delaware Press, 1998), p. 37.

23 William Shakespeare, *The Comedy of Errors*, edited by Stanley Wells (Penguin: Harmondsworth, 1972), I.1.32–3. All further quotations from the play will be taken from this edition and reference will be given in the text.

24 Marie Axton, *The Queen's Two Bodies: Drama and the Elizabethan Succession* (London: Royal Historical Society, 1977), p. 80.

25 On local knowledge of Kent as a possible pointer to Marlovian authorship, see also William Urry, *Christopher Marlowe and Canterbury*, edited by Andrew Butcher (London: Faber & Faber, 1988), introduction, p. xxcvii.

26 See, for instance, Howard and Rackin, *Engendering a Nation*, p. 66.

27 John Bakeless, *The Tragicall History of Christopher Marlowe*, 2 vols (Cambridge, Massachusetts: Harvard University Press, 1942), I, p. 98.

28 Harry Levin points out that 'the episode of the broken alliance' in *Tamburlaine* 'actually happened among the foes of Scanderbeg' (*Overreacher*, p. 54).

29 Both this and the original Harvey reference are quoted and discussed in Samuel C. Chew, *The Crescent and the Rose* (Oxford: Oxford University Press, 1937), pp. 477–8. For an interesting account of Scanderbeg in

relation to *Henry V* (itself clearly influenced by *Tamburlaine*), see Richard Hillman, *Intertextuality and Romance in Renaissance Drama* (Basingstoke: Macmillan, 1992), pp. 34–5. Bakeless too discusses the Scanderbeg question, as well as the also lost *Maiden's Holiday* and the still extant *Lust's Dominion*, both of which are sometimes, though in my view unconvincingly, attributed to Marlowe (*Tragicall History*, pp. 284–5, 206 and 276), Bakeless is inclined to entertain the attribution of the *Maiden's Holiday* on the grounds that Marlowe is likely to have written more plays than now survive.

30   See, for instance, Marilynn Desmond, *Reading Dido: Gender, Textuality, and the Medieval* Aeneid (Minneapolis: University of Minnesota Press, 1994), p. 31.

31   Brooke, *Life*, pp. 393–6; but see Michel Poirier, *Christopher Marlowe* (London: Chatto & Windus, 1951), p. 202.

32   Diana Henderson, *Elizabethan Lyric, Gender, and Performance* (Urbana: University of Illinois Press, 1995), p. 151. For comment on the absence of Marlovian sonnets, see also Alan Haynes, *Sex in Elizabethan England* (Stroud: Sutton, 1997), p. 95. Boas refers to rumours that 16 Marlowe sonnets were found in the last century, but there is no trace of them now (*Christopher Marlowe*, p. 223).

33   Michael J. Warren, '*Doctor Faustus*: The Old Man and the Text', *English Literary Renaissance* 11 (1981), pp. 111–47, p. 145.

34   See, for instance, Leslie Spence, 'The Influence of Marlowe's Sources on *Tamburlaine 1*', *Modern Philolology* 24 (November 1926), pp. 181–200, p. 183.

35   Though Margo Hendricks dates *Dido* to between 1588 and 1592 ('Managing the Barbarian: *The Tragedy of Dido, Queen of Carthage*', *Renaissance Drama* [1992], pp. 165–88, p. 167), mainly, it seems, because she reads it as a post-Armada play (p. 168), and T.M. Pearce argues that '[i]t is inconceivable that he should have written the *Dido* play before the *Tamburlaine* plays, which are almost devoid of the arts of stage technique...Judged by this test, *Dido* stands between the *Tamburlaine* plays and *Dr. Faustus*' ('Evidence for Dating Marlowe's *Tragedy of Dido*', in *Studies in the English Renaissance Drama*, edited by Josephine W. Bennett, Oscar Cargill and Vernon Hall, Jr (London: Peter Owen and Vision Press, 1959), p. 239.

36   See, for instance, Svetlana Makurenkova, 'Intertextual Correspondences: The Pastoral in Marlowe, Raleigh, Shakespeare, and Donne', in Alexandr Parfenov and Joseph Price, eds, *Russian Essays on Shakespeare and his Contemporaries* (Newark: University of Delaware Press, 1998), pp. 185–200, p. 186.

37   Michel Poirier would put the Ovid before the Lucan on the grounds that it has more mistakes (*Christopher Marlowe*, p. 78). Clifford Leech, who also comments on the errors in the Ovid, similarly dates it early (*Christopher Marlowe: Poet for the Stage*, edited by Anne Lancashire [New York: AMS Press, 1986], p. 13).

38   Albeit love inflected in a typically Marlovian way: Harry Levin points out that Marlowe 'translates Ovid's *ambitiosus amor* as "my ambitious ranging minde"' (*Overreacher*, p. 27). He too dates the translations to this period, as does Charles Nicholl, '"At Middleborough": Some Reflections on Marlowe's Visit to the Low Countries in 1592', in *Christopher Marlowe and English Renaissance Culture*, edited by Darryll Grantley and Peter Roberts (Aldershot: Scolar Press, 1996), pp. 38–50, p. 40.

39   Clifford Ronan, '*Antike Roman*' (Athens: University of Georgia Press, 1995), pp. 157 and 156. D.J. Palmer also argues for the relevance of the Lucan translation in particular to the rest of the Marlowe canon ('Marlowe's Naturalism', in *Christopher Marlowe*, edited by Brian Gibbons [London: Ernest Benn, 1968], pp. 153–75, p. 161, and see too James Shapiro, '"Metre meete to furnish Lucans style": Reconsidering Marlowe's *Lucan*', in *A Poet and a Filthy Play-Maker: New Essays on Christopher Marlowe*, edited by Kenneth Friedenreich, Roma Gill and Constance Brown Kuriyama (New York: AMS Press, 1988), pp. 315–26. Douglas Cole sees the twin emphases on love and war in Lucan and Ovid as being mirrored at roughly the same time in *Tamburlaine* and *Dido* (*Suffering and Evil in the Plays of Christopher Marlowe* [Princeton: Princeton University Press, 1962], p. 75).

40   Boas, *Christopher Marlowe*, p. 44. On parallels and affinities between Lucan and Marlowe, see also Steane, *Marlowe*, p. 258, who interestingly points out that both men were innovators in their own times in the contemporaneity of their material, in the *Pharsalia* and the *Massacre at Paris* respectively.

41   See Thomas Wharton [1781], quoted in Millar Maclure, ed., *Marlowe: The Critical Heritage 1588–1896* (London: Routledge, 1979), p. 58, and Rowse, *Christopher Marlowe*, p. 114.

42   Brooke, *Life*, pp. 396, 398, 368–9 and 375.

43   Some critics have concurred with the implication on the title-page that Nashe wrote part of the play: see, for instance, Nicholas Davidson, 'Christopher Marlowe and Atheism', in Grantley and Roberts, *Christopher Marlowe and English Renaissance Culture*, pp. 129–47, p. 130, and Boas, *Christopher Marlowe*, p. 50; see also Leech, *Christopher Marlowe*, p. 15). Others, however, argue that it is all Marlowe's: see, for instance, W. L. Godshalk, 'Marlowe's *Dido, Queen of Carthage*', *English Literary History* 38:1 [March 1971], pp. 1–18, p. 1), Rowse (*Christopher Marlowe*, p. 44), and Brian Gibbons, 'Unstable Proteus: Marlowe's *The Tragedy of Dido Queen of Carthage*', in *Christopher Marlowe*, edited by Brian Morris (London: Ernest Benn Ltd, 1968), pp. 27–46, p. 28. Eugene M. Waith remarks that 'there are no clear evidences of Nashe's work in the play as it stands' ('Marlowe and the Jades of Asia', *Studies in English Literature* 5 [1965], pp. 229–45, p. 233).

44   Brooke, *Life*, pp. 390–1, 382. See, for instance, Steane, *Marlowe*, p. 118, Bakeless, *Tragicall History*, p. 95, Ellis-Fermor, *Christopher Marlowe*, p. 4, who sees it as then followed by *The Jew of Malta*, and Yuzo Yamada,

'The New Actaeon's Fortune, A and B: Giordano Bruno in the Two Texts of *Doctor Faustus*', *Shakespeare Studies (Tokyo)* 29 (1991), p. 3. Harry Levin, however, treats *The Jew of Malta* as *Tamburlaine*'s successor, followed by *The Massacre at Paris* and *Edward II*, and *Doctor Faustus*, with Samuel Rowley as a (perhaps posthumous) collaborator, last (*Overreacher*, pp. 79, 104, and 144). Mark Thornton Burnett's recent Everyman edition (1999) of the complete plays suggests 1588–9 as the likely date (introduction, p. xii). Rowse (*Christopher Marlowe*, pp. 81–2) is unusual in arguing that *The Jew of Malta* immediately followed *Tamburlaine*.

45   Bevington, 'Marlowe and God', p. 13. Leah Marcus points to updating in the B text of the play, presumably in an attempt to maintain contemporaneity (*Unediting the Renaissance* [London: Routledge, 1996], p. 56).

46   Sidney R. Homan, 'Chapman and Marlowe: The Paradoxical Hero and the Divided Response', *Journal of English and Germanic Philology* 68 (1969), pp. 391–406, p. 397.

47   A.D. Nuttall, *The Alternative Trinity: Gnostic Heresy in Marlowe, Milton, and Blake* (Oxford: The Clarendon Press, 1998), p. 46. See also an unsigned article in the 1893 'Temple Bar' which is reproduced in MacLure, *The Critical Heritage*, p. 189. This also refers to a 1587 English translation of the *Faustbuch* (p. 188), but I know of no supporting evidence for this. Martha Tuck Rozett also compares Tamburlaine with Faustus (*The Doctrine of Election and the Emergence of Elizabethan Tragedy* [Princeton: Princeton University Press, 1984], p. 210), as does H. Roehrman (*Marlowe and Shakespeare: A Thematic Exposition of Some of Their Plays* [Arnhem: Van Loghum Slaterus], pp. 5 and 12).

48   Francis R. Johnson, 'Marlowe's "Imperiall Heaven"', *English Literary History* 12 (1945), pp. 35–44, p. 35. See also M.C. Bradbrook, *The School of Night* (New York: Russell & Russell, 1965), p. 117.

49   Kocher, 'Christopher Marlowe, Individualist', p. 119.

50   John S. Mebane, *Renaissance Magic and the Return of the Golden Age* (Lincoln: University of Nebraska Press, 1989), p. 113. On *Tamburlaine* as influenced by Neoplatonism, see also L.T. Fitz, 'Humanism Questioned: A Study of Four Renaissance Characters', *English Studies in Canada* 5 (1979), pp. 388–405, p. 392.

51   Susan Richards, 'Marlowe's *Tamburlaine II: A Drama of Death*', *Modern Language Quarterly* 261 (1965), pp. 375–87, p. 377.

52   Austin K. Gray, 'Some Observations on Christopher Marlowe, Government Agent', *Publications of the Modern Language Association of America* 43 (1928), pp. 682–700, pp. 692–3.

53   Beatrice Daw Brown, 'Marlowe, Faustus, and Simon Magus', *Publications of the Modern Language Association of America* 54 (1930), pp. 82–121, p. 120.

54   See, for instance, Michael Hattaway, 'The Theology of Marlowe's *Doctor Faustus*', *Renaissance Drama* 3 (1970), pp. 51–78, p. 59, n. 23, and Robert Ornstein, 'Marlowe and God: The Tragic Theology of *Dr. Faustus*', *PMLA* 83 [1968], pp. 1378–85, p. 1380). J.P. Brockbank calls it 'the last and finest of Marlowe's heroic plays', though it is unclear to me whether that

means that he also thinks it to be the last of all his plays (*Marlowe: Dr Faustus* [London: Edward Arnold, 1962], p. 23).

55 Edward A. Snow, 'Marlowe's *Doctor Faustus* and the Ends of Desire', in *Two Renaissance Mythmakers*, pp. 70–110, p. 78.

56 See Judith Weil, '"Full Possession": Service and Slavery in *Doctor Faustus*', in *Marlowe, History, and Sexuality: New Essays on Christopher Marlowe*, edited by Paul Whitfield White (New York: AMS Press, 1998), pp. 143–54, p. 149.

57 Irving Ribner, 'Marlowe's "Tragicke Glasse"', in Hosley, *Essays on Shakespeare*, pp. 91–114, pp. 91 and 2.

58 Nicholas Brooke, 'The Moral Tragedy of Doctor Faustus', *The Cambridge Journal* 5 (1952), pp. 662–87, p. 664.

59 Warren, '*Doctor Faustus*', pp. 210, n. 22, and p. 144.

60 Paul H. Kocher, 'The English *Faust Book* and the Date of Marlowe's *Faustus*', *Modern Language Notes* (February 1940), pp. 95–101, pp. 95 and 97. See also Kocher, 'Some Nashe Marginalia Concerning Marlowe', *Modern Language Notes* (January 1942), pp. 45–9, and 'The Early Date for Marlowe's *Faustus*', *Modern Language Notes* (November 1943), pp. 539–42. Davidson ('Atheism', p. 139), suggests that the English Faust Book was 'published for the first time possibly in 1588', but I do not know on what evidence.

61 Curt A. Zimansky, 'Marlowe's *Faustus*: The Date Again', *Philological Quarterly* 41 (January 1962), pp. 181–7, pp. 184 and 185.

62 It might be worth noting that there was a dispute within Canterbury over whether or not the cathedral possessed the body of St Dunstan (see Rowse, *Christopher Marlowe*, p. 4).

63 G.M. Pinciss, 'Marlowe's Cambridge Years and the Writing of *Doctor Faustus*', *Studies in English Literature* 33 (1993), pp. 249–64, p. 254.

64 Michael H. Keefer, ed., *Christopher Marlowe's Doctor Faustus: A 1604-Version Edition* (Peterborough, Ontario: Broadview Press, 1991), introduction, p. lv.

65 Scott McMillin and Sally-Beth MacLean, *The Queen's Men and their Plays* (Cambridge: Cambridge University Press, 1998), p. 158.

66 See, for instance, Poirier, p. 123; Leech, *Christopher Marlowe*, pp. 17–19, who also notes similarities between *Tamburlaine* and *Faustus* (pp. 23 and 128); Constance Brown Kuriyama, *Hammer or Anvil*, p. 135; and William Empson, *Faustus and the Censor*, edited by John Henry Jones (Oxford: Basil Blackwell, 1987), p. 51.

67 See, for instance, N.W. Bawcutt, 'Machiavelli and Marlowe's *The Jew of Malta*', *Renaissance Drama* 3 (1970), pp. 3–49, p. 4.

68 Tucker Brooke, 'The Marlowe Canon', p. 384. He dates the play to 1589.

69 Though Tucker Brooke argued that it was actually more likely to date from 1590 or 1591 ('The Marlowe Canon', pp. 376–8).

70 Harold F. Brooks, 'Marlowe and Early Shakespeare', in *Marlowe*, ed. Morris, pp. 67–94, p. 78. Brooks concludes by tentatively suggesting 1592 for *Doctor Faustus*, and very late 1591 for *Edward II*.

71 See, for instance, Meredith Skura, 'Marlowe's *Edward II*: Penetrating Language in Shakespeare's *Richard II'*, *Shakespeare Survey 50* (1997), pp. 41–55, p. 45, and Gregory W. Bredbeck, *Sodomy and Interpretation: Marlowe to Milton* (Ithaca, NY: Cornell University Press, 1991), p. 58.

72 William Shakespeare, *The Comedy of Errors*, edited by R.A. Foakes (London: Methuen, 1962), introduction, p. xix.

73 Christopher Marlowe, *Edward the Second*, edited by Charles R. Forker (Manchester: Manchester University Press, 1994), I.i.121.

74 *The Comedy of Errors*, ed. Foakes, introduction, p. xxiii.

75 M.C. Bradbrook, 'Hero and Leander', *Scrutiny 2* (1933–4), pp. 59–64, p. 61.

76 Boas also points to similarities between *Dido* and *Edward II*, and similarly conjectures revision (*Christopher Marlowe*, p. 51).

77 Clifford Leech, 'Marlowe's Humor', in Hosley, *Essays on Shakespeare*, pp. 69–81, p. 70.

78 Patrick Cheney, *Marlowe's Counterfeit Profession: Ovid, Spenser, Counter-Nationhood* (Toronto: University of Toronto Press, 1997), p. 4.

79 Richard Rambuss, *Spenser's Secret Career* (Cambridge: Cambridge University Press, 1993), p. 4.

80 See, for instance, Tucker Brooke, *The Life of Marlowe*, p. 51.

81 See, for instance, Michael Hattaway, 'Christopher Marlowe: Ideology and Subversion', in Grantley and Roberts, *Christopher Marlowe*, pp. 198–223, p. 202, Johannes H. Birringer, *Marlowe's 'Doctor Faustus' and 'Tamburlaine': Theological and Theatrical Perspectives* (Frankfurt: Peter Lang, 1984), p. 245, and Steane, *Marlowe*, p. 76.

82 Cheney, *Profession*, pp. 13 and 14; Thomas Healy, *Christopher Marlowe* (Plymouth: Northcote House, 1994), p. 41.

2   1580–1587: Canterbury and Cambridge

1 See, for instance, Tucker Brooke, *Life of Marlowe*, p. 15.

2 See, for instance, Douglas Cole, *Christopher Marlowe and the Renaissance of Tragedy* (Westport, Connecticut: Greenwood Press, 1995), p. 46; Huston Diehl, *Staging Reform, Reforming the Stage* (Ithaca, NY: Cornell University Press, 1997), p. 65; Clifford Leech, *Marlowe: A Collection of Critical Essays* (Englewood Cliffs, NJ: Prentice-Hall, 1964), introduction, p. 9; Jocelyn Powell, 'Marlowe's Spectacle', *Tulane Drama Review* 8 (1964), pp. 195–210, especially p. 197; Marjorie Garber, '"Infinite Riches in a Little Room": Closure and Enclosure in Marlowe', in *Two Renaissance Mythmakers*, pp. 3–21, p. 7; and J.R. Mulryne and Stephen Fender, 'Marlowe and the "Comic Distance"', in *Marlowe*, ed. Morris, pp. 49–64.

3 See, for instance, Max Bluestone, *'Libido Speculandi*: Doctrine and Dramaturgy in Contemporary Interpretations of Marlowe's *Doctor Faustus'*, in *Reinterpretations of Elizabethan Drama*, edited by Norman Rabkin (New York: Columbia University Press, 1969), pp. 33–88, pp. 58 and 70.

4 'The Inheritance of Christopher Marlowe', Part I, *Theology* 47 (1964), pp. 298–305, pp. 302, 304, and 305. See also Joel B. Altman, *The Tudor*

Play of Mind: Rhetorical Inquiry and the Development of Elizabethan Drama (Berkeley: University of California Press, 1978), p. 339.

5 Leech, *Christopher Marlowe: Poet for the Stage*, p. 2.

6 Andrew Butcher, 'onely a boy called Christopher Mowle', in *Christopher Marlowe and English Renaissance Culture*, pp. 1–16, pp. 1, 4 and 3.

7 Kuriyama, *Hammer or Anvil*, p. 218.

8 Urry, *Christopher Marlowe and Canterbury*, pp. 26–7.

9 Butcher, 'onely a boy', p. 5.

10 See Stephen Greenblatt, 'Marlowe and the Will to Absolute Play', from *Renaissance Self-Fashioning: from More to Shakespeare* (Chicago: University of Chicago Press, 1980), pp. 193–221, reprinted in *New Historicism and Renaissance Drama*, edited by Richard Wilson and Richard Dutton (Harlow, Essex: Longman, 1992), pp. 57–82, p. 75.

11 Frank Ardolino, 'The "Wrath of Frowning Jove": Fathers and Sons in Marlowe's Plays', *Journal of Evolutionary Psychology*, 2 (1981), pp. 83–100, p. 83.

12 Hendricks, 'Managing the Barbarian', p. 169.

13 For an acute analysis of the giving of jewels as effecting a reification of relationships, and thus highlighting the power structures inherent in them, see Simon Shepherd, *Marlowe and the Politics of Elizabethan Theatre* (Brighton: Harvester, 1986), pp. 119, 171, 180 and 193–4.

14 David Farley-Hills, 'Tamburlaine and the Mad Priest of the Sun', *Journal of Anglo-Italian Studies* 2 (1992), pp. 36–49, p. 45. I am very grateful to Professor Farley-Hills for sending me a copy of this article.

15 On the way in which patterns in the play are repeated, see also Jackson I. Cope, 'Marlowe's *Dido* and the Titillating Children', *English Literary Renaissance* 4 (1974), pp. 315–25, p. 321, and Sara Munson Deats, *Sex, Gender, and Desire in the Plays of Christopher Marlowe* (Newark: University of Delaware Press, 1997), pp. 99 and 121.

16 Richard Proudfoot, *Marlowe the Playwright* (King's School, Canterbury: King's School Monographs no. 4, 1993).

17 Lawrence Danson, 'Christopher Marlowe: The Questioner', *English Literary Renaissance* 12 (1981), pp. 3–29, p. 13.

18 John Pikeryng, *Horestes*, in *Three Tudor Classical Interludes*, edited by Marie Axton (Cambridge: D.S. Brewer, 1982), ll.952–3.

19 See Stephen Greenblatt, *Marvelous Possessions* (Oxford: The Clarendon Press, 1991), p. 124.

20 On *Tamburlaine* as an Oedipal drama, see, for instance, C.L. Barber, 'The Death of Zenocrate: "Conceiving and subduing both" in Marlowe's *Tamburlaine*', *Literature and Psychology* 16 (1966), pp. 15–24, p. 18, and L.C. Knights, *Further Explorations* (London: Chatto & Windus, 1965), p. 87, note 1.

21 See David M. Bevington, *From Mankind to Marlowe* (Cambridge, Massachusetts: Harvard University Press, 1962), p. 205.

22 See also M.M. Mahood, 'Marlowe's Heroes', in *Elizabethan Drama: Modern Essays in Criticism*, edited by R.J. Kaufmann (Oxford: Oxford University Press, 1961; reprinted 1970), pp. 95–122, p. 102.

23 For a forcible argument that Tamburlaine might in fact be seen as a good father in terms of Renaissance values, see Carolyn D. Williams, '"The Jealousy of Wars": Marlowe's *Tamburlaine* and Renaissance Parenthood', paper read at a conference on Literature, Politics and History, University of Reading, 1995. I am very grateful to Carolyn Williams for sending me a copy of this paper.

24 T.M. Pearce, 'Tamburlaine's "Discipline to his Three Sonnes": An Interpretation of *Tamburlaine, Part II*', *Modern Language Quarterly* 15 (1954), pp. 18–27, p. 20.

25 Paul H. Kocher, 'Marlowe's Art of War', *Studies in Philology* 39 (1942), pp. 207–45, p. 225.

26 Jeremy Tambling, 'Abigail's Party: "The Difference of Things" in *The Jew of Malta*', in *In Another Country: Feminist Perspectives on Renaissance Drama*, edited by Dorothea Kehler and Susan Baker (Metuchen, NJ: The Scarecrow Press, 1991), pp. 95–112, pp. 99 and 103–4.

27 William Blackburn, '"Heavenly Words": Marlowe's Faustus as a Renaissance Magician', *English Studies in Canada* 4:1 (spring 1978), pp. 1–14, pp. 6 and 7.

28 Cutts, *The Left Hand of God*, p. viii.

29 Michael H. Keefer, 'Right Eye and Left Heel: Ideological Origins of the Legend of Faustus', *Mosaic* 22:2 (1989), pp. 79–94, p. 82.

30 Weil, '"Full Possession"', p. 144.

31 Kay Stockholder, '"Within the massy entrailes of the earth": Faustus's Relation to Women', in *'A Poet and a filthy play-maker'*, pp. 203–19.

32 Wilbur Sanders, for instance (*The Dramatist and the Received Idea* [Cambridge: Cambridge University Press, 1968], p. 140), sees Marlowe's treatment of his homosexual characters as informed by 'a neurotic desire for symbolic punishment and expiation'. As will become clear, I disagree.

33 Stephen Orgel, *Impersonations* (Cambridge: Cambridge University Press, 1996), p. 46.

34 See Alan Bray, *Homosexuality in Renaissance England* (London: Gay Men's Press, 1982; reprinted 1988), p. 16; Thomas Laqueur, *Making Sex: Body and Gender from the Greeks to Freud* (Cambridge, Mass.: Harvard University Press, 1990), pp. 63–148; and Bruce R. Smith, *Homosexual Desire in Shakespeare's England: A Cultural Poetics* (Chicago: University of Chicago Press, 1991), p. 215.

35 Claude J. Summers, 'Sex, Politics and Self-Realization in *Edward II*', in *'A Poet and a filthy play-maker'*, pp. 221–40, p. 223.

36 Shepherd (*Marlowe*, p. 119) regards the niece as being essentially a dupe of Gaveston, but I see no evidence for this.

37 Dympna Callaghan, 'The Terms of Gender: "Gay" and "Feminist" *Edward II*', in *Feminist Readings of Early Modern Culture*, edited by Valerie Traub, M. Lindsay Kaplan and Dympna Callaghan (Cambridge: Cambridge University Press, 1996), pp. 275–301, p. 282.

38   Jill L. Levenson, '"Working Words": The Verbal Dynamic of *Tamburlaine*', in *'A Poet and a filthy play-maker'*, pp. 99–115, p. 102.

39   Mahood ('Marlowe's Heroes', p. 113) views Barabas as ambitious to rule, though Catherine Minshull argues that '[s]o small is Barabas's interest in ruling that, when given the opportunity to be governor of Malta, he merely exchanges the position with Ferneze in return for yet more wealth' ('Marlowe's "Sound Machevill", *Renaissance Drama* 13 [1982], pp. 35–53, p. 41).

40   See Shepherd, *Marlowe*, pp. 75 and 156–7, and also David M. Bergeron, *Shakespeare's Romances and the Royal Family* (Lawrence, Kansas: University Press of Kansas, 1985), p. 110, and Lena Cowen Orlin, 'The Fictional Families of Elizabeth I', in *Political Rhetoric, Power, and Renaissance Women*, edited by Carole Levin and Patricia A. Sullivan (Albany: SUNY Press, 1995), pp. 85–110, p. 103.

41   See, for instance, Peter Roberts, 'The Studious Artizan: Christopher Marlowe, Canterbury and Cambridge', in *Christopher Marlowe*, ed. Grantley and Roberts, pp. 17–37, p. 22, and Boas, *Christopher Marlowe*, p. 8.

42   Caroline Spurgeon, *Shakespeare's Imagery and What it Tells Us* (Cambridge: Cambridge University Press, 1935), p. 13.

43   Nina Taunton, 'Biography, a University Education, and Playwriting: Fletcher and Marlowe', *Research Opportunities in Renaissance Drama* 33 (1994), pp. 63–97, pp. 72, 73, 81 and 82. See also Michael H. Keefer, 'Misreading Faustus Misreading: The Question of Context', *Dalhousie Review* 65 (1986), pp. 511–33, p. 518 and Martin Versfeld, 'Some Remarks on Marlowe's Faustus', *English Studies in Africa* 1 (1958), pp. 134–43, p. 134.

44   Ribner, 'Marlowe and the Critics', p. 224.

45   See Lesley B. Cormack, *Charting an Empire: Geography at the English Universities, 1580–1620* (Chicago: The University of Chicago Press, 1997), pp. 14–15.

46   Carroll Camden, 'Marlowe and Elizabethan Psychology', *Philological Quarterly* 8 (1929), pp. 69–78, p. 69.

47   Roma Gill, 'Snakes Leape by Verse', in *Marlowe*, ed. Gibbons, pp. 135–50.

48   Irving Ribner, 'Marlowe's "Tragicke Glass"', in *Essays on Shakespeare*, ed. Hosley, pp. 92 and 94.

49   For a detailed account of the pattern of Marlowe's residence, see Boas, *Christopher Marlowe*, pp. 13–15. Boas also points to the relative absence of an interest in law in Marlowe's plays (p. 17), suggesting that this was something he did not study, in marked contrast to the many legally trained dramatists of the next decade or two.

50   Gray, 'Some Observations', pp. 683–4.

51   Gray, 'Some Observations', pp. 683, 689 and 692–3.

52   Nicholl, '"At Middleborough"', p. 40.

53   John Michael Archer, *Sovereignty and Intelligence: Spying and Court Culture in the English Renaissance* (Stanford: Stanford University Press, 1993),

p. 70. Archer too stresses that it is Burghley rather than Walsingham who seems to have employed him (p. 71).

3   1587–1589: London and the World

1   Irving Ribner, 'Marlowe and Machiavelli', *Comparative Literature* 6 (1954), pp. 348–56, p. 355. See also Philip Edwards, *Threshold of a Nation: A Study in English and Irish Drama* (Cambridge: Cambridge University Press, 1979), pp. 54 and 64.
2   Kuriyama, *Hammer or Anvil*, pp. 22–3.
3   Michael Hattaway, 'Christopher Marlowe: Ideology and Substance', in *Christopher Marlowe*, ed. Grantley and Roberts, pp. 198–223, p. 201.
4   Leech, *Christopher Marlowe: Poet for the Stage*, p. 12.
5   Danson, 'Christopher Marlowe: The Questioner', p. 11.
6   Marjorie Garber, '"Here's Nothing Writ": Scribe, Script, and Circumscription in Marlowe's Plays', *Theatre Journal* 36 (1984), pp. 301–20, p. 303.
7   Roy W. Battenhouse, *Marlowe's Tamburlaine: A Study in Renaissance Moral Philosophy* (Nashville: Vanderbilt University Press, 1947).
8   Constance Brown Kuriyama, 'Dr. Greg and *Doctor Faustus*: The Supposed Originality of the 1616 Text', *English Literary Renaissance* 5 (1975), pp. 171–97, p. 186.
9   Peter Berek, '*Tamburlaine*'s Weak Sons: Imitation as Interpretation before 1593', *Renaissance Drama* 13 (1982), pp. 55–82, pp. 56, 59 and 75.
10   Charles Nicholl, *The Creature in the Map* [1995] (London: Vintage, 1996), p. 169.
11   John Cutts, 'Tamburlaine "as fierce Achilles was"', *Comparative Drama* 6:2 (1967), pp. 105–9, pp. 106–7.
12   Kuriyama, *Hammer or Anvil*, p. 14.
13   Ann Rosalind Jones and Peter Stallybrass, 'Dismantling Irena: The Sexualizing of Ireland in Early Modern England', in *Nationalisms and Sexualities*, edited by Andrew Parker, Mary Russo, Doris Summer and Patricia Yaeger (London: Routledge, 1992), pp. 157–74, p. 162.
14   See, for instance, Ribner, 'Marlowe's "Tragicke Glasse"', p. 93
15   Birringer, *Marlowe's 'Doctor Faustus' and 'Tamburlaine'*, p. 320. See also Cutts, *The Left Hand of God*, p. 89.
16   James Robinson Howe, *Marlowe, Tamburlaine, and Magic* (Athens, Ohio: Ohio University Press, 1976), p. 103.
17   See, for instance, Roy T. Eriksen, *A Study of the Tragedie of Doctor Faustus (1616)* (Oslo and New Jersey: Solum Forlag A/S and Humanities Press International, 1987), p. 193.
18   Rozett, *The Doctrine of Election*, p. 146.
19   Cutts, *The Left Hand of God*, p. 55; see also pp. 75 and 86.
20   Bevington, *From* Mankind *to* Marlowe, p. 210.
21   See, for instance, William J. Brown, 'Marlowe's Debasement of Bajazet: Foxe's *Actes and Monuments* and *Tamburlaine, Part I*', *Renaissance Quarterly* 24 (1971), pp. 38–48, and Roy W. Battenhouse, 'Protestant Apologetics

and the Subplot of *2 Tamburlaine*', *English Literary Renaissance* 3 (1973), pp. 30–43, p. 32.
22 Bakeless, *Tragicall History*, Vol. I, p. 205.
23 See Ethel Seaton, 'Marlowe's Map', in *Marlowe*, ed. Leech, pp. 36–56, p. 40.
24 Hendricks, 'Managing the Barbarian', pp. 166 and 179.
25 See, for instance, Leech, 'Marlowe's Humor', pp. 72–3, and Cutts, *The Left Hand of God*, pp. 10–11. See also Ethel Seaton, 'Marlowe's Light Reading', in *Elizabethan and Jacobean Studies Presented to F.P. Wilson* (Oxford: The Clarendon Press, 1959), pp. 17–35, p. 28.
26 Levin, *The Overreacher*, p. 29.
27 See Jonathan Andrews, Asa Briggs, Roy Porter, Penny Tucker and Keir Waddington, *The History of Bethlem* (London: Routledge, 1997), p. 133.
28 I am grateful to S.P. Cerasano for assistance on Alleyn's background.
29 Quoted in Cole, *Christopher Marlowe*, p. 69.
30 For an account of the brawl in which Marlowe and Watson fought on the same side on 18 September 1589, see Mark Eccles, *Christopher Marlowe in London* (Cambridge, Massachusetts: Harvard University Press, 1934), p. 36. For Watson in general, see for instance Wraight and Stern, *In Search of Christopher Marlowe*, pp. 124–5.
31 Urry, *Christopher Marlowe and Canterbury*, p. 63.
32 On the circle of Chapman and Roydon, see for instance James Shirley, *Thomas Harriot: A Biography* (Oxford: The Clarendon Press, 1983), pp. 66–7.
33 Kyd said merely 'Warner', which could be, and has been, variously identified as either Walter or William. The mathematically-minded Walter seems a more likely candidate than the classicist William, but William also had connections with the Muscovy company, which he celebrated three years after Marlowe's death in *Albion's England*, and if Marlowe was indeed related to Captain Anthony Marlowe, this might have provided a possible link.
34 See Ernest Strathmann, 'The Textual Evidence for "The School of Night"' (*Modern Language Notes* [March 1941], pp. 176–86), Bradbrook, *The School of Night*, and Eleanor Grace Clark, *Ralegh and Marlowe: A Study in Elizabethan Fustian* (New York: Fordham University Press, 1941), p. 251.
35 See, for instance, Hilary Gatti, *The Renaissance Drama of Knowledge: Giordano Bruno in England* (London: Routledge, 1989), pp. 75–7, Richard Dutton, 'Shakespeare and Marlowe: Censorship and Construction', *The Yearbook of English Studies* 23 (1993), pp. 1–29, Eriksen, *Forme*, p. 59, and Farley-Hills, pp. 36–49.
36 Paul H. Kocher pointed out that 'our only evidence of contact between the two men comes in the year 1593' (*Christopher Marlowe: A Study of his Thought, Learning and Character* [New York: Russell & Russell, 1962], p. 240).
37 For a discussion of Harriot's probable religious views, see Ernest A. Strathmann, *Sir Walter Ralegh: A Study in Elizabethan Skepticism* (New York: Octagon Books, 1973), p. 58.
38 Henry Stevens, *Thomas Hariot* [1900] (New York: Lenox Hill, 1972), pp. 146 and 147.

39   William M. Hamlin, for instance, sees elements of Pyrrhonist scepticism in *Doctor Faustus* which he traces back to Giordano Bruno via Hariot and Warner ('Skepticism and Solipsism in *Doctor Faustus*', *Research Opportunities in Renaissance Drama* 36 [1997], pp. 1–22, p. 8).
40   Christopher Devlin, *The Life of Robert Southwell, Poet and Martyr* (London: Longman, 1956), p. 267.
41   See R.B. Wernham, 'Christopher Marlowe at Flushing in 1592', *English Historical Review* 91 (1976), pp. 344–5, p. 345.
42   Jeffrey Knapp, *An Empire Nowhere: England, America, and Literature from Utopia to* The Tempest (Berkeley: University of California Press, 1992), p. 159.
43   Wraight and Stern, *In Search of Christopher Marlowe*, p. 92.
44   Although *A Massacre at Paris* is also set abroad, like *Edward II*, it deals with civil war, rather than confrontations between different nations, and I shall therefore not be discussing it here.
45   On the relation between Scythianness and Irishness here see Roger Sales, *Christopher Marlowe* (Basingstoke: Macmillan, 1991), pp. 56–7.
46   See also Robert Kimbrough, '*1 Tamburlaine*: A Speaking Picture in a Tragic Glass', *Renaissance Drama* 7 [1964], pp. 20–34, p. 30).
47   J.S. Cunningham, ed., *Tamburlaine the Great* (Manchester: Manchester University Press, 1981), introduction, p. 66. See also Peter S. Donaldson, 'Conflict and Coherence: Narcissism and Tragic Structure in Marlowe', in *Narcissism and the Text*, edited by Lynne Layton and Barbara Ann Schapiro (New York: New York University Press, 1986), pp. 36–63, p. 39.
48   See Vivien Thomas and William Tydeman, *Christopher Marlowe: The Plays and Their Sources* (London: Routledge, 1994), pp. 90–2.
49   Note also Stephen Greenblatt's discussion of the use of Scythians as mirroring figures in Herodotus, for 'the discovery of the self in the other and the other in the self' (*Marvelous Possessions*, p. 127).
50   See Jonathan V. Crewe, 'The Theater of the Idols: Theatrical and Antitheatrical Discourse', in *Staging the Renaissance*, edited by David Scott Kastan and Peter Stallybrass (London: Routledge, 1991), pp. 49–56, p. 52.
51   Kocher, 'Marlowe's Art of War', p. 207.
52   Kocher, *Christopher Marlowe*, pp. 190–1.
53   Bakeless, *Tragicall History*, I, p. 52.
54   See also Catherine Belsey, *The Subject of Tragedy* [1985] (London: Routledge, 1991), p. 29.
55   Healy, p. 44. See also Yves Peyré, 'Marlowe's Argonauts', in *Travel and Drama in Shakespeare's Time*, edited by Jean-Pierre Maquerlot and Michele Willems (Cambridge: Cambridge University Press, 1996), pp. 106–23, pp. 113–4.
56   Richard Wilson, 'Visible Bullets: Tamburlaine the Great and Ivan the Terrible', English Literary History 62 (1995), pp. 47–68, pp. 47–8.
57   This is both quoted and discussed in Nicholl, *The Reckoning*.
58   Bartels, *Spectacles of Strangeness*, p. 15.

59 Nick de Somogyi, 'Marlowe's Maps of War', in *Christopher Marlowe*, ed. Grantley and Roberts, pp. 70–95, p. 100.
60 Wilson, 'Visible Bullets', p. 50.
61 De Somogyi, 'Marlowe's Maps of War', p. 104.
62 Wilson, 'Visible Bullets', p. 51.
63 Nicholl, *The Creature in the Map*, pp. 28, 98 and 55. Thomas Cartelli also draws a parallel between the approach of Tamburlaine and that of the conquistadores ('Marlowe and the New World', in *Christopher Marlowe*, ed. Grantley and Roberts, pp. 110–18, pp. 111 and 115), and suggests that Ralegh may have modelled himself on Lope de Aguirre (p. 112).
64 See, for instance, Robert Lacey, *Sir Walter Ralegh* (London: The History Book Club, 1973), p. 54. Anthony Burgess sees Tamburlaine's golden armour as mirroring that of Sir Walter Raleigh, and also links Tamburlaine's killings to the Drogheda massacre (*A Dead Man in Deptford* [London: Hutchinson, 1993], p. 125).
65 See, for instance, Yamada, 'New Actaeon', p. 1, and Keefer, ed., *Christopher Marlowe's Doctor Faustus*, introduction, p. xxv.
66 Lacey, *Ralegh*, p. 117.
67 Strathmann, *Sir Walter Ralegh*, p. 42.
68 Nicholl, '"At Middleborough"', p. 43.
69 *Overreacher*, pp. 104 and 181.
70 Mark Thornton Burnett, 'Tamburlaine: An Elizabethan Vagabond', *Studies in Philology* 94 (1987), pp. 308–23.
71 Danson, 'Christopher Marlowe', pp. 16–17.
72 At the beginning of Part Two events draw nearer to us not only geographically but also chronologically.
73 Pearce, 'Tamburlaine's "Discipline"', pp. 18 and 22.
74 Kocher, 'Marlowe's Art of War', p. 223.
75 Nicholl, *Reckoning*, p. 202.
76 Huston Diehl, 'Inversion, Parody, and Irony: The Visual Rhetoric of Renaissance English Tragedy', *Studies in English Literature* 22 (1982), pp. 197–209, pp. 201 and 202. I am grateful to Derek Roper for drawing this article to my attention.
77 Garber, '"Infinite Riches"', p. 6.
78 Zunder, *Elizabethan Marlowe*, p. 65.
79 Nicholl, *Reckoning*, p. 124.

4 1589–1592: Daring God out of Heaven

1 On the theatricality of these plays, and particularly Ferneze as a dramatist, see, for instance, Roger Sales, 'The Stage, the Scaffold and the Spectators: the Struggle for Power in Marlowe's *Jew of Malta*', in *Christopher Marlowe*, ed. Grantley and Roberts, pp. 119–28, pp. 125–6.
2 Rowse, *Christopher Marlowe*, p. 79.
3 Graham Hammill, 'Faustus's Fortunes: Commodification, Exchange, and the Form of Literary Subjectivity', *ELH* 63 (1996), pp. 309–36.

4 Keefer, 'Misreading Faustus Misreading', p. 517. See also A.N. Okerlund, 'The Intellectual Folly of Dr. Faustus', *Studies in Philology* 74 (1977), pp. 258–78, pp. 265, 268, and 272; Thomas McAlindon, 'Classical Mythology and Christian Tradition in Marlowe's *Doctor Faustus*', *PMLA* 81 (1966), pp. 214–23, p. 219; and Robert Boerth, 'The Mediterranean and the Mediterranean World on the Stage of Marlowe and Shakespeare', *Journal of Theatre and Drama* 2 (1996), pp. 35–58, p. 44.

5 David H. Thurn, 'Economic and Ideological Exchange in Marlowe's *Jew of Malta*', *Theatre Journal* 46 (1994), pp. 157–70, p. 166.

6 Ian McAdam, 'Carnal Identity in *The Jew of Malta*', *English Literary Renaissance* 26 (1996), pp. 46–74, p. 46. See also Arthur Mizener, 'The Tragedy of Marlowe's *Doctor Faustus*', *College English* 5 (1943–4), pp. 70–5, p. 74.

7 Hattaway, 'Theology', pp. 54 and 56.

8 Robert G. Hunter, *Shakespeare and the Mystery of God's Judgments* (Athens, Georgia: University of Georgia Press, 1976), p. 43.

9 Masinton, Christopher Marlowe's Tragic Vision, p. 125.

10 See, for instance, C.L. Barber, '"The Form of Faustus' fortunes good or bad"', *Tulane Drama Review* 8 (1964), pp. 92–119, p. 96; Clifford Davidson, 'Doctor Faustus of Wittenberg', *PMLA* 59 (1962), pp. 514–23, p. 522; David Kaula, 'Time and the Timeless in *Everyman and Dr. Faustus*', *College English* 22 (1960), pp. 9–14, p. 11; Arieh Sachs, 'The Religious Despair of Doctor Faustus', *Journal of English and Germanic Philology* 63 (1964), pp. 625–47, p. 626; Alan Sinfield, *Literature in Protestant England 1560–1660* (Totowa, NJ: Barnes & Noble, 1983), pp. 116–18; Sallye J. Sheppeard, 'Marlowe's Icarus: Culture and Myth in *Doctor Faustus*', in *Subjects on the World's Stage: Essays on British Literature of the Middle Ages and the Renaissance*, edited by David G. Allen and Robert A. White (Newark: University of Delaware Press, 1995), pp. 133–45, p. 134; Richard Waswo, 'Damnation, Protestant Style: Macbeth, Faustus, and Christian Tragedy', *Journal of Medieval and Renaissance Studies* 4:1 (1974), pp. 63–99, pp. 74–5; and John S. Wilks, *The Idea of Conscience in Renaissance Tragedy* (London: Routledge, 1990), pp. 145–51. But see also Ceri Sullivan, 'Faustus and the Apple', *The Review of English Studies*, New Series, 47 (February, 1996), pp. 47–50, p. 50.

11 Pinciss, 'Marlowe's Cambridge Years', p. 259.

12 Mebane, *Renaissance Magic*, pp. 118–19.

13 See, for instance, Rodney Stenning Edgecombe, 'The 'Burning Chair' in the B-Text of *Doctor Faustus*', *Notes and Queries* 241:2 (June 1996), pp. 144–5.

14 Susan Snyder, 'Marlowe's *Doctor Faustus* as an Inverted Saint's Life', *Studies in Philology* 63 (1966), pp. 565–77, p. 565.

15 Brooke, 'Moral Tragedy', p. 669.

16 Garber, '"Infinite Riches"', p. 13.

17 Snow, 'Ends of Desire', pp. 70–1.

18 Marlowe, *The Complete Plays*, ed. Mark Thornton Burnett, p. 538.

19   Empson, Faustus and the Censor, p. 44. He also suggests that the original version included harem scenes (p. 62).
20   Cheney, *Counterfeit Possession*, pp. 193 and 204.
21   Steane, *Marlowe*, p. 119.
22   Garber, ' "Here's nothing writ" ', pp. 312–16.
23   Taunton, 'Biography', p. 70.
24   Keefer, 'Misreading Faustus Misreading', pp. 511 and 512. See also Pauline Honderich, 'John Calvin and Doctor Faustus', *Modern Language Review* 68 (1973), pp. 1–13, p. 5, and James A. Reynolds, 'Faustus' Flawed Learning', *English Studies* 57 (1976), pp. 329–36, p. 332.
25   Robert Rentoul Reed, Jr., *The Occult on the Tudor and Stuart Stage* (Boston: The Christopher Publishing House, 1965), p. 90.
26   Francis R. Johnson, 'Marlowe's Astronomy and Renaissance Skepticism', *English Literary History* 13 (1946), pp. 241–54, p. 241.
27   See, for instance, Leah S. Marcus, *Unediting the Renaissance* (London: Routledge, 1996), p. 42, and Kenneth Muir, 'Three Marlowe Texts', *Notes and Queries* 241:2 (June 1996), pp. 142–4.
28   Roma Gill, ' "... such conceits as clownage keeps in pay": Comedy and *Dr. Faustus*', in *The Fool and the Trickster: Studies in Honour of Enid Welsford*, edited by Paul V.A. Williams (Cambridge: D.S. Brewer, 1979), pp. 55–63, p. 56.
29   See, for instance, Boas, *Christopher Marlowe*, p. 211.
30   Kuriyama, 'Dr. Greg and *Doctor Faustus*', pp. 171 and 172.
31   Warren, '*Doctor Faustus*: The Old Man and the Text', pp. 115 and 117–18. See also Ernst Honigman in 'Ten Problems in *Dr Faustus*', in *The Arts of Performance in Elizabethan and Early Stuart Drama: Essays for G.K. Hunter*, edited by Murray Biggs, Philip Edwards, Inga-Stina Ewbank and Eugene M. Waith (Edinburgh: Edinburgh University Press, 1991), pp. 173–91, p. 183.
32   Bluestone, '*Libido Speculandi*', p. 41.
33   Michael H. Keefer, 'Verbal Magic and the Problem of the A and B Texts of *Doctor Faustus*', *Journal of English and Germanic Philology* 82 (1983), pp. 324–46, p. 325. See also George L. Geckle, 'The 1604 and 1616 Versions of *Dr. Faustus*: Text and Performance', in *Subjects on the World's Stage*, ed. Allen and White, pp. 146–61.
34   See, for instance, Fredson Bowers, 'Marlowe's *Doctor Faustus*: The 1602 Additions', *Studies in Bibliography* 26 (1973), pp. 1–18, p. 2; but see also Eric Rasmussen, 'Rehabilitating the A-Text of Marlowe's *Doctor Faustus*', *Studies in Bibliography* 46 (1993), pp. 221–38, pp. 236 and 234.
35   Brooke, 'Moral Tragedy', pp. 664 and 673.
36   Barber, ' "Forme" ', p. 109. See also Roland M. Frye, 'Marlowe's *Doctor Faustus*: The Repudiation of Humanity', *South Atlantic Quarterly* 55 (1956), pp. 322–8, pp. 324–5; Clifford Davidson, 'Doctor Faustus at Rome', *SEL* 9 (1969), pp. 231–9, p. 231; William W. French, 'Double View in *Doctor Faustus*', *West Virginia University Philological Papers* 17 (1970), pp. 3–15, p. 4, and Warren D. Smith, 'The Nature of Evil in *Doctor Faustus*', *Modern*

Language Review 60 (1965), pp. 171–5, p. 171. Thomas McAlindon interestingly suggests the B-text 'offers the first and in some ways the best interpretation of Marlowe's play' (*Doctor Faustus: Divine in Show* [New York: Twayne, 1994], p. xi; see also p. 87).

37 See also Robert B. Heilman, 'The Tragedy of Knowledge: Marlowe's Treatment of Faustus', *Quarterly Review of Literature* 2 (1945), pp. 316–32, p. 326.

38 Paul H. Kocher, 'Nashe's Authorship of the Prose Scenes in *Faustus*', *Modern Language Quarterly* 2 (1942), pp. 17–40, pp. 17, 19 and 29.

39 See also James Smith, 'Marlowe's Dr. *Faustus*', *Scrutiny* 8 (1939), pp. 36–55, p. 37.

40 Kocher, 'Nashe's Authorship', p. 20; Peter Holland, ' "Travelling hopefully": the Dramatic Form of Journeys in English Renaissance Drama', in *Travel and Drama in Shakespeare's Time*, pp. 160–78, pp. 161–2. See also Celia Daileader, *Eroticism on the Renaissance Stage: Transcendence, Desire, and the Limits of the Visible* (Cambridge: Cambridge University Press, 1998), pp. 6–7.

41 Christopher Highley, 'Wales, Ireland, and *I Henry IV*', *Renaissance Drama* 21 (1990), pp. 91–114, p. 99.

42 Barber, ' "Forme" ', p. 117.

43 Robert H. West, 'The Impatient Magic of Dr. Faustus', *English Literary Renaissance* 4:2 (1974), pp. 218–40, pp. 226–7. See also Barbara Howard Traister, *Heavenly Necromancers: The Magician in English Renaissance Drama* (Columbia: University of Missouri Press, 1984), p. 90.

44 Bluestone, 'Libido Speculandi', p. 34. See also Robert A. Logan, 'The Sexual Attitudes of Marlowe and Shakespeare', *University of Hartford Studies in Literature* 19 (1987), pp. 1–23, p. 5.

45 Barber, ' "Forme" ', pp. 106–7. See Alison Findlay's chapter 'Heavenly Matters of Theology', in *A Feminist Perspective on Renaissance Drama* (Oxford: Blackwell, 1999; I am very grateful to Alison Findlay for allowing me to see this before publication).

46 Masinton, *Christopher Marlowe*, pp. 124–5; Leech, *Christopher Marlowe*, p. 109.

47 See, for instance, G.K. Hunter, *Dramatic Identities and Cultural Tradition* (Liverpool: Liverpool University Press, 1978), p. 75.

48 McAdam, 'Carnal Identity', p. 54.

49 Quoted in Keefer, *Christopher Marlowe's Doctor Faustus*, introduction, p. xxvi.

50 Empson, *Faustus and the Censor*, p. 95.

51 Jonathan Goldberg, 'Sodomy and Society: The Case of Christopher Marlowe', *Southwest Review* 69 (1984), pp. 371–8.

52 See, for instance, W. Moelwyn Merchant, 'Marlowe the Orthodox', in *Christopher Marlowe*, ed. Morris, pp. 179–92, Anne Hargrove, 'Lucifer Prince of the East and the Fall of Marlowe's Dr. Faustus', *Neuphilologische Mitteilungen* 84 (1983), pp. 206–13, p. 212, and Joseph Westlund, 'The Orthodox Christian Framework of Marlowe's *Faustus*', *Studies in English Literature* 3 (1963), pp. 191–205, p. 191, note 1.

53 Keefer, 'History and the Canon', pp. 507–8.
54 Leo Kirschbaum, 'Marlowe's Faustus: A Reconsideration', *The Review of English Studies* 19 (1943), pp. 225–41, p. 229.
55 Brooke, 'Moral Tragedy', p. 670.
56 Danson, 'Questioner', pp. 18 and 26.
57 Mebane, *Renaissance Magic*, p. 117.
58 *Christopher Marlowe*, pp. 150 and 153.
59 Una Ellis-Fermor, 'The Equilibrium of Tragedy', in *Marlowe*, ed. Leech, pp. 108–11, p. 110; she modifies this somewhat in her *Christopher Marlowe* (Hamden, Connecticut: Archon Books, 1967), p. 85.
60 Paul H. Kocher, 'Marlowe's Atheist Lecture', *Journal of English and Germanic Philology* 39 (1940), pp. 98–106, p. 98, and 'Backgrounds for Marlowe's Atheist Lecture', *Philological Quarterly* 20 (1941), pp. 302–24.
61 Kuriyama, 'Dr Greg and *Doctor Faustus*', p. 192.
62 Ornstein, 'Marlowe and God', p. 1379.
63 George T. Buckley, *Atheism in the English Renaissance* (Chicago: University of Chicago Press, 1932), p. 129.
64 Lily B. Campbell, '*Doctor Faustus*: A Case of Conscience', *Publications of the Modern Language Association of America* 67 (1952), pp. 219–39, pp. 219 and 223–4.
65 T.W. Craik, 'Faustus' Damnation Reconsidered', *Renaissance Drama* 2 (1969), pp. 189–96.
66 'History and the Canon', pp. 513–4.
67 Tucker Brooke, 'The Marlowe Canon', p. 385.
68 One might also wonder about textual corruption when Ferneze refers to 'a daily sacrifice of sighs and tears' (III.ii.32), a line also found in *Love's Sacrifice*, a play by Ford, of whose *oeuvre* it is much more representative, which was probably at press in the same year.
69 Howard S. Babb, '*Policy* in Marlowe's *The Jew of Malta*', *ELH* 24:2 (June 1957), pp. 85–94, pp. 86, 88, 92 and 94.
70 Ribner, 'Marlowe and Machiavelli', pp. 351 and 353.
71 Ribner, 'Marlowe's "Tragicke Glasse"', p. 92.
72 Margaret Scott, 'Machiavelli and the Machiavel', *Renaissance Drama* 15 (1984), pp. 147–74, p. 151.
73 Poirier, *Marlowe*, p. 48.
74 See, for instance, N.W. Bawcutt, 'Machiavelli and Marlowe's *The Jew of Malta*', *Renaissance Drama* 3 (1970), pp. 3–49, pp. 4 and 29–30.
75 Catherine Minshull, 'Marlowe's "Sound Machevill"', *Renaissance Drama* 13 (1982), pp. 35–53, pp. 42, 49 and 50. See also Robert C. Jones, *Engagement with Knavery* (Durham, NC: Duke University Press, 1986), pp. 65 and 66.
76 Laura Feitzinger Brown has recently shown that even when Pilia-Borza, Ithamore and Bellamira call Barabas a fiddler, they are insulting him ('When Does a Fiddler not Play the Fiddle? Re-thinking the Musician Interlude in *The Jew of Malta* 4.4', *English Language Notes* [June 1996], pp. 10–18, p. 13).
77 Thomas and Tydeman, for instance, claim that 'it is obvious that *The Jew of Malta* makes no pretence to historical veracity' (*Christopher*

Marlowe: The Plays and their Sources, p. 297). Notable exceptions to the general lack of interest in the specificity of the Maltese setting are Bartels, *Spectacles of Strangeness*, p. 83; Roma Gill, ed., *The Jew of Malta* (Oxford: Oxford University Press, forthcoming), introduction, p. x (I am deeply grateful to Roma Gill for kindly giving me a copy of her introduction before publication); and David Farley-Hills, 'Was Marlowe's "Malta" Malta?', *Journal of the Faculty of Arts*, Royal University of Malta, Vol. III, no. 1 [1965], pp. 22–8, p. 23). I am very grateful to Professor Farley-Hills and to Dr Paul Xuereb, Librarian of the University of Malta, for their assistance in obtaining a copy of this. The University of Malta Library also contains an MA dissertation by Peter Paul Grech on 'Background to *The Jew of Malta*'. For copyright reasons it has been impossible for me to consult this, but I am grateful for the courtesy and helpfulness of the library staff in correspondence about it. Leon Kellner ('Die Quelle von Marlowes *Jew of Malta*', *English Studies* 10 [1886], p. 101) asserts at one point that Marlowe knew Malta better than any other Mediterranean island, but never provides evidence for this statement. I am grateful to my mother for translating this article for me, as well as for obtaining materials from Valletta library. Michael G. Brennan points to one possible source of information in his 'Christopher Marlowe's *The Jew of Malta* and Two Newsletter Accounts of the Siege of Malta (1565)', *Notes and Queries*, Vol. 238 (New Series, Vol. 40), no. 2 (June 1993), pp. 157–60.

78   Claire-Eliane Engel, *Histoire de l'Ordre de Malte* (Geneva: Nagel, 1968), p. 197.

79   Stanley Fiorini, 'Malta in 1530', in *Hospitaller Malta 1530–1798*, edited by Victor Mallia-Milanes (Msida, Malta: Mireva Publications, 1993), pp. 111–98, pp. 141–2.

80   Ernle Bradford, *The Great Siege: Malta 1565* [1961] (Harmondsworth: Penguin, 1964), pp. 180–1.

81   Joseph Attard, *The Knights of Malta* (Marsa, Malta: Publishers Enterprise Group, 1992), p. 69.

82   Cecil Roth, 'The Jews of Malta', *Transactions of the Jewish Historical Society of England*, 12 (1928–31), pp. 187–251, pp. 189 and 188.

83   Farley-Hills, 'Marlowe's "Malta"', p. 24.

84   Dorothy Dunnett, *The Disorderly Knights* [1966] (London: Century, 1984), p. 63. For the belief in Phoenician origins, see D.H. Trump, *Malta: An Archaeological Guide* (London: Faber and Faber, 1972), pp. 22–3.

85   Roma Gill, 'The Jew of Malta', *Scientia*, Vol. XXXVIII (1975–76–77), pp. 74–86, pp. 82–3; I am very grateful to Roma Gill for sending me a copy of this article. There is again an echo of *The Spanish Tragedy*, where Hieronimo is seen fixing up the stage curtain.

86   Roth, 'Jews of Malta', p. 191.

87   Peter French, *John Dee* [1972] (London: Ark, 1987), p. 171 and 49.

88   Roma Gill, 'The Jew of Malta', *Scientia*, p. 84.

89   James R. Siemon, ed., *The Jew of Malta*, second edition (London: A. & C. Black, 1994), introduction, pp. xii.

90   Roth, 'Jews of Malta', pp. 216–17 and 211.

91   Attard, *The Knights of Malta*, p. 29.
92   Francesco Balbo di Correggio, *The Great Siege of Malta*, trans. Major Henry Alexander Balbi (Copenhagen: Capt O.F. Gollcher and Dr Ole Rostock, 1961), p. 70.
93   Frank Felsenstein, *Anti-Semitic Stereotypes* (Baltimore: Johns Hopkins University Press, 1995), p. 162.
94   Paul Cassar, 'Malta's Medical and Social Services under the Knights Hospitallers', in *Hospitaller Malta*, pp. 475–82, p. 480.
95   Niccolo Machiavelli, *The Prince*, trans. George Bull (Harmondsworth: Penguin, 1961), pp. 60–1.
96   Luc Borot, 'Machiavellian Diplomacy and Dramatic Developments in Marlowe's *Jew of Malta*', *Cahiers Elisabéthains*, 33 (1988), pp. 1–11, p. 2.
97   A member of the same family as Scanderbeg, on whom Marlowe is sometimes thought to have written a play.
98   Quoted in Bradford, *The Great Siege*, p. 112.
99   W.H. Prescott, quoted in Bradford, *The Great Siege*, p. 140. See also Brian Blouet, *The Story of Malta* (London: Faber and Faber, 1967), pp. 69–70.
100 Bartels, *Spectacles of Strangeness*, p. 90.
101 Engel, *Histoire de l'Ordre de Malte*, p. 206.
102 Bradford, *The Great Siege*, p. 222.
103 Charles Nicholl, *The Reckoning: The Murder of Christopher Marlowe* (London: Jonathan Cape, 1992), p. 227.
104 Bradford, *The Great Siege*, p. 219.
105 Roth, 'Jews of Malta', p. 208.
106 Coburn Freer, 'Lies and Lying in *The Jew of Malta*', in '*A Poet and a Filthy Playmaker*', pp. 143–65.
107 *The Jew of Malta*, ed. Gill, introduction, p. xiii.
108 Stephen Greenblatt, 'The Will to Absolute Play', p. 118.

5   1592–1593: Tobacco and Boys

1   Irving Ribner points out that Marlowe consulted Stow as well as Holinshed ('Marlowe's *Edward II* and the Tudor History Play', *ELH* 22 [1955], pp. 243–53, p. 245).
2   See, for instance, Mark Thornton Burnett, '*Edward II* and Elizabethan Politics', in *Marlowe, History, and Sexuality*, pp. 91–108, p. 92.
3   Levin, *Overreacher*, p. 37. See also William Keach, *Elizabethan Erotic Narratives* (New Brunswick, NJ: Rutgers University Press, 1977), p. 100, and Georgia E. Brown, 'Breaking the Canon: Marlowe's Challenge to the Literary Status Quo in *Hero and Leander*', in *Marlowe, History, and Sexuality*, pp. 59–76, p. 59.
4   Forker, 'Marlowe's *Edward II*', p. 79.
5   *Overreacher*, p. 181; Dennis Kay, 'Marlowe, *Edward II*, and the Cult of Elizabeth', *Early Modern Literary Studies* 3.2 (September 1997): 1.1–30 (<http://purl.oclc.org/emls/03-2/kaymarl.html>), p. 6; Stephen Orgel, *Impersonations* (Cambridge: Cambridge University Press, 1996), p. 48.

6   Logan, 'Sexual Attitudes', p. 1. See also Harold Bloom, ed., *Modern Critical Views: Christopher Marlowe* (New York: Chelsea House Publishers, 1986), introduction, p. 1.
7   L.J. Mills, 'The Meaning of *Edward II*', *Modern Philology* 32 (1934), pp. 11–31, p. 12.
8   Homan, 'Chapman and Marlowe', p. 406.
9   Thurn, 'Sovereignty', p. 116.
10 Kathleen Anderson, '"Stab as Occasion Serves": The Real Isabella in Marlowe's *Edward II*', *Renaissance Papers* (1992), pp. 29–39, p. 32. See also Betty Travitsky, 'Husband-Murder and Petty Treason in English Renaissance Tragedy', *Renaissance Drama* 21 (1991), pp. 171–98, p. 182.
11 Michael Manheim, 'The Weak King History Play of the Early 1590's', *Renaissance Drama* 2 (1969), pp. 71–80, p. 73.
12 Berdan, 'Marlowe's *Edward II*', p. 197.
13 See, for instance, Zara Bruzzi, 'A Device to Fit the Times: Intertextual Allusion in Thomas Middleton's *Women Beware Women*', in *The Italian World of English Renaissance Drama*, edited by Michele Marrapodi (Newark: University of Delaware Press, 1998), pp. 302–20, p. 314; John M. Berdan, 'Marlowe's *Edward II*', *Philological Quarterly* 3 (1924), pp. 197–207, p. 207; Lawrence Normand, ' "What passions call you these" ': *Edward II* and James VI', in *Christopher Marlowe*, ed. Grantley and Roberts, pp. 172–97. But see also Mario DiGangi, 'Marlowe, Queer Studies, and Renaissance Homoeroticism', in *Marlowe, History, and Sexuality*, pp. 195–212, p. 203.
14 A notable exception is Cheney, *Marlowe's Counterfeit Profession* (see, for instance, pp. 57, 99 and 153); see also Henderson, *Passion Made Public*, pp. 120–1 and 148–9.
15 See, for instance, Roy Battenhouse, 'Chapman's *The Shadow of Night*: An Interpretation', *Studies in Philology* 38 (1941), pp. 584–608.
16 Hendricks, 'Managing the Barbarian', pp. 166 and 185 n.4.
17 Ovid's Elegies, Book II, Elegy XVIII. Elizabeth was also sometimes figured as Aeneas (see Marcus, *Puzzling Shakespeare*, p. 58).
18 John Marston, *Antonio and Mellida*, in *The Malcontent and Other Plays*, edited by Keith Sturgess (Oxford: Oxford University Press, 1997), Induction, 83, and I.I.190–3.
19 Karen Newman, *Fashioning Femininity and English Renaissance Drama* (Chicago: The University of Chicago Press, 1991), p. 97.
20 Christopher Pye, *The Regal Phantasm: Shakespeare and the Politics of Spectacle* (London: Routledge, 1990), p. 60.
21 Hattaway, Theology', pp. 70 and 77.
22 Levin, *Overreacher*, p. 37.
23 Kay, 'Marlowe, *Edward II*, and the Cult of Elizabeth', p. 1.
24 Callaghan, 'The Terms of Gender', p. 283. Thomas Wharton observed in 1781, '[i]t seems somewhat remarkable that Marlow, in describing the pleasures which Gaveston contrived to debauch the infatuated Edward, should exactly employ those which were exhibited before the sage Elizabeth. But to her they were only occasional and temporary relaxations' (quoted in MacLure, ed., *Marlowe: The Critical Heritage*, p. 65).

25 Steane, *Marlowe*, p. 228.

26 Kay, 'Marlowe, *Edward II*, and the Cult of Elizabeth', pp. 3 and 5.

27 Alan Haynes, *The White Bear: Robert Dudley, The Elizabethan Earl of Leicester* (London: Peter Owen, 1987), pp. 14, 55, 43 and 79.

28 I thought at first that this had not previously been noticed, but in fact it has been remarked upon by Thomas McAlindon and Ann Lecercle-Sweet (see William Tydeman and Vivien Thomas, *State of the Art: Christopher Marlowe* [Bristol: The Bristol Press, 1989], p. 85), as well as by Cutts (*The Left Hand of God*, pp. 211–18). John Gillies, in 'Marlowe, the *Timur* Myth, and the Motives of Geography', in *Playing the Globe: Genre and Geography in English Renaissance Drama*, edited by John Gillies and Virginia Mason Vaughan (London: Associated University Presses, 1998), pp. 203–29, points to the importance of river imagery in the *Tamburlaine* plays (p. 214). Ian McAdam points to the presence of the motif in *The Jew of Malta* also ('Carnal Identity in *The Jew of Malta*', p. 60), and see too Cheney, *Counterfeit Profession*, pp. 70–2.

29 Quoted in Steane, *Marlowe*, p. 61. It is suggestive that Izaak Walton should have included 'The Passionate Shepherd to his Love' in *The Compleat Angler* and that John Taylor the Water-Poet should have been fond of *Hero and Leander*.

30 Haynes, *Sex*, p. 81.

31 Thurn, 'Sovereignty', p. 132.

32 Philip Edwards, *Sea-Mark: The Metaphorical Voyage, Spenser to Milton* (Liverpool: Liverpool University Press, 1997), p. 52.

33 Kay, 'Marlowe, *Edward II*, and the Cult of Elizabeth', p. 7.

34 Edwards, *Sea-Mark*, p. 66.

35 Gareth Roberts, 'Necromantic Books: Christopher Marlowe, Doctor Faustus and Agrippa of Nettesheim', in *Christopher Marlowe*, ed. Grantley and Roberts, pp. 148–71, p. 163.

36 Martin T. Williams also draws the parallel between Marlowe's treatment of the sea in *Hero and Leander* and Homer's in *The Odyssey* ('The Temptations in Marlowe's *Hero and Leander*', *Modern Language Quarterly* (1955), pp. 226–31, p. 227, and Erich Segal speaks of the 'Odyssean quality in Barabas' ('Marlowe's *Schadenfreude:* Barabas as Comic Hero', in Bloom, *Modern Critical Views*, pp. 121–36, p. 135.

37 Charles Forker, in the notes on this in his Revels edition of the play (Manchester: Manchester University Press, 1994), thinks the allusions both here and to Juno are from Ovid, but he also points out that Circe here is on her way to Scylla, another character first encountered in the *Odyssey*. *Hamlet*, a play that contains some textual overlap with *Edward II* and some common themes, has a Laertes, which could conceivably suggest that Shakespeare was alert to the presence of an Odyssean parallel in Marlowe's play.

38 Though Forker thinks the allusion this time is to Virgil.

39 Andrew M. Kirk, 'Marlowe and the Disordered Face of French History', *Studies in English Literature* 35 (1995), pp. 193–213, p. 193.

40 Paul H. Kocher, 'François Hotman and Marlowe's *The Massacre at Paris*', *PMLA* 56 (1941), pp. 349–68, p. 365.
41 Potter, 'Marlowe's *Massacre*', p. 70; Archer, *Sovereignty*, p. 91. Potter also points to the links often made between Henri III (whose real name was in fact Alexandre Edouard) and Edward II, and to the fact that the *chargé d'affaires* at the time of the massacre, who seems to be represented in the play as the 'Agent for England', was William Lyly, who may have had a connection with Marlowe's old school (p. 89; see also Archer, *Sovereignty*, pp. 92 and 175).
42 Cheney, *Marlowe's Counterfeit Profession*, p. 186.
43 'The Marlowe Canon', p. 391.
44 'The Reputation of Christopher Marlowe', p. 361.
45 William Keach, 'Marlowe's Hero as "Venus' Nun"', *English Literary Renaissance* 2 (1972), pp. 307–20, pp. 311–12.
46 M. Morgan Holmes, 'Identity and the Dissidence it Makes: Homoerotic Nonsense in Kit Marlowe's *Hero and Leander*', *English Studies in Canada* (1995), pp. 151–69, p. 151.
47 Robert Speaight, 'Marlowe: the Forerunner', *Review of English Literature* 7 (1966), pp. 25–41, p. 41; Leech, 'Marlowe's Humor', p. 79; Holmes, 'Identity', p. 160.
48 See, for instance, Marion Campbell, ' "*Desunt Nonnulla*": The Construction of Marlowe's *Hero and Leander* as an Unfinished Poem', *English Literary History* 51 (1984), pp. 241–68, and W.L. Godshalk, '*Hero and Leander*: The Sense of an Ending', in '*A Poet and a Filthy Playmaker*', pp. 293–314.
49 Tromly, p. 165.

6 A Great Reckoning: From 1593 to Immortaliy

1 Henry Petowe, quoted in Wraight and Stern, *In Search*, p. 329.
2 See J. Leslie Hotson, *The Death of Christopher Marlowe* (London: The Nonesuch Press, 1925).
3 Goldberg, 'Sodomy and Society', p. 372.
4 Robertson, *Marlowe*, pp. 19 and 24.
5 Gray, 'Some Observations', pp. 694, 698 and 699.
6 Urry, *Marlowe and Canterbury*, p. 81; Davidson, 'Atheism', p. 140; Ethel Seaton, 'Marlowe, Robert Poley, and the Tippings', *Review of English Studies* 5 (1929), pp. 273–87, pp. 273 and 87.
7 Curtis C. Breight, *Surveillance, Militarism and Drama in the Elizabethan Era* (Basingstoke: Macmillan, 1996), pp. 127–49. Empson just remarks that Marlowe was 'safely murdered', but does not suggest by whom (*Faustus and the Censor*, p. 63).
8 See Roy Strong, *The Cult of Elizabeth* [1977] (London: Thames & Hudson, 1987), pp. 74 and 79.
9 Paul E.J. Hammer, 'A Reckoning Reframed: the "Murder" of Christopher Marlowe Revisited', *English Literary Renaissance*, 26 (1996), pp. 225–42,

p. 231, 238 and 240. See also Arthur Freeman, letter to the *Times Literary Supplement* (19 June 1992), p. 15.

10 William Dinsmore Briggs, 'On a Document Concerning Christopher Marlowe', *Studies in Philology* 20 (1923), pp. 153–9, p. 153; Frederick S. Boas, 'New Light on Marlowe and Kyd', *Fortnightly Review* (February, 1899), pp. 212–25, p. 217.

11 Roy Kendall, 'Richard Baines and Christopher Marlowe's Milieu', *English Literary Renaissance* 24 (1994), pp. 507–22, pp. 507, 508, 511 and 520.

12 'New Light on Marlowe and Kyd', p. 218.

13 Samuel Tannenbaum, *The Assassination of Christopher Marlowe* (Hamden, Connecticut: The Shoe String Press, 1928), pp. 41–2 and 48.

14 Terry Deary and Neil Tonge, *The Terrible Tudors* (London: Scholastic Children's Books, 1993), pp. 58–63. My thanks to Annaliese Connolly for drawing this to my attention.

15 Holmes, 'Identity', p. 155.

16 Roy Battenhouse, 'Chapman's *The Shadow of Night:* An Interpretation', *Studies in Philology* 38 (1941), pp. 584–608, p. 590, note 19; Homan, 'Chapman and Marlowe', p. 393.

17 See *Antonio and Mellida*, Induction, l.83. Harebrain, in *A Mad World, My Masters*, will not let his wife read *Hero and Leander or Venus and Adonis*. (Thomas Middleton, *A Mad World, My Masters and Other Plays*, edited by Michael Taylor [Oxford: Oxford University Press, 1995], I.2.45.) See also Bruzzi, 'A Device to Fit the Times', pp. 313–14, for the suggestion that *Women Beware Women* contains echoes of *Edward II* (in particular of a moment which is itself echoing Ovid). See also James Shapiro, '"Steale from the deade?": The Presence of Marlowe in Jonson's Early Plays', in *Renaissance Drama as Cultural History: Essays from Renaissance Drama 1977–1987*, edited by Mary Beth Rose (Evanston, Illinois: Northwestern University Press, 1990), pp. 75–107; Stephanie Wright, 'The Canonization of Elizabeth Cary', in *Voicing Women: Gender and Sexuality in Early Modern Writing*, edited by Kate Chedgzoy, Melanie Hansen and Suzanne Trill (Keele: Keele University Press, 1996), pp. 55–68, p. 63; Maurice Charney, 'Marlowe's *Edward II* as Model for Shakespeare's *Richard II'*, *Research Opportunities in Renaissance Drama*, XXXIII (1994), pp. 31–41; Maurice Charney, 'The Voice of Marlowe's Tamburlaine in Early Shakespeare', *Comparative Drama* 31:2 (summer 1997), pp. 213–23, p. 219; and Nicholas Brooke, 'Marlowe as Provocative Agent in Shakespeare's Early Plays', *Shakespeare Survey*, 14 (1961), pp. 34–44.

18 See John Baker, in 'Readers' Queries', *Notes and Queries* 241:3 (September 1996), p. 306.

19 Thomas Heywood, *The Captives, or The Lost Recovered, in Thomas Heywood: Three Marriage Plays*, edited by Paul Merchant (Manchester: Manchester University Press, 1996), II.iii.132–3 and IV.ii.

20 Antony Telford Moore, 'Ford's Parody of Edward Alleyn', *Notes and Queries* 241:2 (June 1996), pp. 190–1; Lisa Hopkins, 'Touching Touchets: *Perkin Warbeck* and the Buggery Statute', *Renaissance Quarterly* 52 (1999), 384–401.

21   Lawrence Danson, 'Continuity and Character in Shakespeare and Marlowe' *Studies in English Literature 1500–1900* 26:2 (1986), pp. 217–34, p. 217; Richard A. McCabe, *Incest, Drama and Nature's Law 1550–1700* (Cambridge: Cambridge University Press, 1993), p. 241.

22   John Ford, *'Tis Pity She's a Whore*, edited by Brian Morris (London: Ernest Benn 1968), I.i.4–8 (all further quotations from the play will be from this edition); Cyrus Hoy, '"Ignorance in Knowledge": Marlowe's Faustus and Ford's Giovanni', *Modern Philology* 57 (1960), pp. 145–54.

23   Ribner, 'Marlowe and the Critics', p. 212. On Marlowe's reputation in the Restoration and Romantic periods, see also MacLure, *Marlowe: The Critical Heritage*, pp. 8–12.

24   Levin, *Overreacher*, p. 63; Edmund Gosse, *Father and Son*, edited by Peter Abbs (Harmondsworth: Penguin, 1983), p. 227; Thomas Dabbs, *Reforming Marlowe: The Nineteenth-Century Canonization of a Renaissance Dramatist* (Lewisburg: Bucknell University Press, 1991), p. 14.

25   Stephanie Cowell, *Nicholas Cooke: Actor, Soldier, Physician, Priest* (London: W.W. Norton, 1993); Liam Maguire, *Icarus Flying: The Tragical Story of Christopher Marlowe* (London: Ormond Books, 1993); Anthony Burgess, *A Dead Man in Deptford* (London: Random House, 1993); Chris Hunt, *Mignon* (London: Gay Men's Press, 1987). I am indebted to Annaliese Connolly for help in researching novelisations of Marlowe's life.

26   Robin Chapman, *Christoferus or Tom Kyd's Revenge* (London: Sinclair-Stevenson, 1993), pp. 88, 107, and 161.

27   Peter Whelan, *The School of Night* (London: Warner Chappell, 1992). For an account of a further fictional encounter between Marlowe and Shakespeare, in D.C. Comics' *The Sandman*, see Michael D. Bristol, *Big-time Shakespeare* (London: Routledge, 1996), chapter 5. Marlowe also occurs as a character in Iain Sinclair's *Slow Chocolate Factory* (London: Phoenix House, 1997), which was reviewed in the *Times Literary Supplement*, 21 November, 1997, p. 23 (with thanks to Martin Wright for alerting me to this).

28   Howard Felperin, *The Uses of the Canon: Elizabethan Literature and Contemporary Theory* (Oxford: The Clarendon Press, 1990), p. 100; Nicholas Brooke, 'Marlowe the Dramatist', in *Elizabethan Theatre: Stratford-upon-Avon Studies* 9 (1966), pp. 87–106, p. 105; Heilman, 'Tragedy of Knowledge', p. 319; Heilman, 'Tragedy of Knowledge', p. 319; Keefer, 'Misreading Faustus Misreading', p. 515; Edwards, *Sea-Mark*, p. 64.

29   Quoted in MacLure, *Critical Heritage*, p. 4.

Index

Abulafia, Abraham   91
Admiral's Men, the   48
Aeneid   57
Aguirre, Elvira de   54
Aguirre, Lope de   54
All Ovids Elegies   15, 37
Allen, Don Cameron   5
Alleyn, Edward   47, 59, 68, 103,
   106–7, 141
Alphonsus Emperor of Germany   7
Amintae Gaudia   103, 118
Amores   15
Anderson, Kathleen   105–6
Antonio and Mellida   110
Archer, John Michael   40, 127
Arden of Faversham   7–8
Ardolino, Frank   24–5
As You Like It   140–1

Babb, Howard S.   84–5
Babington, Anthony   76, 137
Baines, Richard   1, 51, 64, 67, 89,
   94, 135–6, 138–9
Bakeless, John   12, 46, 50
Balbi, Francisco   93
Barber, C.L.   79, 81
Barnes, Barnabe   140
Bartels, Emily   52, 96
Battenhouse, Roy   44
Beaumont, Francis   140
Berdan, John   106
Berek, Peter   44–5
Berlioz, Hector   142
Bevington, David   6, 16, 46
Birringer, Johannes H.   45
Blackburn, William   30
Blount, Sir Christopher   139
Blount, Edward   47
Bluestone, Max   79, 81
Boas, F.S.   15, 138–9

Boke Named the Governour   29
Borgia, Cesare   95
Borot, Luc   95
Bradbrook, M.C.   20, 23
Breight, Curtis   137
Briggs, W.D.   138
Brooke, Nicholas   17, 68, 79,
   83, 145
Brooks, Harold   19
Brown, Beatrice Daw   16–17
Bruno, Giordano   48, 91, 117
Buckley, George T.   83
Bull, Eleanor   135, 140
Burgess, Anthony   143
Burghley, William Cecil, Lord   40,
   53, 137
Burnett, Mark Thornton   x, 56, 69
Butcher, Andrew   24
Byron, George Gordon, Lord   142

Callaghan, Dympna   33, 114
Camden, Caroll   37
Campbell, Lily   83–4
Captives, The   141
Cary, Elizabeth   140
Cecil, Sir Robert   116
Chapman, George   47, 119, 131,
   133, 140
Chapman, Robin   143–4
Charles, V   87
Cheney, Patrick   ix, 21–2, 69, 127
Children of the Queen's
   Chapel   108
Cole, Douglas   5–6, 37
Coligny, Admiral   127
Colluthus   15
Comedy of Errors, The   7, 9, 20
*Contention Between the Houses of York
   and Lancaster*   8, 11
Corkine, William   103

Corpus Christi College,
  Cambridge 1–2, 36, 38–9,
  78, 141
Cowell, Stephanie 143
Craik, T.W. 84
Cunningham, J.S. 50
Cutts, John P. 30, 44, 46

Dabbs, Thomas 142
Danson, Lawrence 28, 43–4, 57,
  83, 141
Davidson, Nicholas 136–7
Davies, John 54
Dee, John 91
Depp, Johnny 142
Devlin, Christopher 48
Dido, Queen of Carthage 3–4,
  13–15, 20–2, 25–7, 31–4,
  37,46,48, 52, 57–8, 61, 68, 90–1,
  106, 108, 124
Diehl, Huston 61
Divils Charter, The 140
Doctor Faustus 3, 6–7, 13–14,
  16–23, 30–1, 37, 40, 48–9,
  51–2, 61–3, 65–84, 87, 91, 104–6,
  112–14, 116–17, 127,
  132, 139–45
Drayton, Michael 47
Drury, Thomas 138
Dyer, Elizabeth 24

Edward II 3–4, 9–10, 12, 15, 17,
  19–22, 32–5, 49, 52, 55, 68–9, 82,
  104–7, 114–27, 130, 139, 144
Edward II (ballet) 144–5
Edward III 7, 10
Edward VI 67
Edwards, Philip 120, 124, 145
Eliot, T.S. 69
Ellis-Fermor, Una 6, 83
Elizabeth I 9–l0, 34, 38, 46, 51, 67,
  l07–16, 118, 137, 139
Elyot, Sir Thomas 29
Empson, William 67, 69, 77, 82
Engel, Claire-Eliane 88
English Mirror, The 50

Essex, Robert Devereux,
  Earl of 118, 135, 137,
  139
Everett Rupert 142

Faerie Queene, The 19, 22, 113
Farley-Hills, David 26, 90
Faust Book, The 17–19, 40, 78
Felperin, Howard 145
Foakes, R.A. 20
Ford, John 171
Forker, Charles R. x, 104, 123–4
Foucault, Michel 74
Foxe. John 45
Freer, Coburn 99
Frizer, Ingram 103, 135, 138–40,
  142

Garber, Marjorie 44, 62, 68–9, 78
Gilbert, Sir Humphrey 29, 59
Gill, Roma 37, 79, 91, 100
Goethe, Johann Wolfgang von 80
Goldberg, Jonathan 136
Golden, Kenneth 145
Gosse, Edmund 142
Gosson, Stephen 29
Grantley, Darryll ix
Gray, Austin K. 16, 39–40, 136
Greenblatt, Stephen 100
Greg, W.W. 17–18, 71, 84
Greene, Robert 3, 47
Grey, Lady Catherine 34
Grey, Lady Jane 34
Grey, Lady Mary 34

Hakluyt, Richard 50
Hamlet 9, 68, 71–2, 74, 81
Hammer, Paul J. 137–8
Hammill, Graham 66
Hammon, Thomas 141
Hannibal 7, 13
Harington, Sir John 54
Hariot, Thomas 48, 54, 136
Harvey, Gabriel 12, 54, 85
Hattaway, Michael 43, 66, 113
Haynes, Alan 119

Healy, Thomas   22, 50
Heilman, Robert B.   145
Henderson, Diana   13
Hendricks, Margo   25, 46, 108
Henri III   127
Henry V   7
Henry VI, Part 1   7–12, 107, 141–2
Henry VI, Part 2   7–8, 10–12, 107, 141–2
Henry VI, Part 3   7–8, 10–12, 107, 141–2
Henry VIII   23, 67, 72, 87
Henslowe, Philip   18–19
Hero and Leander,   2–4, 14, 19–21, 36, 47, 65, 69, 104, 113–14, 119, 124, 129–33, 140, 141–2
Herodotus   45
Heywood, Thomas   7, 141
Highley, Christopher   80–1
Hoffman, Calvin   7
Holinshed's Chronicles   123
Holland, Henry   18
Holland, Peter   80
Holmes, M. Morgan   130, 140
Homan, Sidney   16, 105, 140
Horestes   28
Hotson, Leslie   38–9
Howard, Sir Charles, Lord Admiral   48
Howe, James Robinson   45
Hunt, Chris   143
Hunter, Robert G.   66
Hutten, Philip von   62

Ivan the Terrible   51
Ive, Paul   19

James VI and I   34, 107
Jarman, Derek   105, 118, 120, 144
Jew of Malta, The   3, 8, 19–22, 30, 33–4, 48, 52, 61, 63–6, 68–9, 81–2, 85–101, 106, 139, 141
Johnson, Francis   16, 78
Jonson, Ben   2, 47, 140
Jones, Ann Rosalind   45
Julius Caesar   7

Kay, Dennis   104, 114, 116–17, 120
Keach, William   130
Keefer, Michael   19, 31, 66, 78–9, 82, 84, 145
Kendall, Roy   138–9
King John   8
King's School, Canterbury   1, 29, 36, 141
Kirk, Andrew   127
Kirschbaum, Leo   82
Knack to Know a Knave, A   18
Knapp, Jeffrey   48
Kocher, Paul   5–6, 16, 18, 29, 50, 79–80, 83, 127, 138
Kuriyama, Constance Brown   24, 43–4, 79–80, 83
Kyd, Thomas   7–8, 47, 70, 82, 85, 89, 103, 107, 135–6, 138

La Valette, Jean de   87–9, 93, 95–6, 99
'Larum for London, a   7
Law, Jude   142
Leech, Clifford   20, 43, 81, 130
Leicester, Robert Dudley, Earl of   116–8
Levenson, Jill   33
Levin, Harry   x, 6, 55, 104, 114
Locrine   7
Logan, Robert A.   105
Loncraine, Richard   142
Looking Glass for London and England, A   17
Lord Strange's Men   103, 106
Love's Labour's Lost   11
Love's Sacrifice   171
Lucan   3, 14, 21, 37
Lust's Dominion   8

Macbeth   7, 68, 145
Machiavelli, Niccolò   85, 94–5
Maguire, Liam   143
Manheim, Michael   106
Manwood, Sir Roger   8, 117
Marlowe, Anthony   50

Marlowe, Edmund   54
Marlowe, John   24
Marprelate tracts   79
Marston, John   110, 140
Mary I   67
Mary, Queen of Scots   10, 40, 67, 98
Masinton, Charles   67, 81
Massacre at Paris, The   3, 7, 15, 17, 19, 21–2, 30, 32–5, 37, 52, 69, 82, 106, 127–9, 139, 142
McAdam, Ian   66, 82
McCabe, Richard   141
MacLean, Sally-Beth   19
McMillin, Scott   19
Mebane, John   16, 67, 83
Merchant of Venice, The   7, 141
Merry Wives of Windsor, The   141
Meyrick, Gelly   137
Middleton, Thomas   140
Mills, L.J.   105
Milton, John   2
Minshull, Catherine   85–6
Mirror for Magistrates   50
More, Sir Thomas   129
Mowle, Christopher   24
Muscovy Company, The   50

Nashe, Thomas   15, 47, 79–80, 140, 145
Newman, Karen   111
Nicholl, Charles   40, 54–5, 137–8
Northumberland, Henry Percy, Earl of   48, 136
Novak, Kim   145
Nuttall, A.D.   16

Odyssey, The   126
Orgel, Stephen   x, 32, 104
Ornstein, Robert   83
Ovid   3, 15, 21, 37, 105, 108, 114
Owens, Margaret E.   8

Parker, John   36
Parker, Matthew   36, 38, 88

'Passionate Shepherd to his Love, The'   3, 13–14, 119, 123, 142
Pearce, T.M.   29, 59
Pembroke, Mary Herbert, Countess of   103
Pembroke's Men   117–18
Perkin Warbeck   171
Perkins, William   18–19
Petowe, Henry   133, 140
Pharsalia   15
Phillips, Edward   2
Pikering/Puckering, John   28, 136–7
Pinciss, G.M.   18, 67
Poirier, Michel   85
Poley, Robert   76, 136–40
Polybius   38
Potter, David   127
Prince, The   85
Proudfoot, Richard   27

Ralegh, Sir Walter   51, 54–5, 60, 108, 113, 119, 135–7, 139
Rambuss, Richard   21
Ramus, Peter   37, 127
Randolph, Thomas   13
Ribner, Irving   4–6, 17, 37–8, 43, 85, 142
Richard II   7, 141
Richard III   7–8, 141
Richards, Susan   16
Roberts, Gareth   124
Roberts, Peter   ix
Robertson, J.M.   6–7, 14, 136
Romeo and Juliet   7
Ronan, Clifford   15
Roth, Cecil   89–92
Rowse, A.L.   65, 83
Royden, Matthew   47, 107
Roydon, John   24
Rozett, Martha Tuck   45–6

Sannazaro, Jacopo   119
Scanderbeg   7, 12–13
School of Night, the   48
Scott, Margaret   85

Seaton, Ethel   137
Sewell, Rufus   143
Shakespeare, William   1, 4, 7–13, 16, 36, 86, 141–2
Shakespeare in Love   16, 142
Shelley, Percy Bysshe   142
Shepherd, Simon   34
Sher, Antony   53
Sidney, Sir Philip   117
Sidney, Sir Robert   48, 117, 138–9
Skeres, Nicholas   137–40
Snow, Edward   17, 69
Snyder, Susan   68
Somogyi, Nick de   52–3
Southwell, Robert   48
Spanish Tragedy, The   7, 70
Speaight, Robert   130
Spenser, Edmund   13, 19, 21–2, 49, 104
Spies, Johann   78
Spira, Francis   84
Spurgeon, Caroline   36–7
Stallybrass, Peter   45
Stanley, Sir Edward   97–9
Stanley, Sir William   40, 137
Steane, J.B   8, 71, 116
Stockholder, Kay   31
Strange, Ferdinando Stanley, Lord   48, 98–9, 103, 106, 135
Strathmann, Ernest A.   54
Strong, Sir Roy   137
Stuart, Lady Arbella   3, 34
Summers, Claude J.   33

Taine, Hippolyte   5
Tambling, Jeremy   30
Tamburlaine Part One   2–4, 6, 9, 13–16, 20, 22–3, 26–9, 32, 34, 37–8, 43–62, 65, 68–9, 71–3, 81–2, 85, 104–10, 119, 137, 141
Tamburlaine Part Two   2–4, 6, 9, 12–13, 15–16, 19–20, 22–3, 26–7, 29–30, 32–3, 43–7, 49, 52–4, 60–2, 65, 68, 71–3, 81–2, 85, 110–12, 117, 128
Taming of a Shrew, The   7–8

Tannenbaum, Samuel   139
Taunton, Nina   37, 78
Tempest, The   17, 75, 86, 141
Terrible Tudors, The   140
Theatrum Orbis Terrarum   46
Thurn, David H.   66, 105, 119
'Tis Pity She's a Whore   141
Titus Andronicus   7, 142
Toledo, Don Frederic de   97
Toledo, Don Garcia de   96–7
Tromly, Fred B.   ix, 131
Troublesome Raigne of King John, The   7–8, 19
True Tragedie of Richard Duke of York   8, 11
Tucker Brooke, C.F.   8, 13, 15–16, 19, 84, 129–30
Tyrone, Hugh O'Neill, Earl of   8l, 116

Urry, William   24, 136

Venus and Adonis   141
Villiers de l'Isle Adam, Grand Master,   87
Virgil   21, 25, 27, 47, 57
Voltaire   87

Waith, Eugene   6
Walsingham, Audrey   137
Walsingham, Sir Francis   40, 48, 103, 117, 127, 139
Walsingham, Thomas   2, 40, 47, 103, 117, 135, 137, 142
Warner, Walter   47
Warren, Michael   14, 17, 79–80
Watson, Thomas   15, 47, 103
Weil, Judith   31
Whelan, Peter   144
Whetstone, George   50
White, Paul Whitfield   x
Williams, Carolyn   29
Wilson, Richard   51, 53
Wood, Antony à   48

Zimansky, Curt   18
Zunder, William   62